The Consilient Brain

The Consilient Brain

The Bioneurological Basis of Economics, Society, and Politics

Gerald A. Cory, Jr.

Senior Fellow, Graduate Studies and Research
San Jose State University
San Jose, California

Kluwer Academic/Plenum Publishers
New York, Boston, Dordrecht, London, Moscow

Library of Congress Cataloging-in-Publication Data

ISBN: 0-306-47880-3

©2004 Kluwer Academic / Plenum Publishers, New York
233 Spring Street, New York, New York 10013

http://www.wkap.nl/

10 9 8 7 6 5 4 3 2 1

A C.I.P. record for this book is available from the Library of Congress

Permissions for books published in Europe: *permissions@wkap.nl*
Permissions for books published in the United States of America: *permissions@wkap.com*

Printed in the United States of America

**To my parents
Alice and Gerald**

PREFACE

The present work is the third in a series constituting an extension of my doctoral thesis done at Stanford in the early 1970s. Like the earlier works, *The Reciprocal Modular Brain in Economics and Politics, Shaping the Rational and Moral Basis of Organization, Exchange, and Choice* (Kluwer Academic/Plenum Publishing, 1999) and *Toward Consilience: The Bioneurological Basis of Behavior, Thought, Experience, and Language* (Kluwer Academic/Plenum Publishing, 2000), it may also be considered to respond to the call for consilience by Edward O. Wilson. I agree with Wilson that there is a pressing need in the sciences today for the unification of the social with the natural sciences. I consider the present work to proceed from the perspective of behavioral ecology, specifically a subfield which I choose to call interpersonal behavioral ecology.

Ecology, as a general field, has emerged in the last quarter of the 20th century as a major theme of concern as we have become increasingly aware that we must preserve the planet whose limited resources we share with all other earthly creatures. Interpersonal behavioral ecology, however, focuses not on the physical environment, but upon our social environment. It concerns our interpersonal behavioral interactions at all levels, from simple dyadic one-to-one personal interactions to our larger, even global, social, economic, and political interactions.

Interpersonal behavioral ecology, as I see it, then, is concerned with our behavior toward each other, from the most obvious behaviors of war among nations, to excessive competition, exploitation, crime, abuse, and even to the ways in which we interact with each other as individuals in the family, in our social lives, in the workplace, and in the marketplace. It is about more, however, than just damage control, adjustment, and repair to the structure and behavior of our interpersonal lives. It seeks to go further—to understand and apply the dynamics of interpersonal behavior with a view to improving the larger social, economic, and political systems that shape our lives.

This present book seeks to identify and explore the basic algorithms of our evolved brain structure that underlie and shape our economic, social, and political institutions, as well as our thought, and behavior within them. In the quest to unify the social with the natural sciences, we must inevitably turn to evolutionary neuroscience as the bridging discipline. There is no where else to go. Although our brain evolved under constraints of the laws of physics and chemistry, the evolutionary process itself involved chaotic and random factors, as well as natural selection processes. The algorithms of our brain, then, which are the foundation of our social sciences, can never have the immutability and predictability of the laws of physics and chemistry. These algorithms, although dynamic, shaping factors of our behavior, are, to a degree, innately variable and experientially modifiable. This fundamental difference between the natural and social sciences precludes a simplistic reduction, but indicates, rather, the establishment of linkages and bridges.

ACKNOWLEDGMENTS

The ideas presented in this book evolved over a period of a half-century during which I accumulated many intellectual debts. My early interest in the brain goes back to my employment at Tidewater Hospital, a private psychiatric institution (1950–1951) in Beaufort County, South Carolina. Under the supervision of psychiatrist, A. K. Fidler, I participated extensively in patient care and studied the greats of psychiatry and brain science. I have pursued my interest in neuroscience unflaggingly since that time. I also wish to acknowledge Robert H. Wienefeld, former chair of history at the University of South Carolina, who, during my undergraduate years in the early 1950s helped me to begin thinking historically and economically.

I wish especially to thank Kurt Steiner of Stanford University for his guidance and encouragement. His support of the ideas and concepts of this work has been of great value to me over the years since we first met at Stanford in 1970. Also I wish to thank Robert North, Nobutaka Ike, Hans Weiler, Peter Corning, Donald Kennedy, Charles Drekmeier, Tilo Schabert, Alexander George, Richard Fagen, Daryl Bem, and Robert Packenham, all of Stanford University, who gave their advice and support in the development of these ideas many years ago. I owe special and more recent thanks to Paul D. MacLean of the National Institute of Mental Health, for his review, helpful comments, and continuing encouragement; and to Elliott White, now emeritus of Temple University, for his review of a related manuscript, his encouragement, and his many valuable comments. I also wish to thank Edward O. Wilson of Harvard University for his acknowledgment of my work and his encouragement.

For their review and endorsement of earlier, related works, I wish to thank Russell Gardner, Jr., clinical professor of Psychiatry, Medical College of Wisconsin, Daniel Levine, Department of Psychology, University of Texas Arlington, Kent Bailey, Emeritus Professor of Psychology, Virginia Commonwealth University, Gary Lynne, Professor of Economics, University of Nebraska, Detlev Ploog, Professor of Psychiatry, Max Planck Institute for Psychiatry, Munich, Germany, Alice Scheuer, of University of Hawaii (and the WHO Field Psychiatric Center), Brian Barry, Department of Psychology, Rochester Institute of Technology, Andre Fiedeldey, Department of Psychology, University of Pretoria, Arthur Sementelli, Department of Political Science, Stephen Austin State University, Nacogdoches, Texas, and Trudi Miller, Department of Political Science, University of Minnesota. Paris Arnopoulos, of Concordia University, who shares an interest in algorithms bridging the natural and social sciences, also generously reviewed an earlier related work. Simon Rodan and Robert C. Wood of the College of Business, San Jose State University provided thoughtful comments and opportunities for discussion. I wish also to thank Richard Mapplebeckpalmer, Rector of Grace North Church, Berkeley, California for the opportunity to present some of my thoughts to the challenging group at the Grace Institute for Religious Learning and for his encouraging review of an earlier manuscript.

I appreciate very much the opportunity to pursue my research as a senior fellow in Graduate Studies and Research, San Jose State University, made possible with encouragement and support of Nabil A. Ibrahim, Associate Vice-President and Joe Pesek, Associate Dean. My special thanks go to Susan Hoagland, Rochelle G. Baloca, Ruth Bermea, Andy Hernandez, Sara Javid, Eona Lewis, Mattie Lewis, Yen Li, De'An Marr, Randy Nunez, Geeta Patel, Samantha Rodriguez, Brenda Sanchez, Candy Simel, and Loan Vu, the support and evaluative staff of Graduate Studies and Research, for their helpful comments and participation in the refinement of the teamwork development program during which we explored many of the ideas presented in this book.

David Conrath, Dean, S. Lee Jerrell, Associate Dean, College of Business, Burton Dean and Abdel El-Shaieb, past and present chairs of the Department of Organization and Management, and Sylvia Peaker, departmental Executive Assistant created a supportive and encouraging academic environment for teaching and research.

Vic and Adrienne Hochee, John Lightburn, David McKenna, and Peter Lynch were my valued colleagues over many years and provided their criticisms and support with generosity and thoughtfulness. My thanks also go to my many seminar colleagues and students, who were an inspiration and a challenge over the years. I also wish to thank my wife Mary, my daughter Catherine, and my granddaughters Davida and Rachel for their support and inspiration.

Kathleen P. Lyons, senior editor, and Marissa Kraft editorial assistant at Kluwer Academic/Plenum, were my patient guides and supporters through the production of this book.

As appropriate, I remain responsible for any errors or misinterpretations that may appear in the present work.

CONTENTS

CONTENTS   xiii

1

INTRODUCTION

This book is an effort at bridging disciplines. It responds to the call for consilience (1998), a concerted effort toward unifying the natural and social sciences, by sociobiologist Edward O. Wilson. The human brain is essentially a *social* brain. As such, it *creates* the social sciences. The human brain, thus, is the necessary unifying or bridging mechanism to achieve consilience between the natural and the social sciences. Therefore, I think the title, *The Consilient Brain*, is appropriately chosen. Although the title has changed, this book may be considered, in part, a revision and expansion of my earlier work, *The Reciprocal Modular Brain in Economics and Politics* (1999).

The study of the brain is advancing rapidly. This book, and its predecessor, could not have been written ten years ago. Perhaps not even five years ago. Brain study got a great boost when the U. S. government declared the 1990s to be the decade of the brain. More federal funding became available for brain research. And neuroscience, the scientific study of the brain, became increasingly important on our university and college campuses. That situation continues to the present day.

But the new emphasis on neuroscience built on a body of research and experimentation that had been accumulating for several decades before. Most important to the study of the consilient social brain was the work of Paul D. MacLean. MacLean was the longtime chief of the Laboratory of Brain Evolution and Behavior of the National Institutes of Health. Unlike mainstream behavioral and cognitive neuroscientists, MacLean studied the brain from the standpoint of evolution. This is the only way to truly understand it—to trace it through a long, long period of history and development going back into deep time—to the beginning of life itself. This book, while drawing on all areas of neuroscience, builds on the evolutionary perspective pioneered by MacLean and others like him.

The book is divided into four parts. The first part, made up of six chapters, is foundational. I first place the brain in evolutionary context. MacLean (1990) refers to the primary function of the human brain as the preservation of the individual self and the human species. Although this may be said of the nervous system of any organism which must survive to reproduce, MacLean leads us to consider not just automatisms or automatic, tightly wired instinctual mechanisms but the evolved social architecture of the human brain upon which choices are made.

In line with MacLean's insight, I develop the Conflict Systems Neurobehavioral (CSN) Model from the major evolutionary spurts that took us from primitive vertebrates to mammals, then to primates, and ultimately to our human status. A dynamic set of global-state neural algorithms express the conflict and resulting reciprocity between earlier self-preserving circuitry and later affectional or other-preserving circuits. Our higher brain centers developed, in part, in response to the special problems of social adaptation created by our conflicting neural network architecture. The understanding and management of the resulting conflict becomes possible with the development of newer brain structures that also permit the emergence of reciprocity, voluntary choice, language and abstract thought. The dynamic algorithms of our neural architecture are expressed in three ways: graphically, by precise verbal description and, finally, by a mathematical equation representing their interactive social dynamic. The neural dynamic pervades all aspects of our lives.

The second part, made up of nine chapters, explores the applications of the CSN model with its neural equation to economics and free enterprise. The new findings in brain science have a profound message for these disciplines. We have incorrectly defined the basis of economics and free enterprise over the past two centuries as based on a sole self-interest motive. This inaccurate definition derives from a Newtonian perspective adopted long before the emergence of brain science. This still lingering Newtonian perspective sees the shaping dynamic of the market and society in terms analogous to the forces of physics. It, thereby, misses the organic nature of the neural algorithms and ignores the very prominent mammalian affectional circuitry of the brain that drives a second primary motive of empathy or other-interest.

The market could never have evolved or continued without empathy. We would not know what to do or how to do it to respond to the needs of others. Without empathy we simply would lack the neural equipment to be engaged—we would not care. The market evolved out of family giving and sharing motivated by the dynamic of our neural architecture—the tug and pull between the dual primary motives of self-preservation and affection, ego and empathy, or self- and other-interest. The omission of empathy as a balancing primary motive in the structure and behavior of the market is not only inaccurate scientifically, it has produced negative side effects. The omission of empathy has skewed market behavior toward greed and cynicism, damaging public trust in the commercial market system. It has further given our very valuable democratic free enterprise system an inaccurate and unfavorable press among developing nations as fundamentally materialistic, exploitative, and non-caring. We need to correct both the inaccurate science as well as the accompanying negative side effects.

The chapters of part three examine the role of the consilient social brain in the management and creation of scarcity from the perspective of political economy and institutional economics. Human society, to include the economic and political aspects, is a product of the human brain interacting with like brains under environmental constraints. There is no other possible source. There are no social, economic, or political essences or universals existing out there in a positivist, mechanical world waiting to be discovered. The human brain functions, among other things, as a normative, evaluative, and environment-shaping organ based upon its evolved mechanisms to assure survival of the individual and the species within the existing constraints. All aspects of human society, then, are normatively based. There is no such thing as a positivist, value-free human politics, economics, or any other aspect of society.

The brain evolved as a scarcity-coping organ in a primarily kinship based foraging society where sharing or reciprocity was essential to survival and which reinforced the adaptive evolution of the mammalian characteristics of self-preservation and affection. The reciprocal neural algorithms of behavior are a scarcity-coping mechanism. Reinforced, however, by emphasis on the self-interested logic of a limitless productivity as an end in itself, the brain becomes a scarcity-generating mechanism. The greater part of scarcity, therefore, is self-generated and reinforced by our prevailing politico-economic paradigm. A limitless productivity as an end in itself, then, unless modified and properly managed, threatens to take us to the brink of extinction by exhausting the carrying capacity of the environment. Our institutions, our derived environmental constraints, are devised to order the reciprocity dynamic. To the extent that they provide order (regulate), and they invariably do, the institutions are political. To the extent that they impact reciprocity, and they invariably do, they are economic. Institutions, then, are concerned with ordering reciprocity in some way. In that sense they are politico-economic.

Chapters 19 and 20 in part three examine the new institutional economics from the perspectives of Oliver Williamson and Douglass North. Although both scholars attempt to deal with the problem of cooperation within a self-maximizing paradigm, they both fall short of the mark. Beneath the assumptions of both scholars lies the implicit, unarticulated dynamic of the reciprocal algorithms of our evolved neural architecture. This shaping reciprocal dynamic is driven by behavioral tension. Transaction costs, added by institutions to the process of exchange, can be linked to and understood in terms of behavioral tension, thus establishing further the dynamic link between brain science and economics. The costly paradox of transaction cost economics is that its emphasis on self-interested opportunism as fundamental has the effect of increasing rather than decreasing such costs.

The chapters, making up part four, apply the new findings in evolutionary neuroscience and the CSN model to the issues of social stratification, political democracy, and global trade. The neural dynamic drives the tendency to reciprocity expressed at the foundation of our social structure, our democracy, as well as their projection into the global arena made both virtual and urgent by the new information technology. The CSN model and the equation of our consilient social brain provide a dynamic framework for explaining and predicting the necessary movement toward a global society.

The final chapters move the analysis into the somewhat softer, but equally important areas of humanity—our sense of justice, our moral consciousness, and ethics. Again, the model and equation of our consilient social brain provide an organizing, illuminating, and guiding framework to explicate these less tangible aspects of our human sociality so important to the rapidly developing global society.

PART I

THE DYNAMIC
OF OUR CONSILIENT SOCIAL BRAIN

2

THE MASLOW HIERARCHY OF NEEDS
VS. MACLEAN'S TRIUNE BRAIN

Confronted with recent advances in the study of the genome, molecular biology, and evolutionary neuroscience, scholars have increasingly challenged the long–prevailing so-called standard social science model of human nature that sees our brain as a *tabula rasa* or blank slate. In political science, Elliott White (1992), acknowledged the end of the empty organism perspective that had prevailed for the greater part of the 20th century in the form of behaviorist psychology. Focusing on the importance of neurobiology as a necessary foundation for the sciences of human action, to include the science of politics, he wrote: "A science of human life that ignores the brain is akin to a study of the solar system that leaves out the sun."(1992: 1). Primatologist Shirley Strum and social scientist Bruno Latour in their article "Redefining the Social Link from Baboons to Humans," (1991), argued for a performative model of social interaction in which society is continually constructed or performed by active social beings. Popular writer and cognitive scientist Steven Pinker of Massachusetts Institute of Technology, brought the debate into the public forum in his *The Blank Slate: The Modern Denial of Human Nature* (2002).

In an earlier work *How the Mind Works* (1997), Pinker sought to bring together the computational theory of the mind and the emerging discipline of evolutionary psychology with emphasis on information processing as the primary function of an evolved, adaptive modular brain. The concept of the brain, as a set of information-processing modules evolved independently to cope with specific adaptive problems as set out by Pinker and others, has become the standard for cognitive as well as evolutionary psychology (see, especially Barkow, et al., 1992; Cosmides & Tooby, 1989; Tooby & Cosmides, 1989; Tooby & Devore, 1987). Cognitive science, combining the insights of evolutionary psychology, seeks to discover how the mind works by, in Pinker's words, "reverse engineering." That is, it identifies adaptive behaviors in the evolutionary environment and then back engineers them to postulate specific modules in the brain to deal specifically with the identified environmental challenges. Although "reverse" or "back engineering" sounds technical and scientific, it often amounts to no more than the mere assertion of highly dubious neural connections or substrates. This approach may have its utility but it must be used with care. Its rather indiscriminate usage has led to a proliferation of imaginary modules existing in the brain (e.g., see Panksepp and Panksepp, 2000; de Waal, 2002) without adequate foundations in actual neural circuitry or in keeping with sound evolutionary principles. In fact the "identify a behavior, posit a brain module" approach has been likened to the pseudo-science of phrenology which in the 19th century sought to identify personality traits by examining lumps on cranium (from the perspective of neuroscience, see especially, Friston, 2002).

The new approaches, however, have progressively filled the former empty organism or blank slate concept of the brain and have given us the theoretical and empirical foundations for an active, performing organism. Owing to the overemphasis on cognition as information processing, however, there has been a notable neglect of emotion, consciousness, and subjectivity. In very recent years a complementary literature has emerged that includes the neglected areas of feelings and emotions. Such feelings and emotions must arise from the innate reward and response systems (or modules) that must necessarily exist to give pure cognition or information processing its subjective quality, value, or affective meaning (e.g., Cory, 1999, 2000b; Cory & Gardner, 2002; Edelman & Tononi, 2000; Panksepp, 1998; Damasio, 1994, 1999; LeDoux, 1997; Restak, 1994; Edelman, 1992).

This book carries on this theme of the active, performing organism. It is an effort to further clarify and define the shaping dynamic that proceeds from our evolved modular brain structure to influence our social, economic, and political lives and institutions. It attempts further to integrate the findings of these new approaches with the earlier influential and more vintage insights of psychologist Abraham Maslow and neuroscientist Paul MacLean.

Models from the psychological (to include neuropsychological) sciences, however, have seldom been widely applied to issues of social, economic, and political theory. Among the reasons for this lack of applicability is that psychological models usually focus on the individual. They are constructed at a level of generalization and analysis that makes them unsuitable for theorizing at the higher altitude or level of generalization of these social science disciplines. The Maslow hierarchy of needs and the triune brain concept of MacLean have both been with us for a long time (Maslow's hierarchy for the better part of five decades, MacLean's for the better part of three) and are generally familiar.

MASLOW'S HIERARCHY

In Maslow's theoretical structure, needs are usually organized from bottom to top in the form of a staircase, or stepladder as follows: physiological needs (hunger, thirst), safety needs, belonging or social needs; esteem needs; and the self-actualizing need. Maslow theorized that these needs were emergent: That is, as we satisfied our basic needs of hunger and thirst, our safety needs would then emerge. As we satisfied our newly emerged safety needs, the next level, the belonging or social needs, would come into play. Next came esteem needs, and finally, as these were satisfied, the self-actualizing need at the top of the hierarchy emerged (Maslow, 1943, 1970, 1968).

Maslow's hierarchy has appeared in every basic text on psychology and behavior for the past four decades. It also appears in most texts on organizational behavior. Its influence has been widespread as a behavioral scheme of ready and easy reference. It has also been popularized in casual and impressionistic writing about motivation. Maslow's well-known concept represents one of the earliest comprehensive efforts to develop a model of the human biological inheritance.

The Maslow hierarchy has, however, serious shortcomings that limit its utility for conceptualizing the genetic inheritance. For one thing, it lacks an evolutionary perspective. The hierarchy of needs is presented as a given, disconnected from the evolutionary process which produced it. Secondly, the concept of hierarchy is not fully developed. It does not allow sufficiently for interaction of the levels of hierarchy and does not account for those cases that violate the normal priority of needs (Cory, 1974: 27–29, 85–86; Corning, 1983: 167–172; Maddi, 1989: 110–118; Smith, 1991). Maslow's hierarchy has also been criticized for being culture bound, fitting neatly with particularly the U.S. concept of material achievement and success as a steady stair-step progression of higher development (Yankelovich, 1981). It thereby tends to ignore or diminish the great accomplishments in thought, morality, and service to humanity of many of the great figures of human history (Maddi, 1989). Maslow's hierarchy, with its almost exclusive focus on the individual, affords little insight into the dynamics of social interaction. In its rather long history, despite some attempts, it has failed to become a major influence in socialization or political theory (Zigler and Child, 1973: 33–35; Knutson, 1972: 168–172, 261–263. Davies, 1963, 1991, has made the most consistent effort to apply Maslow's concepts to politics).

MACLEAN'S MODULAR CONCEPT: MISMEASURED AND MISUNDERSTOOD

MacLean's triune brain concept is one of the earliest modular concepts of the brain. Although it has been acknowledged to be the single most influential idea in brain science since World War II (e.g., Durant in Harrington, 1992: 268), it has largely been overlooked by cognitive psychology. In an extreme case it has been summarily and undeservedly rejected as wrong by Steven Pinker in his 1997 book noted earlier. This anomalous situation—in which the pioneering modular statement of brain organization coming from neuroscience itself and providing a natural match with aspects of the modular cognitive approach—has been brought about by a couple of seriously flawed reviews of MacLean's work that appeared in the influential journals *Science* (1990) and *American Scientist* (1992).

The effect of these faulty reviews has been to deny the use of MacLean's very significant research and insights to the researchers in the cognitive psychological as well as the social science community, who relied upon the authority of these prestigious journals. In fact Pinker bases his unfortunate and mistaken rejection of MacLean's thought solely on a reference to the review in *Science* which is the most prejudicial and grossly inaccurate of the two (Pinker, 1997: 370, 580). The detailed and documented rebuttal of these reviews is reported in Appendix I. A considerable, well-deserved, and important resurgence of interest in MacLean's work has occurred in very recent years (e.g. see Damasio, 1999; Lieberman, 2000; Cory, 1999, 2000a,b; Cory and Gardner, 2002; Panksepp, 2002). MacLean's concepts of the limbic system and the triune brain, when properly represented, are soundly grounded in evolutionary neuroscience, and with some clarifications, are the most useful concepts for linking neuroscience with the more highly integrated concepts of the social sciences. The presentation that follows here is adjusted to accommodate criticisms which raise valid questions.

MacLean sees behavior as essentially irrational—motivated and validated by earlier nonverbal brain structures. In fact, this irrationality is a frequent theme of concern to MacLean (1990, 1992). Accordingly, in the few instances when MacLean's triune brain concept has been applied to society and politics, this factor of irrationality has been given major play (e.g., Peterson, 1981, 1983; Pettman, 1975: 153–175). This emphasis on irrationality, however, has obscured much of the potential value of the concept. Extended, elaborated, and applied thoughtfully, MacLean's concept provides the neuroscientific basis for a better understanding of the structure and dynamics of our social, economic, and political lives.

THE INTERCONNECTED, THREE-LEVEL (TRIUNE) BRAIN

In a thoroughgoing, encyclopedic summary of the previous fifty years of brain research, MacLean (1990) documents the human brain as an evolved three-level interconnected, modular structure (Figure 1). This structure includes a component of self-preservational circuitry reflecting gene-based continuity from our ancestral reptiles. The human ancestral line split off from the dinosaur ancestral line during the Permian and Triassic periods between 225–250 million years ago.

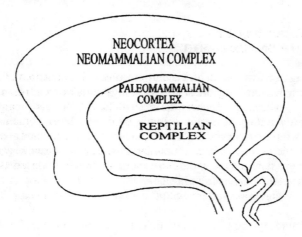

Figure 1. A simplified, modified sketch of the triune brain structure (After MacLean). As represented here the three brain divisions do not constitute distinct additions but rather modifications and elaborations of probable preexisting homologues reflecting phylogenetic continuity.

MacLean called this early ancestral circuitry the R-complex or the protoreptilian complex. In his three-part scheme, MacLean also included a later modified and elaborated mammalian affectional complex, and a most recently modified and elaborated neocortex representing the higher centers of the human brain.

THE EVOLUTION OF INTERCONNECTED TRIALITY

As brain evolution continued in the branching vertebrate line leading to humans, simple protoreptilian brain structure was not replaced. It was modified and elaborated. The protoreptilian structure, then, gave us the substructure and DNA or gene-based continuities (called homologues) for later brain development. It did this while largely retaining its basic character and function. The mammalian modifications and neocortical elaborations that followed reached the greatest development in the brain of humankind. We must understand the qualitative differences of the three levels to appreciate the dynamics of human social experience and behavior.

The protoreptilian brain tissues in humans mainly do the same job they did in our ancestral vertebrates. They run the fundamentals, or daily master routines, of our life-support operations: blood circulation, heartbeat, respiration, basic food getting, reproduction, and defensive behaviors. These were functions and behaviors also necessary in the ancient ancestral reptiles as well as earlier amphibians and fishes. These earlier vertebrates had to do these things to stay alive, reproduce, and become our ancestors.

The next developmental stage of our brain comes from rudimentary mammalian life. MacLean called it the paleo-or "old" mammalian brain. This set of circuits is also known as the limbic system. These limbic tissue-clusters developed from gene-based continuities preexisting in the protoreptilian brain. They included significant elaboration of such physiological structures as the hypothalamus, the amygdala, the hippocampus, the thalamus, and the limbic cingulate cortex.

Behavioral contributions to life from these modified and elaborated paleo-mammalian structures or limbic system included, among other things, the mammalian features (absent in our ancestral vertebrates) of warmbloodedness, nursing, infant care, and extended social bonding. These new characteristics were then neurally integrated with the life-support functional and behavioral circuitry of the protoreptilian brain tissues to create the more complex form of mammals.

The neocortex, which MacLean called the neo- or "new" mammalian brain, is the most recent stage of brain modification and elaboration. This great mass of hemispherical brain matter dominates the skull case of higher primates and humans. It gained its prominence by elaborating the preexisting gene-based continuities present in the brain of earlier vertebrates. Gradually, it overgrew and encased the earlier ("paleo") mammalian and protoreptilian neural tissues. It did not, however, replace them. As a consequence of this neocortical evolution and growth, these older brain parts evolved greater complexity and extensive interconnected circuitry with these new tissue clusters. In that way, they produced the behavioral adaptations necessary to life's increasingly sophisticated circumstances.

REFINING AND DEFINING HUMAN UNIQUENESS

The unique features of our human brain were refined over a period of several million years in a mainly kinship based foraging society where sharing or reciprocity was necessary to our survival. Such sharing and reciprocity strengthened the adaptive evolution of the now combined mammalian characteristics of self-preservation and affection.

Ego and empathy, self-interest and other-interest, are key features of our personal and social behavior. To connect these features to MacLean's concept we need, at this point, a behavioral vocabulary rather than a neurophysiological one. We need a vocabulary that will express what the presence of our protoreptilian self-preserving mechanisms and our paleomammalian affectional brain structures mean for our day-to-day, subjectively experienced, behavioral initiatives and responses to one another and the world we live in. I will draw the behavioral vocabulary from analogy with information and computer technology.

THE SELF-PRESERVING AND AFFECTIONAL PROGRAMMING

Our early vertebrate or reptilian ancestors were cold-blooded and they did not have brain structures for any extended parental caring. Their care of offspring was, in most cases, limited to making a nest or digging a hole to lay eggs in. The eggs were, then, left to hatch on their own. Some reptiles, not knowing their own offspring, would cannibalize them. It was not much of a family life. But the reptiles continued to exist because they produced large numbers of eggs—enough to make sure some offspring survived to reproduce again and continue the species line.

This basic reptilian neural network, plus a group of neural structures clumped together at the forward end of the brain stem and called the basal ganglia, essentially make up our human brain stem. From the mainly survival-centered promptings of these ancestral circuits, as elaborated in our human brain, arise the motivational source for egoistic, surviving, self-interested subjective experience and behaviors. Here we have the cold-blooded, seemingly passionless, single-minded, self-serving behaviors that we have generally associated with the present-day lizard, the snake, and that most maligned of fishes, the shark. And intuitively, we call our fellow humans who behave this way such names as snakes, geckos, and sharks.

Here is a world revolving almost exclusively around matters of self-preservation. The protoreptilian brain structures, then, will be called, following our high tech vocabulary, our self-preservation programming or circuitry.

But we humans are mammals. We not only got the self-preserving circuitry of our early vertebrate ancestors, we got also the circuitry for infant nursing, warmblooded, passionate, body-contacting, behaviors that we share with the lion, the wolf, the primates. The motivational source for nurturing, empathetic, other-interested experiences and behaviors arises from such circuitry.

Here is a world in which nearly single-minded self-preservation is simultaneously complemented and counterpoised by the conflicting demands of affection. The early mammalian modifications, then, will be called our affectional programming or circuitry.[1]

---

[1] Positing the affectional programming draws not only upon current neuroscience but also the extensive literature on the concepts of social bonding and attachment, especially the work done on higher primates and man. For fundamental work on lower animals see the pioneering work of the Austrian ethologist and Nobel prize winner Konrad Lorenz (1970 & 1971). Particularly relevant here would be the work of psychologist, Harry F. Harlow on the nature of love and attachment in rhesus/macaque monkeys (1965, 1986). Harlow described five affectional systems in monkeys—maternal, mother-infant, age-mate, heterosexual, and paternal

OUR EVOLVED BRAIN AND BEHAVIORAL CONFLICT

These core behavioral programs within us are built up of many contributing subroutines of our neural architecture. Neuroscientist Jaak Panksepp calls such programs global-state variables. He states that a network doctrine is needed to grasp such system-wide emergent dynamics (2002: xiv). These global-state circuits act as dynamic factors of our behavior. They are energy-driven by our cellular as well as overall bodily processes of metabolism, or energy production, as mediated by *hormones, neurotransmitters, and neural architecture.* And each is an inseparable part of our makeup, because each is "wired into" our brain structure by the process of evolution.

The degree of gene control, however, does vary. Older brain parts, like the brain stem and parts of the limbic system, long established and necessary for survival, are under tighter gene control. Other more recent tissues, especially the higher centers of the neocortex, depend a lot on development and experience.

We are set up for behavioral conflict simply by the presence of these two global-state energy-driven modular programs in our lives—up and running, perhaps, even before birth. Their mere physical presence sets us up for a life of inner and outer struggle, as we are driven by and respond to their contending demands.

Conflict is more than an externally observed, objective ethical, moral, or decision-making dilemma as much modern science tends to see it. We also feel it very strongly within ourselves. That is, inwardly or *subjectively,* we get feelings of satisfaction when we can express our felt motives. On the other hand, we get feelings of frustration when we cannot express our self-preservation or affectionate impulses in the behavioral initiatives and responses we wish to make.

Behavioral tension then arises. We experience such behavioral tension as frustration, anxiety, or anger. And it arises whenever one of our two fundamental behavioral programs—self-preservation or affection—is activated but meets with some resistance or difficulty that prevents its satisfactory expression. This subjective tension becomes most paralyzing when both programs are activated and seek contending or incompatible responses *within a single situation.* Caught between "I want to" and "I can't"—for example, "I want to help him/her, but I can't surrender my needs"—we agonize. Whether

---

(1986). In this chapter I have proposed one all- inclusive affectional program. It is personally interesting to me that Crews (1997) argues that affiliative behaviors evolved from reproductive behaviors. This is a position that I took in 1974 in the first version of the conflict systems neurobehavioral model (Cory, 1974) presented in this chapter. There has been a recent resurgence of interest in the evolutionary biological basis of affection and empathy, especially in primates (e.g., Goodall, 1986; de Waal, 1996, Boehm, 1999). In the case of humans, the work of Spitz (1965) and British psychiatrist John Bowlby (1969, 1988) is of special interest. All the foregoing reflect field observations, experimental behavioral observations and clinical work. None of them penetrate the brain itself. More recent work in computer modeling of neural processes has focused primarily on cognition and avoided dealing with the more complex issues of affiliation and emotion. For example, Churchland and Sejnowski in their extensive and well-known work on the computational brain acknowledge the neglect of these critical areas (1992: 413). From the standpoint of neuroscience, it is also notable that Kandel, Schwartz, and Jessell, authors of the most widely used text on introductory neuroscience also show this neglect (1995). See also Damasio (1999). Extensive research has been done on the role of the amygdala in emotion, but such research has generally focused on the emotion of fear (LeDoux, 1997). The neglect is not difficult to explain. Research on such complex pathways within the brain, in spite of great progress in recent years, is still in its early stages. The unknowns are still very vast. Currently the best summary of research in neuroscience on the nurturing, caring, family-related behavior are contained in Panksepp (1998); Carter (1997); Numan & Sheehan (1997); Fleming, et al., (1996); MacLean (1990: 380–410; 520–562). For a popular treatment see Taylor (2002).

this tension arises through the blocked expression of a single impulse or the simultaneous but mutually exclusive urgings of two competing impulses, whenever it continues unresolved or unmanaged it leads to the worsening condition of behavioral stress.

THE BLESSING OF TENSION AND STRESS

The evolutionary process by which these two opposite global-state promptings of self-preservation and affection were combined in us gave us a great survival advantage. Their combined dynamic binds us together in social interaction and provides us with a wide range of behavioral responses to our environment. Our naturally conflicting programs are a curse, then, only to the extent that we fail to recognize them as a blessing. Our self-preservation and affection programs allow us a highly advanced sensitivity to our environment. They keep our interactive social behaviors within survival limits by giving us the ability to understand and appreciate the survival requirements of others. Ironically, the accompanying behavioral tension—*even the stress!*—is an integral part of this useful function. It allows us to more quickly evaluate our behavior and the effect it is having on ourselves and others.

Behavioral tension serves as an internal emotional compass that we can use to guide ourselves through the often complicated and treacherous pathways of interpersonal relations.

Behavioral stress tells us that we are exceeding safe limits for ourselves and others, and even for our larger social, economic, and political structures.

At this point we have the fundamentals of our behavioral dynamic. But if we are to manage this conflicting circuitry, we need to add another element. We need a certain level of consciousness. Maybe we should best think of it as self-aware consciousness.

CONFLICT OR CHOICE: THE MULE'S DILEMMA

Self-aware consciousness gives us the ability to talk about and generalize our internally felt motives. If all we had were the conflicting programs of self-preservation and affection, we would, be among the animals whose behaviors are run automatically by instinct. We would be driven by the urgings of fight, or flight, or bondedness and the decision would be made for us by preset neural priorities.

With self-conscious awareness, however, we face the dilemma of choice. Perhaps, every so often, we would, nevertheless, be like the conflicted mule of southern farmland tradition, who looked back and forth between water and hay, unable to move or make a choice. We, too, might be caught in the conflict of those urgings, unable to make a decision.

What gives us the power to rise above the mule's dilemma—to overcome it? What makes the difference between instinctual conflict and the power of choice? These questions take us to the next chapter.

3

THE CONFLICT SYSTEMS
NEUROBEHAVIORAL MODEL

As scientists we don't know whether kindred mammals—cats, dogs, mules, elephants, dolphins, chimpanzees, and others—with paleomammalian brain structures, with self-preservation and affection circuitry, just act on preset neuronal priorities or whether they experience conscious conflict and must choose among such conflicting behavioral priorities. We may suspect that these mammals have conflict. Or we may protest from the perspective of *homo arrogance* that they do not. It's a tough question for scientists. Science has not yet developed good interviewing techniques for these other mammals.

There is, however, absolutely no doubt about us humans. We certainly do. We can reflect and generalize not only upon our choices, but upon the meanings they have for our personal lives as well as our species' existence and significance.[2] And it is in that capacity to reflect, to self-consciously experience, generalize, and decide upon the tug-and-pull of our conflicting urgings, that we come to third stage of brain development in MacLean's model: the neomammalian or "new" mammalian brain structures—what I call the executive programming or circuitry.[3]

THE CONFLICT SYSTEMS NEUROBEHAVIORAL (CSN) MODEL

The neural circuitry that produces consciousness is still not well understood. For

---

[2] In cognitive neuroscience brain modules are commonly seen as competing and also cooperating (e.g., see Crick, 1994; Baars, 1997). Several researchers have also posited the dynamic of conflicting modules, vying for ascendancy in behavior and consciousness (e.g., Edelman & Tononi, 2000; Edelman, 1992; Dennett, 1998; Pinker, 1997: 58, 65).

[3] The evolution of the neocortex, our big brain, was in all probability greatly enhanced by the tug and pull of our conflicting programs. Humphrey (1976) sees the function of the intellect providing the ability to cope with problems of interpersonal relationships. See also the discussion in Masters (1989: 16–26) and Erdal and Whiten (1996). Cummins (1998) argues that interpersonal relationships, competing and cooperating with conspecifics for limited resources, is the chief problem confronting social mammals. Cummins concentrates on dominance hierarchies which she sees as dynamic rather than static.

most of the twentieth century scientists avoided taking up the question. It was simply too difficult and there were no good tools for studying it. In the last couple of decades, however, new techniques like brain imaging have been developed. Besides, sometimes scientific ideas just have to wait their time to become fashionable. The time is ripe at long last for consciousness. The study is now fashionable and many scientists are doing it very seriously.

Although the emerging circuitry producing consciousness is still unclear, I follow the position here that there is no homunculus—meaning from the Latin, "little artificial person"—or other Cartesian dualistic process involved. Such ideas as a little observer inside our heads have plagued writers on consciousness for centuries. It still does today. Even hard-nosed scientists occasionally get caught up in it. After all, there has to be someone in there to see and experience what is going on.

The French Renaissance philosopher, René Descartes (1596–1650), left us a legacy of mischief when he separated body from mind in the 17th century. Descartes, with his famous phrase *cogito ergo sum*—I think therefore, I am—saw the only certain reality as mind. Mind, as the only certain reality, thus, became separated from the body, to include the brain. Body and brain, these physical or material manifestations, from Descartes' view, had a more dubious reality status. Descartes' split of mind and body at that time also fit well the church's doctrine of the soul as existing separately from the body. Descartes, in the early Renaissance, was unable to detach himself from the church tradition.

Descartes, then, bequeathed us the duality of mind and body that still haunts us today when we try to come to grips scientifically with the question of consciousness. Like Descartes, we all *know* we have consciousness. But we, as scientific moderns, cannot stand firmly and convincingly on his *cogito ergo sum*. The assertion from intuition simply doesn't meet the standards of empirical evidence that we demand today. On the other hand, it is pretty easy to prove that bodies and brains have reality.

The neural substrate of consciousness is still a matter of considerable speculation and debate (e.g., see Edelman & Tononi, 2000; Cory, 2000a; Damasio, 1999, 1994; Searle, 1997; Smith, 1996). Nevertheless, it seems that our expanded and elaborated neocortex (or isocortex), anchored in and interconnected with our earlier mammalian and protoreptilian brain systems, is part of the "dynamic core" (Edelman & Tononi, 2000; cf. Dennett, 1998) necessary to our *self-aware* or *self-reflective* consciousness.

As well, our elaborated neocortex provides us with the evolutionarily unique and powerful ability to use verbal and symbolic language.[4] We can, thus, create concepts and ideas by which to interpret our consciousness. We can describe the feelings, motives, and behaviors that arise within us and in response to our social and environmental

---

[4] A language module did not, of course, pop out of nowhere and appear in the neocortex. The capacity for spoken language involved modifications of supporting anatomical structures including the laryngeal tract, tongue, velum (which can seal the nose from the mouth) and the neural connections that tied in with motor areas necessary for the production of speech. These all evolved relatively concomitantly from the hominid ancestral line and, combined with the elaboration of the neocortical structures of thought and syntax, made language possible. This example of the complexity of language development provides a caveat to avoid overly simplistic one for one specialized module for specific behavioral or functional adaptation positions. The work of Philip Lieberman, a linguistic psychologist at Brown University, is especially relevant for the understanding of this very complex language capability. See the up-to-date treatment of these issues in Lieberman' s *Eve Spoke* (1998).

experiences. It is with this so-called executive programming that we acquire the ability to name, to comment upon, to *generalize*[5] and to *choose* between our contending sets of behavioral impulses. Self-preservation is commonly called, at a high level of cognitive generalization, "egoistic" or "self-interested" behavior. We call affection, at an equally high level of cognitive generalization, "empathetic" or "other-interested" behavior. *Empathy allows us the critical social capacity to enter into or respond emotionally to another's self-interest as well as other emotional states.*[6]

Although the positioning of ego and empathy in Figure 2 (facing the reader) is primarily for illustrative purposes only and is not intended to suggest a definitive lateralization, there is evidence to suggest that the right hemisphere is favored for emotion and the left for more analytical self-preserving behaviors (e.g., see Damasio, 1994; Tucker, Luu, & Pribram, 1995; Brownell & Martino, 1998). However, Heller, et al. (1998), after noting that it is well established that particular regions of the right hemisphere are specialized to interpret and express emotional information, argue that the total experience of emotion is not lateralized but involves dynamic interactions between forward and posterior regions of both hemispheres as well as subcortical (limbic) structures. Such complex, highly generalized capacities as ego and empathy should more safely be thought of as engaging the interaction of both hemispheres. Davidson (1995),

---

[5] The ability to self-consciously generalize is apparently a unique gift of the neocortex with it billions of neurons interconnected into hierarchical networks. The level of generalization issue in all our disciplines likely springs from this. That is, we can move from parts to wholes in generalizing and from wholes to parts in analyzing freely up and down throughout our neural networks. Generalizing (and implicitly analyzing) has been recognized by scholars in many disciplines as perhaps the defining characteristic of the human brain (e.g., Hofstader, 1995: 75; Einstein, 1954: 293). This generalizing capacity loosens up the tight wiring of routines and characteristics of earlier brain structures and allows us to manage and, to some degree, overcome the mechanisms that we inherited in common with kindred species (e.g., see Panksepp, 1998: 301). In other words, the generalizing, analyzing capacities of the neocortex change the rules of the game for us humans by freeing us up from the blind tyranny of primitive mechanisms. This capacity must always be weighed when trying to apply findings in, for example, even primate ethology to humans. One of the reasons our feelings and motives are so difficult to verbalize and communicate to others is probably because the earlier evolved brain(reptilian and limbic) systems are nonverbal. Their input enters the neocortex through neural pathways as inarticulate urgings, feelings. It falls to the neocortex with its verbal and generalizing ability to develop words and concepts to attempt to understand, represent, and convey these inarticulate urgings. MacLean (1992: 58) states that the triune brain structure provides us with the inheritance of three mentalities, two of which lack the capacity for verbal communication.

[6] My use of the term empathy here includes the affectional feelings of sympathy which are dependent upon empathy, plus cognitive aspects (Hoffman, 1981, 2000). Losco has noted that empathy, amplified by cognitive processes, could serve as an evolved mediator of pro-social behavior (1986: 125). Empathy and sympathy are frequently used inclusively, especially in more recent writing (Eisenberg, 1994; Batson, 1991). For this reason, in order to suggest the inclusion of sympathy, I have chosen to use the term empathetic rather than the more usual empathic. The positing of the ego and empathy dynamic goes back to the historical juxtaposition of self-interest or egoism and sympathy or fellow-feeling in the thought of David Hume, Adam Smith, and Schopenhauer (Wispe 1991). The present articulation goes back to my doctoral thesis done at Stanford University (1974). The conflict systems neurobehavioral model was applied in several programs which I authored for corporate management training through the education and consulting corporation United States Education Systems during the period 1976–85. Roger Masters (1989) has also noted the possible innate roots of contradictory impulses to include selfishness and cooperative or altruistic behavior in human nature. Trudi Miller (1993) has also drawn our attention to this historical duality and suggested its applicability for today. Neither Hume, Smith, Schopenhauer, Wispe, Masters, nor Miller, however, attempted to articulate a model of behavior based upon this duality, or as MacLean calls it "triality," acknowledging the role of the neocortex in articulating the otherwise nonverbal urgings (1993).

for example, hypothesizes that the left and right anterior regions of the brain are key components of an affective regulatory system for approach and avoidance behaviors.

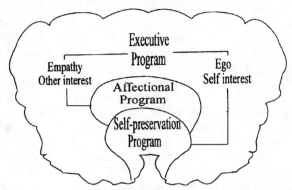

Figure 2. The Conflict Systems Neurobehavioral Model. A simplified cutaway representation of the brain showing the behavioral programs and the derivation of Ego/self-interested and Empathy/other-interested motives and behaviors. I should note that earlier models, e.g., Freud (id, ego, and superego) postulated three-part conflictual models. Freud, however, was unable to tie his model to brain circuitry and it remained ungrounded in neural science because brain research had simply not advanced to that point.

In other words, our executive programming, especially our frontal cortex,[7] has the capability and the responsibility for cognitively representing these limbic and protoreptilian brain connections and inputs and making what may be thought of as our moral as well as rational choices among our conflicting, impulsive, and irrational or nonrational motivations. This self conscious, generalizing, choosing capacity accompanied, of course, with language, is what differentiates us from even closely related primate species and makes findings in primate behavior, although highly interesting and unquestionably important, insufficient in themselves to fully understand and account for human behavior.

EXECUTIVE PROGRAMMING AND NEURAL NETWORKS

According to Joaquin Fuster, of the Neuropsychiatric Institute, UCLA, the frontal cortex constitutes the highest level of a hierarchy of neural structures—reaching down to the motoneurons and anterior roots of the spinal cord—that represents and executes the actions of the organism. Because of its topmost position in this neural hierarchy, the frontal cortex has been named the "executive of the brain and the organ of creativity." (1999: 187; see also Goldberg, 2001).

---

[7] The frontal neocortex especially has long been recognized to be involved in executive functions. See the excellent summary and discussion of findings in Miller & Cummings (1999), Fuster (1997: 150–184). See also Pribram (1973, 1994). Although executive function is frequently equated with frontal cortex function, Eslinger (1996) reminds us that the neural substrate of executive functions is better conceptualized as a neural network which includes the synchronized activity of multiple regions, cortical and subcortical (1996: 392). Eslinger also notes the usual neglect of critically important affectively based empathy and social and interpersonal behaviors in neuropsychological, information-processing, and behavioral approaches (390–391).

Fuster, thus, designates the frontal neocortex as the neural substrate for executive functioning (cf. Pribram, 1973, 1994). There are, however, a number of competing models for executive functioning, some tied to neural substrate, some not. Bernard Baars and colleagues of the Wright Institute have proposed a Neural Global Workspace Model (GW), which combines the concepts of attention, working memory, and executive function into a theater metaphor. Baars and colleagues (Newman, et al., 1997; cf., Harth, 1997) review other neuroscience and neural network models that deal with attention, binding, resource allocation, and gating that share significant features with their own GW model for conscious attention (for an alternative model based on an evolutionary and clinical approaches and which draws upon MacLean's triune concept, see Mirsky, 1996).[8] The authors acknowledge that the models they present implement only partial aspects of their GW theory. Notably neglected are the influences of memory and affective systems upon the stream of consciousness (1997: 1205). The CSN model presented in this paper attempts to incorporate the affective (generalized into empathy) neural substrate necessary to initiate and maintain sociality.

It is noteworthy that distributed artificial intelligence (DIA) models more closely approximate interpersonal behavior in that they seem to reflect an effort at intelligent balance between the competitive self-interest and cooperation which is necessary to the operation of complex social organizations (Newman, et al. 1997: 1196; Durfee, 1993).

Underpinning the CSN model, the neural substrate for self-survival (generalized as ego) mechanisms may proceed from circuits in the basal ganglia and brain stem (protoreptilian complex) through connections with the amygdala, other limbic structures (early mammalian complex), and probable cortical representations which add emotion or passion (see Kandel, et al., 1995: 595–612), ultimately to be gated into the frontal cortex by thalamocortical circuitry (e.g., see Sherman & Guillery, 2001; Baars, 1997, 1988; LaBerge, 1995; Crick, 1994).

Likewise, the mammalian nurturing (affectional) substrate and its associated motivation, a fundamental component underlying empathy, may originate in the septal and medial preoptic limbic (see Fleming, et al., 1996; Numan,1994; Numan & Sheehan, 1997) areas, proceed through hippocampal and amygdaloid circuitry (Bachevalier, 2000; Brothers, 1989) as well as other limbic structures, and in turn, be gated into the orbital and frontal cortex by neuromodulating thalamocortical circuits (to include the cingulate cortex), where the conflict with egoistic inputs is resolved in the executive or Global Workspace of conscious self-awareness. The neuromodulating and gating of *affect* as well as cognition by the thalamocortical circuitry is supported by neurologists Devinsky and Luciano (1993), who report that the limbic cingulate cortex, a cortical structure closely associated with the limbic thalamus, can be seen as both an *amplifier* and a filter, which joins *affect* and *intellect* interconnecting the *emotional and cognitive components of the mind* (1993: 549).

Tucker, Luu, and Pribram (1995) speculate that the network architecture of the frontal lobes reflects dual limbic origins of the frontal cortex. Specifically, the authors speculate that two limbic-cortical pathways apply different motivational biases to direct the frontal lobe representation of working memory. They suggest that the dorsal limbic mechanisms projecting through the cingulate gyrus may be influenced by hedonic evaluations, *social*

---

[8]   Levine (1986) has also considered MacLean's triune modular concept as a useful tool in network modeling.

attachments, initiating a mode of motor control that is holistic and impulsive. On the other hand, they suggest that the ventral limbic pathway from the amygdala to the orbital frontal cortex may implement a more restricted mode of motor control reflecting the adaptive constraints of *self-preservation* (1995: 233–234). The orbital frontal cortex via its connections to the anterior cingulate gyrus, amygdala and other limbic structures seems especially important to the interaction of ego and empathy (Eisler & Levine, 2002; Weisfeld, 2002; Schnider & Gutbrod, 1999; Fuster, 1999; Damasio, 1994). Such findings are consistent with the CSN model in which ego and empathy represent conflicting subcortical inputs into the cortical executive. As noted, several researchers have posited the dynamic of conflicting modules, vying for ascendency in behavior and consciousness (e.g., Edelman & Tononi, 2000; Dennett, 1998; Pinker, 1997; Edelman, 1992;).

Although it is beyond the scope of this chapter to attempt to deal with the as yet partially understood detailed electrochemical physiology of such egoistic/empathetic conflict, it is appropriate to acknowledge that such behavior is made possible in part by the complex electro-chemical excitatory and inhibitory interactions among groups of interconnected neurons (e.g., see the discussions in Koch, 1999; Cowan, et al., 1997; Fuster, 1997: 102–149; Gutnick & Mody, 1995).

The role of hormones and neurotransmitters must also be acknowledged in any complete analysis. For instance, from the egoistic perspective, testosterone is associated with competitiveness and power urges. Serotonin levels in humans seem related to confidence and self-esteem. On the empathetic side, oxytocin, arginine vasopressin, and prolactin are important to pair bonding and maternal as well as paternal caring behavior. Opioids (endorphins and enkaphalins) seem important to positive social relationships. For readers interested in more detail, two recent and wide-ranging volumes update the research focusing specifically on affiliation and affection: Carter, et al., (1997), *The Integrative Neurobiology of Affiliation*, and Panksepp (1998), *Affective Neuroscience*. Panksepp especially speculates on the contrast between testosterone-driven power urges and oxytocin and opioid mediated affectional behavior (1998: 250–259; see also Toates 2001). Damasio reminds us, however, that there is a popular tendency to overemphasize the efficacy of hormones by themselves. Their action depends upon neural architecture and their effects may vary in different brain regions (1994: 77–78; cf., Kolb, et al., 2003, 1998).

THE MAJOR RANGES OF
RECIPROCAL, CONFLICT BEHAVIOR

The two master programs of self-preservation and affection that have been wired into our brain structure operate dynamically according to a set of behavioral rules, procedures, or algorithms. We experience the workings of these algorithms internally. We also express them externally in our interpersonal behavior. We need to understand the workings and applications of these algorithms to grasp the role of conflict, tension, and stress in our personal and interactive lives.

The major ranges of the CSN model (Figure 3) show graphically the features of this ego-empathy dynamic. In the display, both internally felt as well as interpersonal behavior is divided from right to left into three main ranges. From right to left, they are the egoistic range, the dynamic balance range, and the empathetic range. Each range represents a varying mix of egoistically and empathetically motivated behaviors. The solid line stands for ego and pivots on the word "ego" in the executive program of the brain diagram. The broken line stands for empathy and pivots on the word "empathy" in the diagram.[9]

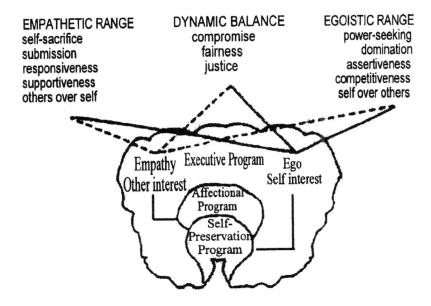

Figure 3. The Major Ranges of Reciprocal, Conflict Behavior.

The Egoistic Range

The egoistic range indicates behavior dominated by our self-preservation circuitry. Since the two behavioral programs are locked in inseparable unity, empathy is present here, but to a lesser degree. Behavior in this range is self-centered or self-interested. It may tend, for example, to be dominating, power-seeking, or even attacking, where empathy is less. When empathy is increased, ego behavior will become less harsh. It may, then, be described more moderately as controlling, competitive, or assertive. As empathy is gradually increased, the intersection of the two lines of the diagram will move toward the range of dynamic balance. That is, ego behavior will be softened as empathy is added. But the defining characteristic of the egoistic, self-interested range is *self-over-others.* Whether we are blatantly power-seeking or more moderately assertive, in this range we

---

[9] The dynamic of the model, the tug and pull of ego and empathy, self- and other-interest allows the expression of the mix of motive and behavior as a range or spectrum. The usual dichotomizing of self-interest and altruism is seen only at the extremes of ranges. All or most of behavior is a mix of varying proportions. Jencks (1990: 53–54) also notes that every motive or act falls somewhere on a spectrum or range between the extremes of selfishness and unselfishness. Teske (1997) sees a blend of self-and other-interest in his identity construction concept. For a neural network modeling of the dynamic see Levine & Jani (2002).

are putting ourselves, our own priorities, objectives, and feelings, ahead of others.

The Empathetic Range

The empathetic range represents behavior weighted in favor of empathy. Ego is present, but is taking a back seat. When ego is present minimally, empathetic behavior may tend to extremes of self-sacrifice and submission. When ego is increased, empathetic behaviors are moderated. We can then describe them as supportive, responsive, or any of a variety of "others first" behaviors. As the influence of ego is gradually added, empathetic behavior will approach the range of dynamic balance. In the empathetic range, the key phrase to remember is *others-over-self* or others first. Whether we are at the extreme of self-sacrifice or more moderately responsive, we are putting the priorities of others ahead of our own.

The Dynamic Balance Range

The range of dynamic balance represents a working balance between ego and empathy. At this point our behavioral circuitries are operating in roughly equal measure. I speak of "working," "rough," or "dynamic" because the tug-and-pull between the two programs continues ceaselessly. The dynamic nature of the neural architecture means that "perfect" balance may be a theoretical point, unattainable in practice. Our more balanced behavior tends to express equality, justice, sharing, and other behaviors that show respect for ourselves and others. In fact, respect for self and others is the keynote of the range of dynamic balance.

Behavioral Tension and Energy or Activity Level

The extent to which the circuits of self-preservation and affection, ego and empathy, are out of balance, or pulling against each other, is a measure of our behavioral tension. We experience this behavioral tension, both internally and between ourselves and others, in any relationship or interaction. Unmanaged or excessive tension becomes, of course, behavioral stress.

But that is not all. Important also is the amount of energy we give to the interaction or the relationship. The amount of energy we put into any activity depends mostly upon how important we think it is. Or how enthusiastically we feel about it. In competitive sports or contests, we can easily see the differences in energy. In intellectual contests, like chess, the energy invested may be intense, but much less obvious.

From the descriptions given above we can put together the reciprocal algorithms of our social behavior. These algorithms are detailed in the next chapter.

4

THE GLOBAL-STATE ALGORITHMS
OF RECIPROCAL BEHAVIOR

In beginning this chapter, I feel obligated to clarify the meaning of algorithm. Although unfamiliar to many of my generation, the word *algorithm* has come into popular parlance with the rise of computers and information technology. In a sense it is a buzzword, a word of currency and sophistication. When you use it, you let everyone know that you are "in the know"—technologically "cool," perhaps. Let's look deeper.

THE ORIGIN OF ALGORITHM

Because of its recent and current celebrity, some people think of algorithm as a new word. Some even see it as a possible acronym put together from parts of other words. Looking back into the history books a couple of millennia, however, we find that the honors must go to a Persian mathematician of the ninth century. His name is recorded as Mohammed al-Khowarizmi. Through twists and turns of fate plus the vagaries of translation, his name has come down to us in the present form that the venerable Persian would probably not recognize.

But al-Khowarizmi gave us the formal procedures for solving standard problems of arithmetic: addition, subtraction, multiplication, and division. Procedures or processes that every schoolchild takes for granted today. At the time, however, it was a significant achievement.

Algorithm, then, originated as a way or method of solving math problems, usually by breaking them down into simpler sequential steps. Its usage, however, has now become extended. In computer science we use the word to describe the various step by step procedures for solving problems so that they can be programmed into computers.

Some writers, however, have taken the meaning even further. David Harel of the Weizmann Institute of Science in Israel, for instance, applies algorithms to human decision-making in most areas of life. Harel sees algorithms applicable not only in business, science, and technology, but also to such ordinary things as looking up a telephone number, filling out a form—even cooking. Algorithms have, in fact, been compared to recipes that provide a step by step process for making dishes for the family dinner (Harel 1987).[10]

Algorithm, then, has become a flexible term that can tame many variable processes. That is why I have chosen to use it in describing the interactive dynamic of our neural architecture. In an earlier 1992 publication, *Rescuing Capitalist Free Enterprise for the Twenty-First Century*, I called the neural dynamic the *laws* of reciprocal behavior. This was, of course, by analogy with the laws of the physical sciences. Although the laws of physics and the interactive dynamic of our neural architecture are undoubtedly linked, the neural dynamic as the product of organic evolution is more variable. This variability makes the use of the word *laws* somewhat misleading. Algorithm offers the better choice to reflect the variability of the neural dynamic. I will return to this subject in more detail in a later chapter.

THE ALGORITHMIC NEURAL DYNAMIC

From Figure 3, representing the major ranges of behavior, we saw the dynamic of our neural architecture displayed graphically. Here, I will supplement that visual reference by a precise verbal description of that global-state, interactive dynamic.

From the dynamic interplay of ego, empathy, and activity level come a series of algorithmic rule statements.

The first algorithm describes the egoistic range:

1.   Self-interested, egoistic behavior, because it lacks empathy to some degree, creates tension within ourselves and between our selves and others. The tension increases from low to high activity levels. And it increases as we move toward the extremes of ego.

Within ourselves, the tension created by the tug of neglected empathy is experienced as a feeling of obligation to others or an expectation that they might wish to "even the score" with us.

Within others, the tension created by our self-interested behavior is experienced as a feeling of imposition or hurt, accompanied by an urge to "even the score."

Children often reveal the dynamic of such behavior in a clear, unsophisticated form. Imagine two children playing on the living-room floor. One hits the other. The second child hits back, responding in kind. Or the children may not hit each other at all. One might instead call the other a bad name. The second child reciprocates, kicking off a round of escalating name-calling. One child may eventually feel unable to even the score and will complain to a parent to intervene. Most of us have experienced such give-and-take as children. Surely, we have seen it countless times in our own children and grandchildren.

Similar behavior is embarrassingly observable among adults. It can be seen in husband and wife arguments, bar fights, hockey games, political campaigns, even in sophisticated lawsuits. The rule operates not only in such highly visible conflict situations, but also in very subtle interactions—in the small behavioral exchanges, the ongoing give-and-take of all interpersonal relations.

---

[10] See Berlinski (2000) for a readable treatment of algorithms in computers.

Expressive of the underlying conflictual excitatory/inhibitory dynamic of the neural architecture, we can say that

The reactions that build in ourselves and others do so potentially in proportion to the behavioral tension created by egoistic, self-interested behavior.

That is, the harder I hit you, the harder you hit me in return. Or the fouler a name you call me, the fouler a name I call you in return. Or perhaps with more sophistication, I resolve the tension in me by an act of visible "superiority." I ignore you—although I *could* call you an even fouler name, if I chose.

The second algorithm describes the empathetic range—behavior on the other side of the scale:

2.   Empathetic behavior, because it denies ego or self-interest to some degree, also creates tension within ourselves and others. This tension, likewise, increases as activity levels increase and as we move toward extremes of empathy.
     Within ourselves, the tension created by the tug of the neglected self-interest (ego) is experienced as a feeling that "others owe us one" and a growing need to "collect our due." This tension, especially if it continues over time, may be experienced as resentment at being exploited, taken for granted, not appreciated, or victimized by others.
     Within others, the tension created is experienced as a sense of obligation toward us.
     The reactions that build in ourselves and others, again, are in proportion to the behavioral tension created. And again, the unmanaged, or excessive tension is experienced as behavioral stress.

When we do things for others—give them things, make personal sacrifices for them—it can make us feel righteous, affectionate, loving. But we *do* want a payback. That's the tug of self-interest. It can be very slight, hardly noticeable at first. But let the giving, the self-sacrifice, go on for a while, unacknowledged or unappreciated (that is, without payback to the ego), and see how we begin to feel.

The tension, the stress, starts to show. We complain that others are taking advantage of us, taking us for granted, victimizing us. Self-interest cannot be long short-changed without demanding its due. We may eventually relieve the stress by blowing up at those we have been serving—accusing them of ingratitude, withdrawing our favors, or kicking them out of the house. Or we may sandbag the stress, letting it eat away at our dispositions, our bodies.

On the other hand, when we do things for others, they often feel obliged to return the favor in some form to avoid being left with an uneasy sense of debt. Gift-giving notoriously stimulates the receiver to feel the need to reciprocate. Think of the times when you have received a holiday gift from someone for whom you had failed to buy a gift. Sometimes the sense of obligation prompted by the empathetic acts of others can become a nuisance.

The third algorithmic rule statement describes the range of dynamic balance; that is, the relative balance between our contending motives:

3.   Behavior in the range of dynamic balance expresses the approximate balance of ego and empathy. It is the position of least behavioral tension. Within ourselves and others, it creates feelings of mutuality and shared respect.

For most of us it is an especially satisfying experience to interact with others in equality, with no sense of obligation, superiority or inferiority. To work together in common humanity, in common cause, is to experience behavioral dynamic balance. Of course, there are many versions of the experience of dynamic balance: the shared pride of parents in helping their child achieve, the joy of athletes in playing well as a team, the satisfaction of coworkers in working together successfully on an important project.[11]

RECIPROCITY THROUGH CONFLICT

These algorithms of behavior operate in the smallest interactions, the vignettes, of everyday personal life. The dynamic of behavioral tension provides that for every interpersonal act, there is a balancing reciprocal. A self-interested act requires an empathetic reciprocal for balance. An empathetic act, likewise, requires a balancing self-interested reciprocal. This reciprocity goes back and forth many times even in a short conversation. Without the reciprocal, tension builds, stress accumulates, and either confrontation or withdrawal results. If not, and the relationship continues, it becomes a tense and stressful one of inequality or domination/submission, waiting and pressing for the opportunity for adjustment.

These, then, are the basic interpersonal algorithms of our three-level brain. These algorithms show how we get to reciprocity through conflict. They shape the conflict and reciprocity, the give-and-take, at all levels of our interactive, social lives.

Overemphasis on either self-interest or empathy, exercise of one program to the exclusion of the other, creates tension and stress in any social configuration—from simple dyadic person-to-person encounters up to and including interactions among members of the workplace, society at large, social groups, and entire economic and political systems.[12]

---

[11]   See Eckel and Grossman (1997). Without making any connection with brain science or the reciprocal algorithms of behavior, the authors use a typology of fairness (for me, for you, for us) which expresses the conflict systems neurobehavioral model and the reciprocal algorithms of behavior.

[12]   Somit and Peterson (1997) see that evolution has provided us with a predisposition for hierarchically structured social and political systems, in other words, a tendency to hierarchy. I would suggest that this may be seen as an alternative perspective of the same dynamic of the tug and pull of ego and empathy of the triune brain structure that underlies reciprocity. Reciprocity, although more often than not seemingly unbalanced, in social and political relationships, is nevertheless always there to some degree. Even the range of dynamic balance of the conflict systems model is an approximate and shifting balance with some degree of hierarchy of dominance and submission. In its purest form, ceteris paribus, the innate dynamic only tends, rather imperfectly toward a balanced reciprocity. It does not and cannot achieve it deterministically, but only probabilistically. When other things are not equal, i.e., there are differences in personal strength, talent, ability, and intelligence, such differences will allow some individuals or groups to control more resources and thereby create hierarchies. Such hierarchies may be accepted by the less capable, but not without behavioral tension. The hierarchies are inherently unstable because of this behavioral tension. That is, as soon as the unequal capacities become less unequal, those on the lower end almost invariably move to contest and alter the hierarchy. Somit and Peterson acknowledge this tendency to unbalanced reciprocity or hierarchy as regrettable. And they devote their book to helping us understand how we may achieve the desired, balanced or non-hierarchical political system. Salter (1995) has pulled together a considerable quantity of naturalistic

PREDICTABILITY AND THE CSN MODEL

The scientific worth of a model is often said to be its ability to make predictions. The CSN model meets that standard. Each of the algorithmic rule statements can be phrased as a testable prediction. As a homey example, try behaving in an egoistic, domineering manner toward a family member or friend. That is, if you dare to risk the consequences.

The CSN model predicts that both you and the family member or friend will experience behavioral tension and will report such feelings. This has been tried many times and has produced consistent results. It's really not recommended. If, on the other hand, you prefer to try empathetic, serving behavior, especially over a period of time, you may find the model's predictions of behavioral tension likewise hold.

The CSN model's predictive and explanatory powers go far beyond such straightforward, intuitive examples. The predictive power will be explicit in the extraordinary range of its explanatory power demonstrated in the succeeding chapters of this book.

---

observation on the genetically-based communicative signaling in human and nonhuman species involved in the negotiating and maintenance of hierarchies.

5

THE DYNAMIC EQUATION
OF OUR NEURAL ARCHITECTURE

In past chapters I have presented the dynamic of our neural architecture in two forms: the CSN model of the major ranges of behavior and the descriptive algorithms of reciprocal behavior. Here, I will introduce a third form—the mathematical expression or equation that represents the dynamic. If math is not your favorite subject, don't let the math I use intimidate you. I will keep it simple. I won't use a lot of the usual confusing math symbols or Greek letters. Instead I will use abbreviations of the actual English words. You won't have to hold a bunch of numerical abstractions in the frontal part of your neural architecture while you try to follow the reasoning.

Keep in mind something that is easy to forget. The math is *not* the dynamic. Nor is it the reality. Math *represents* the dynamic and the reality. Math is a tool we invented that helps us clarify and simplify. Symbols are used because they are easier to manipulate than word descriptions. They also help us to see relationships more sharply. In the equation, I will *represent* the previous graph of the major ranges as well as the written description of the algorithms. I will try to capture very simply the dynamic of our social neural architecture.

Here goes.

$$BT = \frac{Ego}{Empathy} \quad or \quad \frac{Empathy}{Ego} = \pm 1 \text{ (dynamic balance, approx. equilibrium or unity)}$$

There it stands: the dynamic equation of our consilient, social brain expressed as a dynamically-balanced equation or an equation approaching equilibrium.

Pretty straight forward really. In the equation BT stands for behavioral tension and is a function of the ratio of ego to empathy or vice versa. It represents our self-preservation and affection circuitry tugging and pulling against each other. Because of the nature of the dynamic—the varying tug and pull of forces against each other—we can make either ego or empathy the numerator or denominator to avoid the inconvenience of fractions. The switching back and forth of the numerator and denominator to avoid fractions does not affect the utility or accuracy of the equation. It is the *magnitude* of divergence or convergence between the two forces that we are interested in expressing by the equation.[13] This short equation gives basic mathematical expression to the social architecture of our evolved brain structure. As the conflicting circuits of our social brain approach equilibrium or dynamic balance, behavioral tension/stress are minimized.

I use the symbolic notation, ± 1 (plus or minus one) to represent dynamic balance for two reasons:

First, the plus or minus notation represents approximate, but not perfect unity, equilibrium, or dynamic balance. Perfect unity, equilibrium, or balance, would be 1 or unity without the plus or minus. Perfect unity is a theoretical point impossible to attain because of the ongoing tug-and-pull of the dynamic circuitry.

Second, the notation represents the minimal range for behavioral tension. Since the dynamic tug and pull goes on ceaselessly, there is never zero tension. Also there is never zero ego or empathy because they are locked together in inseparable unity in our neural architecture.

On the other hand, as the ratios diverge more and more toward the extremes of ego or empathy, behavioral tension increases. For example, if we have an empathy magnitude or numerical value of 8 and an ego magnitude of 4, or vice-versa, we have a behavioral tension magnitude of 2.

At a minimum the neural dynamic works generally to keep our social behavior within survival limits. This is its most important function. On the other hand, at the level of optimal functioning, the algorithms, driven by behavioral tension, tend to move us toward dynamic balance of ego and empathy or self- and other-interest—that is, toward balanced reciprocity, or equality. The equation, therefore, is very simple, but deceptively so, because it can be quite variable and can ramify in many ways.

---

[13] The issue of magnitudes in economics as opposed to precise numerical calculation has been acknowledged at least since the time of the French economist Jean-Baptiste Say (1767–1832). Concerning the application of mathematics to economics he wrote:"The *values* with which political economy is concerned, admitting of the application to them of the terms *plus* and *minus*, are indeed within the range of mathematical inquiry; but... they are not susceptible of any rigorous appreciation, and cannot, therefore, furnish any *data* for absolute calculations. In political as well as in physical sciences, all that is essential is a knowledge of the connexion between causes and their consequences. Neither the phenomena of the moral or material world are subject to strict arithmetical computation" (1855, xxvi; italics in the original).

Another French mathematician and economist, Antoine Augustin Cournot (1801–1877) considered by some to be the first to apply mathematics successfully to political economy, had thoughts similar to Say. Cournot affirmed that simple numerical calculation of magnitudes is not the point of mathematization in economics. The purpose of such presentation is the elaboration of form and structure. Cournot was concerned with the demonstration of functional relationships which could be expressed by the functions of calculus. He was not concerned with numerical calculation and felt some events were resistant to precise numerical calculation except in trivial situations or games of chance. He wrote: "those skilled in mathematical analysis know that its object is not simply to calculate numbers, but that it is also employed to find relations between magnitudes which cannot be expressed in numbers...." (1838: 2–3).

Later on, French economist Léon Walras (1834–1910) attempted to solve the issue by dividing economics into three classes: pure science, applied science, and practical science. In the first two, mathematical formulas should be abstract and general in order to apply to all cases. Pure theory is concerned with the relationships and functions of magnitudes not precise numerical calculation. On the other hand, in practical economics, under limited conditions, one can hope to achieve instances of precise numerical calculation (see Jaffé, 1983: 27–28; also Walras, 1954: 64).

For instance, we can experience, even control or direct, by effort of our frontal executive, a different mix of ego and empathy in every one of our relationships and interactions. Some of our relationships may be quite dynamically-balanced or harmonious. Some may be tension-filled. Some may be quite unbalanced and stressful.

In one day—even in one hour of an exciting day—we may be jerked reactively back and forth all over the ego-empathy spectrum. Or we may move back and forth more self-consciously. Perhaps the average of all our relationships and interactions is a measure of our personal social health. I will get back to this thought later in the book. In the meantime I want to point out a couple of ways the social equation is different from others you may be more familiar with.

THE NEURAL SOCIAL EQUATION: SOME DIFFERENCES

The neural social equation is not a simple reciprocal. Don't let this confuse you. Simple reciprocals, which we see a lot of in math, merely show a proportional relationship. They compare the amount of something to the amount of something else. Or they compare a part to a whole. They have no dynamic similar to the social equation. There is no behavioral tension. On the contrary, the social equation is dynamic. It is driven by tension. The numerator and denominator tug and pull against each other, straining toward dynamic balance or equilibrium.

Don't confuse the equation with the resultant or outcome of a simple intersection of forces like you see often in the physical sciences. Such forces impact each other but they do not varyingly tug and pull against each other dynamically.

The organic equation is different. It represents a dynamic, living process. And that difference makes all the difference in the world.

SIMPLE, BUT POWERFUL

Indeed the equation is simple. But it does what has never been done before. It captures the central dynamic of our neural architecture. It captures a vitally important living, organic algorithm in very simple terms. It allows us to see and express relationships in many areas of our lives. Relationships we have seen only dimly and, perhaps, as fragmented up to now.

In the chapters that follow I will show these relationships. They extend from our social relationships to the dynamics of the market to the workings of our social and political worlds.

Scientists use the words *elegant* and *beautiful* to describe such equations. There are a number of them in physics. There are none so far in the social sciences. If you choose to follow me through to the end, you too may judge it to be the elegant or beautiful equation of our social neural architecture.

Before going into the personal and societal applications of the social equation, I want to deal with one other important, distinctly biological feature of the neural dynamic—its homeostatic quality.

6

THE HOMEOSTATIC REGULATION
OF OUR SOCIAL NEURAL ARCHITECTURE

Living things, from the single cell on up, have remarkable regulating mechanisms. They must. If they didn't they would fall apart. They would simply die and breakdown into their many component parts. In physiology, this ability to regulate, to keep all parts working together within set limits, was first described by Claude Bernard, a French physiologist of the 19th century. However, it was Walter B. Cannon, an American physiologist, who gave these regulating processes the name "homeostasis."[14]

The year was 1929 and the name stuck. The word Cannon chose comes from two Greek words. *Homeo* means similar and *stasis* means standing. As used by Cannon, and other scientists who followed him, homeostasis does not mean something rigidly set in concrete, unshakable, or immovable. It describes a condition that varies yet at the same time is relatively constant. For the organism it describes a condition that is kept within survival limits. When the homeostatic limits are exceeded the mechanism either self-corrects or the organism gets dysfunctional. That is; it either gets out of whack, sick, or dies.

Like all other creatures, our human vital processes are homeostatic. Built-in controls keep them generally within healthy and, ultimately, within survival limits. Familiar examples are our body temperature which must be kept within a rather narrow range around 98.6 degrees Fahrenheit. Above that we have a fever. Below that we risk hypothermia. Our body must act to correct both indicated conditions to stay healthy or alive. Another example is our blood pressure which varies rather widely to accommodate our changing levels of physical activity. Nevertheless our blood pressure must remain within limits or we're in for big trouble.

The list of homeostatically controlled physical processes is very long indeed. I could go on and on. Practically every bodily process is regulated within certain varying limits.

---

[14] Cannon (1871–1945) used the name homeostasis in his 1929 work and developed it fully in his seminal *Wisdom of the Body* (1932). See the summary article by Lapeyre and Lledo in *Encyclopedia of Human Behavior* (1994).

Even the hormones and neurotransmitters that mediate behavior within our neural architecture are regulated homeostatically. When the regulation fails, ours moods, our feelings, and ultimately our behaviors get out of sorts. A huge pharmaceutical industry exists to help us keep our bodily and behavioral processes in relative homeostasis—from blood pressure medications, to diet pills, to mood regulators.

These homeostatic processes, from the vital activities of the smallest cell up to the integrated functions of our body as a whole, can all be described by algorithms. They can likewise be represented by mathematical equations. Despite sometimes mind-boggling complexity, they all function within necessary survival limits.

HOMEOSTASIS, CYBERNETICS, AND INFORMATION THEORY

The discovery and study of homeostasis in the vital processes of living organisms led to the science of control systems, cybernetics, and information theory. Biological systems gave us both the model and the inspiration for these technological advances. The computer or information revolution depends upon modeling of our physical regulating processes.

When we build computers, software, and information control systems, we are creating partial analogs of ourselves out there. And then we're interacting with them to support our daily lives. Information, computers, controlled mechanical processes—all model the organic algorithms that regulate living processes.

Homeostatic systems, whether biological or fabricated, require certain essentials. At a minimum, they must have standards or limits, the ability to monitor and evaluate those standards and limits against performance, and the capacity to initiate corrective action. They must also have sensors to get input for comparison, and effectors that can act to carry out the needed adjustments.

The concept of feedback is one of the most important ideas to come out of the study of homeostasis and its human made information control sciences. Feedback refers to the information for comparison and evaluation that sensors both internal and external bring us. Homeostatic systems need feedback to tell them how they are doing. When to start corrective action. When to stop it.

HOMEOSTASIS OF THE SOCIAL ARCHITECTURE

The word homeostasis usually refers to the regulation of the internal environment of living organisms. Can we legitimately apply the concept to the workings of our social neural architecture?

Absolutely. All the elements for homeostatic regulation are present—standards, the ability to monitor and evaluate, sensors and effectors. In fact, our autonomic nervous system through its connections with the hypothalamus has primary involvement in behavioral homeostasis. The hypothalamus is closely linked with neural structures in the both the affectional and self-preservational circuitry located in the limbic system and the brain stem (e.g., see Herbert & Schulkin, 2002; Kandel, et. al., 2000: 871–997; Nelson, 2000, esp. pp. 447–494; Becker, et al., 1992).

Like other bodily processes, our social neural architecture is regulated within limits. All the sensory systems of our body feed information into the monitoring neural centers.

Many cues—from happy, sad, angry facial expressions to vocalizations of tenderness, frustration, surprise, and anger—are genetically wired and fine-tuned through development and experience. The muscles of our body act to carry out adjustments to our social as well as physical environment.

What we experience as behavioral tension is the generic regulator. It tells us when we are deviating from balance. Behavioral stress warns us that we're exceeding safe limits (e.g., see Przewlocki, 2002). The behavioral spectrum set out in Chapter 3 illustrates the necessary behavioral range and limits. The algorithms of reciprocity in Chapter 4 describe the social regulatory process. The social equation formulated in Chapter 5 represents the process mathematically.

HOMEOSTATIC VARIABILITY, NEURAL PLASTICITY, AND LEARNING

Homeostatic regulations, as noted, can vary quite a bit in the ranges permitted. Some are tighter, some are looser. Our social architecture is one of the looser kind. This is to be expected. The brain, in its higher centers, is the most plastic of our organs. It is designed for learning—to respond to new experience. Learning plays an important role in the variability among individuals of the neural dynamic (on neural plasticity, see Kolb, et al., 2003; Shaw & McEachern, 2001; Kolb, 1995; Greenough & Chang, 1989).

In addition, the higher executive centers can also assert a considerable control. Such control can never be absolute, but it can be strengthened or weakened by learning or experience. There would be no point in writing this book if this were not so. By self-consciously exercising our executive architecture we can vary the expression of our behavior across the spectrum of ego and empathy quite widely. As long, that is, as we can handle the behavioral tension we create in the process. That is to say, to a considerable extent, we can control the heat in our own kitchen.

BUT VARIABILITY HAS ITS LIMITS

Despite the variability our social architecture is, nevertheless, set within clear outer limits. When we act too egoistically. When we nearly totally suppress empathy. For instance, when we engage in attacking behavior, we approach the outer limits. And clearly somebody can get hurt. Perhaps we even get hurt ourselves.

Behavior at the extremes of either ego or empathy can be life threatening. We see examples of the egoistic extreme in street crime, gang wars, bar fights, and even in domestic violence. We see the relentless and deadly reciprocity of extremes at a societal level—in war, in the conflict between Israel and the Palestinians, between Pakistan and India over Kashmir. The examples are countless.

On the other hand, we see the empathetic extreme when parents sacrifice themselves for their children. We also see it when firefighters rush into blazing, collapsing buildings to rescue trapped citizens. In the summer of 2002 empathy was demonstrated on television for all to see as extraordinary efforts were made to save trapped miners in Somerset, Pennsylvania.

HUMAN SOCIAL LIFE: A RESOUNDING HOMEOSTATIC SUCCESS

In the face of so much violence reported daily in the news, we may seem most inclined to exceed homeostatic limits and create mainly death and destruction in our social world. This, however, is a distortion—perhaps based on our natural tendency to see the disturbing exception, rather than the comforting rule. It is an illusion encouraged by mass media reporting in a global society.

Much more often the controls of behavioral tension and stress keep us well within survival limits. Mostly we cooperate, help each other out, obey the law. Mostly we live together in reasonable harmony or dynamic balance.

Over history, despite the emphasis on violence in the written record, cooperation has prevailed overwhelmingly. In truth, we seldom exceed homeostatic limits. The historical evidence speaks to us loudly in confirmation. Our homeostatic neural social architecture is an undeniable success. It has brought us to a population success or explosion of over six billion. Crispin Tickell, a longtime advisor to British prime ministers and former president of the Royal Geographical Society, makes this point in a well-read article titled *The Human Species: A Suicidal Success?* (1993).

Of course this collaborative success of our social brain has created other challenges to the maintenance of social homeostasis that we must yet confront adequately—like overpopulation, exhaustion of resources, pollution, global warming. Nevertheless, there is no denying the evidence of success so far.

THE QUESTION OF SCIENCE:
PHYSICS VS. SOCIAL

The major ranges of behavior, the algorithmic rules of reciprocal behavior, the social equation—all describe *central behavior tendencies* of our social brain. That is, they don't explain all the detail about our behavior but only the general dynamic. They also operate rather *imperfectly*. I suspect that this will be true of any behavioral algorithms or principles we try to describe at this level of generalization (cf. Maynard Smith, 2002: 193). These behavioral algorithms, then, can only approximate, but not fully match, the precision of the laws of classical physics or even quantum mechanics.

This is partly because they come about through the process of organic evolution. Organic evolution is by its very nature quite variable in its outcomes. It involves some random change and shuffling of DNA, some mixing up of the DNA-bearing gene packets themselves, all acted on in an unpredictable way by natural selection. Even if we could track DNA changes as they happen, we could not be sure what changes natural selection would eventually choose to keep.

If the falling objects of Galileo's famous experiments acted like these organic algorithms, his laws would not be so mathematically neat and specific. Instead gravity would vary from moment to moment. Objects would fall fast at times, slower at others, and sometimes take short detours, before finally reaching the ground. Getting to the ground would be the outcome of a general tendency to fall. The reciprocal algorithms of our social brain, therefore, cannot operate as immutable universal physical laws but as generalized algorithms with degrees of variation. Probability gets into the calculus.[15]

---

[15] Even the early developers of the application of statistics to economics were aware of the limitations of such application. For example, William Newmarch, of Yorkshire, England, wrote in 1861 that in statistics there was no body of laws comparable to the physical sciences. He commented that statistics as applied to man in society amounted to no more than carefully recorded observations of events that take place under certain conditions. He considered that the element of free will (or perhaps choice as presented by the dynamic of the reciprocal algorithms) would prevent the appearance in the social sciences of regularities or laws comparable to physics (1861: 459–461; Perlman & McCann, 1998).

SOURCES OF PROBABILITY AND THE CSN MODEL

The CSN model, then, because of its organic, variable nature, depends on probabilities for a great deal of its predictability. The idealized, or rather statistically generalized, tug and pull of ego and empathy may be further probabilized in actuality by other contributing factors. Among such factors are: genetic variation, gender and developmental differences, individual experience and learning, and other environmental shaping and reinforcing influences.

In other words, *genetically speaking,* given the individual differences in genetic inheritance that we see in such obvious things as in hair, skin, or eye color, some individuals *behaviorally* may be more or less as strongly wired for self-preservation and affection as others. But granting *gender, developmental, experiential, and learning* differences, every human being is, nevertheless, similarly wired with the fundamental brain architecture unless he/she has very serious genetic defects indeed.

WE TAKE OUR COMPATIBILITY FOR GRANTED

We generally take the commonality of our human brain architecture for granted. We interact with each other socially without questioning our general compatibility. Indeed, without a common architecture our social life would be impossible. A good deal of early childhood research backs us up.

Influential developmental psychologists like Jean Piaget (1965) of Switzerland and Lawrence Kohlberg (1984) of Harvard, operating from a behavioral perspective, have built and tested theories of childhood moral development. In the theories of both scholars moral stages of development emerge much the same in all cultures when the child experiences anything approaching a normal family life. Such generalized moral stages could not be found across cultures if they were not genetically based on the species-wide brain structure and its associated behavioral potentialities.

DEVELOPMENT AND LEARNING INTERACT WITH OUR GENES

From the standpoint of *individual learning, socialization,* and other *environmental* factors, modifications in gene activity and expression occur in early development and throughout life. The higher brain centers, especially, develop in an interactive social context producing some variation in gene expression. Our *individual* life experiences may facilitate, suppress, strengthen, or otherwise modify the expression of these DNA based neural circuits. Other environmental factors, to include the physical conditions under which we live, as well as our socially and scientifically accepted institutions and paradigms, may also shape and reinforce the expression of the evolved algorithmic dynamic. Recent research has revealed considerable plasticity in our neural development (Kolb, et al., 2003; Shaw & McEachern, 2001; Kolb, 1995).

Individual learning, experience, or environmental factors of our individual lives *cannot,* however, *eliminate* the fundamental gene-based structure and programming of the brain. That is, not without radical injury, surgical, or genetic intervention. And the behavioral tension of our dynamic architecture will be there to both resist the changes and to shape the experience, even shape the environment itself, in a dynamic manner. That is, we resist radical manipulation of the human genome and we work assiduously to support and create physical and social environments for our healthy gene expression.

PHYSICS, GENES, AND BEHAVIOR

Because of these factors, the behavioral algorithms are *statistical—much in* the same way as are the second law of thermodynamics and quantum theory of physics. That is, they *generally do not allow precise* prediction of specific behavior at the basic unit of analysis—the individual, molecular, or subatomic levels respectively—but only on the aggregated basis of statistical probability.

The algorithmic rules of reciprocal behavior may, nevertheless, very well prove to be *equally* as valid and useful to social science as the laws of physics are to physical science. They do not and cannot, however, have the immutable quality of physical laws such as gravity. As products of organic evolution and developmental processes, they inevitably involve *more probabilities* because of individual differences, genetic and learned, in the evolved basic units.

THE BEHAVIORAL WAVE FUNCTION

We can make an admittedly loose, but interesting, analogy between the inclusive spectrum of possible behaviors of the CSN model and the particle wave function of quantum physics. The wave function of a particle is defined to include all the possible values of a particle according to probability.

Similarly, we can think of the "wave" function of behavior as including all possible internal and interpersonal behavioral probabilities (mixes of ego and empathy) spreading across the egoistic, empathetic, and dynamic balance ranges. We could write a mathematical wave formula to represent this, but predictability on an individual basis would be challenging because of the high rate of individual variability. I will avoid the temptation of such a detour from my main undertaking and get on to developing the insights and applications of the dynamic equation of our global-state neural algorithms.

But first a few final observations. Viewed from the outside, behavior is predictable from the CSN model, as is quantum behavior—only on a probability basis specified by the metaphorical wave function. The behavioral "wave" function, like that of particle physics, collapses or reduces to one behavior in a decision, action, or observation. If it doesn't collapse, we see frustration, tension, and indecisiveness—ambiguous behavior stalled in uncollapsed waveform.

Upon observation by an *external* observer, the wave function of behavior can be said to collapse to a specifically observable behavior by the individual and that is the end of it. But this would be an overly simplistic "objective" perception somewhat more characteristic of the now largely superceded perspective of radical behaviorism.

Internally, subjectively, we experience a much more complex process because we have conscious access to the dynamic. We know in our conscious self-awareness the tension, the difficulty, the struggle we go through in important issues of ego and empathy conflict. Even yet, in the surely much simpler processes of quantum physics we still do not fully understand what set of dynamics leads to the wave function collapse. In behavior, the dynamic lies in the complexities of subjective preconsciousness and/or self-aware consciousness.[16]

---

[16] That is, in physics it is not known exactly why and how wave function collapses or reduction occurs and how eigenstates are determined (e.g., see Hameroff & Penrose, 1996: 311). The standard Copenhagen Interpretation sees collapse as occurring at randomly measured values when the quantum system interacted with its environment, was otherwise measured, or consciously observed; (e.g., see Stapp's (1972) well-known article on the Copenhagen Interpretation). Penrose (1994) and Hameroff and Penrose (1996) introduce a new physical ingredient they call objective reduction (OR) which becomes guided and tuned into orchestrated OR, in which quantum systems can self-collapse by reaching a threshold related to quantum gravity.

PART II

NEURAL ARCHITECTURE, RECIPROCITY, AND THE MARKET

8

RECIPROCITY AND
THE EVOLUTION OF THE MARKET

The graphic of the CSN model, its descriptive algorithms, and the equation of our social brain represent a dynamically reciprocal neural architecture. Our social brain is structured for give and take—for social exchange. In this chapter I show how the market evolved from this dynamic.

THE NORM OF RECIPROCITY

The norm of reciprocity has long been a major theme in anthropology and sociology. More recently economists have been picking it up. This universally observed norm is found in all societies, primitive and modern.

The literature on reciprocity is extensive and still growing. L. T. Hobhouse (1906: 12) called it "the vital principle of society." Richard Thurnwald (1932: 106) described it as a principle "which pervades every relation of primitive life." Anthropologist Bronislaw Malinowski (1922, 1926) and sociologist Georg Simmel (1950: 387) have considered it the sine qua non of society. Harvard sociologist Talcott Parsons (1951: 21) viewed it as "inherent in the nature of social interaction." Alvin Gouldner (1960) wrote an extensive review article in the *American Journal of Sociology* citing much of the previous literature. French anthropologist Claude Levi-Strauss (1969: 98) has referred to it as a "trend of mind." J. van Baal (1975: 12) has considered it a "part of the human condition." More recently reciprocity has become of interest in economics (e.g., see Fehr & Gachter, 2000; Cory, 2002, 1999; Bowles & Gintis 1998: esp. Ch. 17).

So universally has reciprocity been observed that leading anthropologists and sociologists have long suspected that it must have a psychological or biological origin (e.g., see Levi-Strauss, 1969 and Homans, 1950; 1961: 317). That is, reciprocity must ultimately rest upon mechanisms within the human brain. The dynamic of our evolved neural architecture provides these mechanisms. A closer look at some of the dynamics of exchange will bear out the empirically observable workings of these algorithmic processes.

The prevalence of reciprocity means that in society, everywhere we look, we find social relations of give and take. The relations are sometimes informal, sometimes formal. But spoken or unspoken, written or not, they tell each member that what is received must be returned in some form at some time. The tension binding these give-and-take relations produces the web work of obligation that holds the society together.

In evolutionary theory, scholars account for reciprocity by such concepts as kin selection, inclusive fitness (Hamilton, 1963, 1964), reciprocal altruism (Trivers, 1971, 1981; Alexander, 1987), and game theory (Maynard Smith, 1982; Axelrod & Hamilton, 1981; Bendor & Swistak, 1997). These accounts draw upon so-called selfish gene perspectives, which see such reciprocity as basically selfish.

More recently, however, researchers have reported widespread reciprocity in the behavior of rhesus monkeys and chimpanzees based not upon selfishness, but empathy. Two excellent books that present the extensive evidence for empathy among primates are de Waal (1996) and Boehm (1999).

The observation of empathy in our primate cousins is a welcome approach that tries to escape the selfishness of traditional approaches. All these approaches, however, are based on the outside observation of behavior. They have not tried to identify or even speculate about the neural circuitry within the animal that must necessarily have been chosen by the evolutionary process to accomplish the work of motivating, maintaining, and rewarding such observed reciprocal behavior.

The CSN Model, building upon the evolutionary neuroscience of Paul MacLean, goes to the heart of the question of brain circuitry substrating reciprocity. The social brain, driven by the tug and pull of ego and empathy, is the motive source of human reciprocity. The circuitry lies within the self-preservation and affection structures of our evolved neural architecture. From these insights, we can easily understand the evolution of market exchange.

THE EVOLUTION OF THE MARKET

To understand the behavior of the modern day free enterprise market as it is shaped by the circuits of our social brain, it helps to go back to early times—to reconstruct as best we can the days before the market appeared.

The Family or Group Bond

In those times, when our ancestors consumed what they produced, the excess that they shared with, gave to, or provided for the needs or demands of the family or community was in the nature of natural affection or empathy. The reward for the empathetic, supplying act was emotional—there was not a specific, but a diffuse value assigned to it.

It also had social effects. The givers, providers gained status in the group. The emotional and the social effects were both directly governed by the reciprocal algorithms of behavior.

Let us look more closely. The provider, say the warrior, brought meat from the hunt or the wife brought berries and fruits from the field, tanned skins, and so on, to give to the family or group. The act of providing created behavioral tension in the giver, who acting with empathy denied ego to some degree. This ego denial required a response of acknowledgment—an expression of gratitude, respect, affection, or some other reaffirmation of ego. This providing or giving also created behavioral tension in the receivers. It was a service to their ego, their needs or demands—to their own preservation. The tension created required an offsetting empathetic response, a thank-you, an expression of appreciation or respect.

In any family or close group, even now, this dynamic flows constantly, even in the smallest activities. In the small group, the rewards, the reciprocations, are mostly not quantified, but are diffuse. They become obligations—bonds—that hold the group together for protection or mutual survival. Nevertheless, they must reach some approximation of balance or the unresolved tension will build within the group and become disruptive.

Expressions for *thank you* and *you're welcome*, found in all known human languages, reflect this reciprocity and the behavior needed to relieve it. We call it courtesy. It greases the social skids. Without courtesy daily life would be unbearable. We would have to swallow all that tension or be at each other's throats.

The Gift

From these primitive, familial exchanges, emerged the gift: an empathetic act of providing or serving that followed the same algorithmic behavioral rules that governed provision for survival. It created tension in the giver—an expectation of reciprocity—and tension in the receiver, who was bound to reciprocate. The rewards associated with the gift were at first diffuse, unspecified, unquantified—except by some subjective measure of feeling, emotion, or behavioral tension. A gift to a warrior or chief might vaguely obligate his protection. A gift to a prospective mate might vaguely obligate his or her attentions.

In 1950 the Presses Universitaires de France published anthropologist Marcel Mauss's, path-breaking earlier study about exchange practices in primitive and ancient societies called *Essai sur le Don*. It was most recently translated into English by W. D. Halls (1990) and given the title, *The Gift*.

Mauss was the nephew of Emile Durkheim, an influential figure in establishing the academic discipline of sociology. Mauss was not a neuroscientist, and from all indications had no interest in brain function. And considering the state of neuroscience at the time of his study more than a half century ago, knowledge of the discipline would probably have been of little or no help.

Mauss's study was done in the field. That is, he lived with the peoples he studied so that he could observe their customs and practices closely at firsthand. The quality of his fieldwork set a mid-century standard for such work among anthropologists. Mauss's findings of pervasive reciprocity in gift-giving in all of its varied forms throughout these seemingly primitive societies powerfully confirm the algorithmic dynamic tug and pull of ego and empathy of our neural architecture.

In his introduction, Mauss tells us clearly of his intent. He sets himself the task of discovering of what rule, legal or informal, compels members of ancient or pre-market societies to reciprocate gifts received (1990: 3). He seeks to identify the power resident in the object given that causes its beneficiary to pay it back. This binding power, Mauss finds expressed in powerful feelings and emotions, sanctified by ritual and even having religious overtones (cf., Godelier, 1999). Gift exchange, then, is the essence of social life itself. It is no mere formality of practice.

At one point he identifies the compelling "force" as both mystical and practical (1990: 73). The "power" or the "force" Mauss seeks, but which he can not identify in terms of neural science, is, of course, the reciprocal dynamic of our neural architecture. The compelling power or force is no less than the homeostatically-driven behavioral tension that mandates the give and take of interpersonal reciprocity.

There were serious social, economic, and political consequences attending the exchange of gifts. Generous giving brought honor and prestige. Failure to return an approximately equal gift brought a loss of status. Among the peoples he studied the failure or refusal to engage in exchange of gifts was tantamount to a declaration of war (1990: 13).

To further confirm his findings among living tribes, Mauss searched the literature of ancient peoples—Romans, Germans, even the Hindu Vedic literature of ancient India. Through their legal codes, customs, practices, and myths he found the give and take of exchange central to the lives of all known human societies.

Such universality of practice and custom—worldwide—in all known peoples, cannot be explained away by cultural contact or dispersion. Reciprocity in all its forms is driven by neural algorithms etched into the amino acid sequences of our genes early in human prehistory.

The anthropological literature on gift-giving has expanded greatly since Mauss's work. It continues to the present day. Such literature overlaps with the literature on reciprocity. Although the total volume of work is too extensive to deal with here, I will point out some more recent works that show the continuing interest in this fundamental social phenomenon. For example:

Titmuss (1972) examined the commercial blood acquisition system of the U.S. with the voluntary one in Great Britain with the finding that the latter system was less contaminated, less wasteful, and less costly that the U.S. system.

French scholars have continued their interest in reciprocity and giving following the work of Levi-Strauss, Malinowski, and Mauss. Rather than the positivist, self-interest approach of Mauss, recent scholars have taken the perspective of altruism (e.g., see, Gérard-Varet, Kolm, and Mercier Ythier, 2000). Davis (2000) reports on the altruism in gift in sixteenth century France. Fennell (2002) is of special interest to the presentation here because she reports that empathetic, nurturing dialogue characterizes the gift even in modern society.

From Gift to Transaction

From the gift in all its varied expressions evolved the transaction—namely, the gift with the reciprocal specified or quantified.

The evolution of the transaction from the gift is widely supported by the anthropological literature (e.g., Polanyi, 1957; Gregory, 1982; Mauss, 1990). The *Dictionary of Anthropology* in distinguishing the commodity from gift states that a commodity exchange creates a relationship between things (that is, it is impersonal) as opposed to gift exchange which creates a relationship between people (Seymour-Smith 1986: 44). Gregory (1982) holds that commodity exchange is an exchange of alienable objects between persons who are in a state of reciprocal independence which establishes a quantitative (i.e., specified) relationship. Gift exchange, on the other hand, is an exchange of inalienable objects between persons who are in a state of reciprocal dependence that establishes a qualitative relationship between the persons involved in the exchange (see also Barfield, 1997: 73). Bohannan defines market exchange or the market transaction as the exchange of goods at prices governed by supply and demand under a free and casual contract. On the other hand, reciprocity or gift exchange is seen most clearly in kinship relations (1963: 231–232). Since kinship reciprocity precedes market transactional relations in human affairs, the latter clearly evolved from the former. Hunt (2002) discusses human mammalian sharing in child-rearing, as well as sharing in small unit situations even in modern contexts, and other forms of exchanges or transfers. His approach has a quasi-evolutionary framework and may be compared with the approach I have chosen in this chapter. Appadurai (1986), in line with my presentation, has shifted from the standard anthropological focus on objects to the nature of the transaction itself.

A large body of evidence, then, clearly establishes the case that the transaction evolved from the gift. The transaction probably evolved in groups larger than family or extended kinship units. It is here that we begin to deal with strangers. The transaction is the beginning of the contract, perhaps of the commercial market itself. The transaction operates, however, by the same algorithms of behavior as the gift—except that it attempts to head off the residual, unresolved behavioral tension that creates a condition of obligation or bonding.

After all, in the commercial market, we may be dealing with complete strangers. We may wish to avoid any future obligation to them from our exchanges. We have not seen these strangers before and we may never see them again. Further, we are naturally suspicious of them. They are not family or close neighbors. We feel it wise to avoid the left over tension that might oblige us to invite them home for dinner—to share the feast as our ancestors did.

In such market transactions, then, both the gift object transferred and the reciprocal are specified to the satisfaction of giver and receiver. The exchange deal is done in equal or balanced return. There is no behavioral tension binding us socially and economically in a cycle of mutual obligation. Nevertheless, despite these considerations, the transaction itself retains its essential mammalian characteristics. It is an act of empathy, of nurturing, which requires a balancing reciprocal act in payment to ego.

When we encounter its equivalent in the seemingly impersonalized market economy of today, how often do we feel the subjective experience of the transaction? We take our sick child to the physician, who with empathy and care applies the knowledge it took 10 years and a fortune to gain. We pay the bill—that is, we make a return gift with money that represents a portion of our accumulated education and labor. The scenario is repeated in transactions with the plumber, the carpenter, the computer maker. The behavioral algorithms still apply, but the feeling, the subjective experience has to a large degree been lost.

BEHAVIORAL TENSION YET DRIVES THE TRANSACTION

But wait! Let the transaction go wrong, the expected reciprocals not be forthcoming and the behavioral tension becomes immediately and personally felt. The reality of the transaction—the market—reveals itself with clarity and intensity.

Ask yourself, for instance, the following. If you responded to an ad from a local electronics store for a top of the line TV set with all the bells and whistles—at the unbelievable bargain price of $ 99.00. You rushed down ad in hand before supplies were sold out and paid your money. You received your unopened box and hurried proudly home with it. Pulling your prized purchase eagerly from the box in front of the waiting family, you discover that it is a cheap model with only channel and volume buttons and a set of squatty rabbit ears.

Would you feel behavioral tension at the unexpectedly unbalanced reciprocal? What would you do? Would you laugh it off? Or would you pack it back up and return it with a set of choice comments reflecting your behavioral tension in unmistakable terms? Likely, you would do the latter.

No one likes to be cheated or short-changed. And most of us will be motivated to take some action to correct the imbalance. The small claims courts of the nation have their dockets crammed full, primarily with issues of unbalanced reciprocity in the marketplace. If we don't get satisfaction in expected reciprocity, we may very humanly harbor the behavioral tension indefinitely, hoping to get even in the future.

Our neural architecture assures this reaction.

9

THE MISREPRESENTATION
OF ADAM SMITH

The market evolved from the tug and pull of ego and empathy, the dynamic of our social brain. The market was created by the human brain—by like brains interacting with like brains. There is simply no other possible source. If markets were established and run on the basis of Newtonian mechanics, as once thought by most economists in the 19th century and some in the 20th century, we should expect to find them ready and waiting for us on the moon and Mars. After all, Newtonian principles apply there also. All we would have to do is move in and start using them. The thought is, of course, absurd. Markets are the expression of human social exchange activity. And they don't exist independently of that activity.

For the last two hundred plus years the orthodox theory of free enterprise and economics has similarly inaccurately claimed that self-interest is the *sole primary motive* of the market. How did we get it so wrong?

Open almost any basic economic textbook and you will find that we blame Adam Smith (1723–1790). Smith was a moral philosopher at the University of Glasgow, Scotland back in the 18th century. He earned the reputation as founder of economics and the capitalist free enterprise system by publishing the *Wealth of Nations* in 1776. The source for the venerated self interest motive was a quote from Book I, Chapter 2 of that volume. It goes as follows:

It is not from the benevolence of the butcher, the brewer, or the baker, that we expect our dinner, but from their care for their own interest. We appeal not to their humanity but to their self-interest, and never talk to them of our own necessities, but of their advantages.

But this often cited quote is taken completely out of context. On the same page and on either side of the famous quote, yet never included, are two clear references to the importance of benevolence or empathy. Just two short paragraphs above the quote Smith reminds us that

...man has almost *constant need* for the *help* of his brethren (italics added).

And, immediately following the famous quote he tells us

Thus nobody but a beggar chooses to *depend chiefly* upon the *benevolence* of his fellow-citizens....(italics added).

When properly understood, then, Smith, in the celebrated quote, is not saying that there is only self-interest, but that there is both self-interest and empathy and that we should show an empathetic concern for the self-interest of the butcher, the baker, and the brewer, in requesting their products and services. That is, we should not seize them unjustly, but we should expect to compensate their labors. In fact he makes this absolutely clear—again on the same page—when he says in the line directly above the celebrated quote

Give me what I want, and you shall have what you want, is the meaning of every such offer.

Adam Smith, in the above phrasing, has virtually stated the algorithms of reciprocity, the dynamic tug and pull of ego and empathy, self-and other interest. Both you and I get what we need from the exchange. Nobody gets ripped off. In everyday parlance in our modern times, we call this intuitively—*win-win*. Everyone gets what they want and everyone is satisfied. The exchange as Smith saw it, then, more accurately aimed at a balance of self- and other-interest. And Smith didn't know anything about brain science or neural architecture. He was operating intuitively from common sense. After all he had the same neural architecture we have—although he had no concept of it as such.

But the evidence goes even further. Smith wrote another book—a magnum opus called *The Theory of Moral Sentiments*, which he first published in 1759 well before the *Wealth of Nations*. The second book, almost entirely ignored for two centuries, was for Smith the more important of the two. It emphasized morality, sympathy, and fellow-feeling. Smith considered this book so important he revised it six times—the last time shortly before his death in 1790. Smith's two volumes capture the tug and pull of ego and empathy, the algorithms of reciprocity. Their titles, in all their glory, may accurately be placed above the graph of the major ranges of the CSN model (Figure 4).

How did such a historical oversight or misinterpretation occur? I think there is a reasonable explanation. It goes along the following lines. The businessmen and entrepreneurs of that day were chafing under the excessive and invasive restrictions of the British mercantile system. The crown's bureaucracy was micromanaging everything, stifling trade and business in general. The businessmen saw what they needed to break the restrictive bonds of mercantilism in the self-interest motive and in the hands off (laissez-faire) approach advocated by Smith. They pounced on the two like a fumbled football and off they went. After all, they were practical men interested in making money, not in theory. The empathy—the moral concerns—of Smith got lost in the shuffle.

THEORY OF MORAL SENTIMENTS   WEALTH OF NATIONS

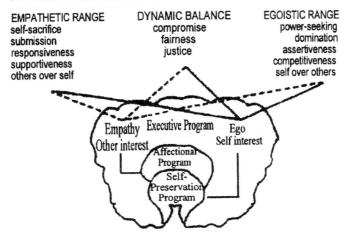

Figure 4. The Works of Adam Smith and the Major Ranges of Reciprocal Behavior.

The overemphasis on self-interest that followed, however, had its negative side effects. It skewed business behavior toward egoism by its denial of empathy. It often led to excess and greed—as in the 1890s, 1920s, the 1980s, and the greed epidemic of the late 1990s and the early 2000s. The excesses periodically gave the free enterprise system a bad press and led to public reaction and regulation in the public interest to counter the negative tendencies.

Adam Smith, when properly understood, got it right. The free market, as an expression of our neural architecture, depends upon the interplay of ego and empathy, self- and other-interest. Not just self-interest alone. A look at the everyday presentation of the business marketplace bears this out further.

EMPATHY IN THE MARKETPLACE

The overemphasis on self-interest and the lack of an adequate behavioral model have prevented us from seeing how the marketplace derives from brain structure, and how empathy or altruism plays an equal role with ego or self- preservation. But the role of empathy is clearly present in the language, if not the practice, of the marketplace. The everyday language of marketing *is* the language of empathy. Let's take a look.

Advertisements, almost without fail, emphasize service or benefit to the customer. Customer service is, in fact, the keynote of most businesses. Every retail store of any size has a customer "service" department in a prominent location. Never once have I seen a company "self-interest" department so proudly and prominently displayed.

Almost nowhere else are we treated with more exaggerated empathy, even obsequiousness, than in some retail businesses. In marketing, as any good salesperson can tell you, empathy works. People respond to it. The features-and-benefits approach to selling is built entirely on empathy. I was told long ago when I worked as a salesperson: "When you talk features, you're bragging; when you talk benefits to the customer, you're selling." Empathy rules. Depending on the skill and sincerity of the salesperson, the genuine feeling may or may not be convincingly displayed, but the basic empathetic behavior is there.

For another example, turn on the TV set at any time of day and count the appeals to empathy—what great benefit of health, wealth, joy, and entertainment the products and services huckstered will bring you. In the Fall of 2002, with corporate greed and a losing stock market, I listened especially to the ads of the brokerage companies. They were very revealing about the nature of their business. How they wished to have it perceived. A leading discount broker, openly stated you must get the self-interest out of the transaction in order to properly advise the customer. A prominent non discount broker claimed to identify with your dreams—to make your dreams their own. The list of companies appealing to empathy and other-interest as their primary purpose in the market goes on and on. Even if we choose to view such ads cynically, they nevertheless indicate the crucial importance of empathy and other-interest in the exchange process.

The act of selling, therefore, clearly demonstrates not only the role of empathy, but also the reciprocal algorithms of behavior. The saleperson's serving behavior toward the customer creates tension in the salesperson, who, acting empathetically, denies his or her own ego to some degree, thereby producing the expectation of reciprocity, a reward. The salesperson's empathetic behavior also creates tension in the customer—a sense of obligation to buy. The sales process not only demonstrates these algorithms of behavior; but it depends upon them.

We, thus, see clearly the contending forces of our neural architecture at work in the daily activity of selling and buying. Anyone who focuses only on self-interest sees only one side of this socio-economic equation. The dynamic of economic exchange, when properly understood is an expression of the dynamic of our neural architecture—the equation of our social brain.

The trick or deception of assigning a self-interest motive to everything—even to the most empathetic or altruistic acts—is made plausible by the fact that the reciprocal is always there. There is always an egoistic reciprocal to any empathetic act; and, likewise, there is always an empathetic reciprocal to any egoistic act.

The dynamic of our social brain supports the protesting observation by Nobelist Amartyr Sen in his well-known article "Rational Fools." Sen writes that one can "define a person's interests in such a way that no matter what he does he can be seen to be furthering his own interests in every isolated act of choice"(1979). The equation also exposes the most glaring and socially distorting deficit of so-called rational choice theory which attempts inaccurately to account for all exchange behaviors in terms of quantifiable self-interest.

RATIONAL CHOICE THEORY CONTRA THE HUMAN MAMMAL

Since the subject came up, let's take a brief, revealing, look at current rational choice theory in the light of our indisputable mammalian heritage. Rational choice and exchange theory in sociology deal with the issues of power and social integration. Sociologist Peter Blau (1964) hits at the heart of reciprocal exchange when he sees its two general functions as creating bonds of friendship and establishing relationships of subordination or domination. Of course, domination and subordination carry inevitable behavioral tension which is at the root of the underlying implicit assumption of all exchange theory—the tug and pull tendency toward equalization of value among all social relationships.

The work of sociologist James S. Coleman illustrates the distortion, however, that appears in the work of some of our most capable theorists when our mammalian heritage, is not fully grasped. Coleman bases his theory of action on the overt premise of rational, self-interested humans, unconstrained by morality, norms, or altruism. He apparently is unaware of, or else assumes erroneously that we lack, our very prominent and significant limbic septal (to include our medial pre-optic area), thalamocingulate brain structures, and our orbital frontal cortex—and that we are only wired innately for self- interest when he writes:

To assume that persons come equipped with a moral code would exclude all processes of socialization from theoretical examination. And to assume altruism or unselfishness would prevent the construction of theory about how persons come to act on behalf of others...when it goes against their private interests (1990: 31–32).

The above quoted statement is, of course, patently not true. If we recognize that the programming for ego and empathy, self- and other-interest—although admittedly undefined by specific social content—is innate in our mammalian neurological structure, we are certainly not thereby prevented from constructing theories about socialization. The focus of such theorizing would, of course, shift from the one-sided view of exclusively self-interested, half-humans to a more correctly balanced view. Our theory could then appropriately focus on how these two innate potentialities of ego and empathy achieve social expression and how they are blended in balanced or unbalanced reciprocity over history in the particular moral codes and norms of any specific culture or society.

Exchange theorist Karen Cook and her associates appropriately see exchange as the ubiquitous structuring activity of societies. Drawing on a metaphor of James Coleman, Cook writes that theories of social structure alone "provide a chassis but no engine." Concerning the unique contribution of exchange theory, she goes on to claim:

A major strength of exchange theory is that in making explicit the reciprocal nature of social interaction it provides a theoretical engine of action to power the chassis that is our understanding of social structure (Cook, O'Brien, & Kollock, 1990: 164).

Cook correctly sees the reciprocal nature of social interaction as the dynamic process of social action and society-building. She remains, however, within the rational choice, self- interested framework and thereby misses the essence of reciprocity—the tug and pull of ego and empathy, concern for ourselves, and recognition and concern for the interests of others. Her "engine", being universal, inevitably implies a grounding in biology or human nature. She does not, however, provide such a grounding.

EQUITY THEORY

Equity theory, a recent direction in sociology and social psychology, is closely akin to exchange theory. Equity theory purports to be a general theory that provides insights into social interactions of all kinds—from industrial relations to issues of justice in more general social encounters. Walster, Walster, and Berscheid (1978) provide a thorough statement of equity theory and bring together the previously scattered research as of the year of publication. More recently, it has been extended to the most personal relationships of marriage and other relationships of intimacy. Hatfield and Traupmann (1981:165–178) summarize the application of equity theory to intimate relationships, a focus in social psychology that has emerged in the last couple of decades.

Equity theory, by the very use of the term equity, reveals its implicit grounding in an intuitive perception of neural dynamic as it tends toward balance in our behavior. Equity theory's four propositions, proclaimed apparently from faulty intuition or generalized observation, are otherwise ungrounded. According to theorists, Walster and colleagues, the four propositions require that:

1. Individuals will try to maximize their outcomes.
2. Groups will try to maximize collective rewards by creating systems of equity and will encourage member adherence. Groups will reward equitable behavior and punish members who don't conform.
3. Members in inequitable relationships will become distressed to the extent of the inequity.
4. Members in an inequitable relationship will try to eliminate their distress by restoring equity. The greater the inequality, the greater the distress, and the harder they will work to restore equity. (Walster, et al., 1978: 6; see also, Donnerstein & Hatfield, 1982).

Walster, et al., state unequivocally that equity theory rests upon what they consider "the simple, but eminently safe assumption that man is selfish" (1978: 7). Except for the fact that the theorists remain in the rational choice, self-interested framework, their propositions, as asserted, are expressive of the reciprocal algorithms of behavior. The dynamic is also run by behavioral tension as reflected in the distress experienced by members.

The apparent logical inconsistency of proposition 1, maximizing outcomes, with proposition 4, restoring equity, is glaring under the assumption that man is selfish and seeks to maximize. If man selfishly seeks to maximize, why should she/he be satisfied with merely restoring equity rather than seeking to reverse the situation to one of dominance in his own favor? This logical inconsistency of the propositions becomes resolved when the tug of empathy is added to self-interest. According to the reciprocal algorithms of behavior, empathy is what permits us to settle, without excessive distress, for a position of equity rather than a reversal of the inequities of the relationship which would be required under a concept of maximizing.

I might reiterate with confidence, then, that reciprocity, proceeding from the evolved structure of our human brain, is the basic structuring dynamic of our social lives. Anthropological and social research have convincingly shown that reciprocity underpins our most primitive and basic social relations, from family interactions, to gift exchange, to the foundations of more complex economic life. It continues to do so in a less obvious, but no less pervasive manner in our modern systems of exchange.

10

THE NEURAL FOUNDATIONS
OF THE INVISIBLE HAND

In this chapter the consilient social brain takes on an icon of economic lore—the invisible hand. As a staple of economic theory, it appears in every economics textbook and in many books on free enterprise and business. We even hear about it on television talk shows. Libertarians, conservative Republicans, and even Democrats invoke it, sometimes reverently and mysteriously. It is generally reported to go back to Adam Smith.

Actually it goes back a little further. No one knows exactly who first thought it up, but the principle is probably first clearly anticipated by the Englishman, Bernard de Mandeville (1670–1733). In 1714 Mandeville published a book called the *Fable of the Bees* in which he argued that individuals in pursuit of their own purely selfish goals, nevertheless, unintentionally produced benefits for society. This is known as the doctrine of "unintended consequences." It is the forerunner of the invisible hand.

Adam Smith, seemingly repelled by Mandeville's excessive emphasis on human selfishness in the then famous *Fable*, sought a more balanced interpretation. His teacher and predecessor at the University of Glasgow, Scotland, Francis Hutcheson, as well as his friend, the famed British philosopher David Hume and others of his circle, followed more in the footsteps of philosopher John Locke (1632–1704). They believed that mankind had an innate concern or sympathy for others which led to a moral sense. Smith states his position in the ongoing debate in his *Theory of Moral Sentiments* (1759).

Smith opens Section 1 Chapter 1 of his moral masterwork, with the following paragraph:

How selfish soever, man may be supposed, there are evidently some principles in his nature, which interest him in the fortune of others, and render their happiness necessary to him, though he derives nothing from it, except the pleasure of seeing it...like all the other original passions of human nature, [it] is by no means confined to the virtuous and humane, though they perhaps may feel it with the most exquisite sensibility. The greatest ruffian, the most hardened violator of the laws of society, is not altogether without it.

Thus, Smith described fellow-feeling or sympathy as he called it. And such is empathy as I call it.

As we saw in the previous chapter, Smith, our economic forefather, then, saw not one but two great natural motives somehow rooted in human nature—self-interest, the desire to accumulate wealth and better one's personal circumstances, and sympathy or fellow-feeling, the source of benevolence and morality.

Smith, we noted, had no access to the findings of modern neuroscience. He knew nothing about brains or neural architecture. He sensed these two motives as somehow built into the nature of human beings by the invisible hand of Deity.

Smith felt that given freedom from government restriction, which was very extensive and invasive at that time, the dynamics of human nature in pursuit of wealth would produce more wealth and a better distribution of it than any deliberate system statesmen could devise. But unlike Mandeville, he saw the benefits proceeding from both self-interest and sympathy.

In Moral Sentiments he writes further on:

[the rich] are led by an *invisible hand* (emphasis added) to make nearly the same distribution of the necessaries of life, which would have been made, had the earth been divided into equal portions among all its inhabitants, and thus without knowing it, advance the interests of society.

Here we have the idea of *unintended consequences* clearly expressed by Smith as the *invisible hand*. In other words, left to operate freely, the dynamics of human nature, driven by the principle motives of self-interest and fellow-feeling, will somehow work to create an approximate equality of distribution, at least at the level of the necessities of life.

Smith could see how fellow-feeling could work effectively to provide moral stability and provisioning among neighbors, but he was troubled when he tried to visualize its working at the higher level of nations and among nations. To fill this gap, then, and following the thinking of some of his predecessors and contemporaries, he invoked the aforementioned deus ex machina, or miracle machine, of the invisible hand. It was essentially an undefined, semi-mystical concept taken more on intuition or faith than any empirical evidence or observation. Among nations as among individuals, Smith saw divine intervention providing a corrective when human nature or natural law fell short of the job.

Smith went on from there to develop his famous economic principles of supply and demand as the dynamic forces that drive the marketplace. These principles, now inappropriately elevated to the status of laws, have served as the foundation of economics up to the present day. In fact, the invisible hand is now taken to be the natural outcome of the workings of the so-called laws of supply and demand. Even Alan Greenspan, head of the Fed, and economic psychologist in residence for the nation, can be heard to invoke the laws of supply and demand and by implication, the invisible hand.

DEMAND AND SUPPLY: EXPRESSIONS OF THE SOCIAL BRAIN

Let's go back for a moment. From the evolution of the market traced in Chapter 8, we can easily see that demand and supply are expressions of our dynamic neural architecture. Ego demands. Empathy provides or supplies. Without empathy there could be no market. We wouldn't know what to offer or how to offer it to respond to the demands or needs of others. We probably wouldn't even care to be bothered.

When ego and empathy meet in dynamic balance, *fairness* and *cooperation tend* to emerge in exchange activity. When ego (demand) and empathy (supply) intersect freely in the marketplace, we *tend* to have equitable exchange. Since the evolved algorithmic dynamic works imperfectly, I use the word *tend*.

Figure 5 sums up the discussion of the evolution of the market I began in Chapter 8. The figure also illustrates the emergence of the economic concepts of demand and supply as an expression of our neural architecture. Demand expresses our egoistic, survival-centered needs. Supply or providing proceeds from empathy and is fundamentally an act of mammalian nurturing. Let's go over it in more detail.

In the sharing, egalitarian culture of early kinship hunting and gathering bands, the reciprocal obligation, mandated by our neural architecture, was, like in the smaller family unit—not specified, but diffuse. That is, the obligation was not clearly quantified, but had a general somewhat formless effect of social bonding and obligation. The emotions of gratitude, affection, respect, esteem, and prestige evoked or expressed in the exchange were the biological glue that held such units together for survival. Such emotions, of course, are expressions of our ego/empathy neural dynamic.

As we proceed to the level of social organization that we call a tribe, the mandatory exchange of gifts takes on a qualitative change. The reciprocal is no longer diffuse but becomes anticipated. A roughly equal return gift kept the balance of prestige and obligation roughly equal. Behavioral tension was minimized. An unequal exchange, however, left a residual of unsatisfied obligation or behavioral tension. Unequal exchange led to contests of status and power always underpinned by the dynamic corrective tendency of behavioral tension.

THE GIFT ECONOMY VS. THE MARKET ECONOMY

It is perhaps at the tribal level that we find what anthropologists describe as the *gift-economy*. The gift economy was a total social system of gift exchange in which the distribution of goods and services was open to public scrutiny. Judgments of fairness and equity were community-shared—there for all to see. Gift exchanges, and their balance or imbalance, defined the essential structure of the society.

Gifts were the sources of prestige, honor, and came to be backed up even by social sanctions of ceremony and religion. Canadian researcher David Cheal sees that the gift economy of today is based mainly upon a feminine perspective of relationships and love (1988: 183). This may very well hold true for early societies. Cheal's point is reinforced from an extreme feminist viewpoint by Genevieve Vaughan (1997). Whatever the faults of Vaughan's one-sided emphasis, she accurately sees giving as based on mammalian mothering. The mammalian affectional architecture from which empathy arises is, of course, shared by men as well as women. The exchange market evolves as distance from the family and its sharing relationships increases and the relationship factors become rarefied or depersonalized. This finding of giving as based upon mammalian affection goes against the widespread image of the bullying, overpowering alpha male who ruled by sheer physical power. Physical power may have given an edge but prestige, status, and leadership in the gift economy were based upon the capacity to give away more than other contenders.

The gift economy is the forerunner of the commercial or transaction economy.[17] Changes in the manner of social exchange mark this transition and justify our calling them differently. But what are the differences that distinguish the two?

There are at least three. First, in the gift economy you get the gift whether or not you can reciprocate equally. The relationship is much more personal, bonded, and inclusive. You are not left to starve or die of exposure because you cannot return an equal amount of valued goods. Of course, you make payback in loss of status and residual obligation to your benefactor. There is no free gift.

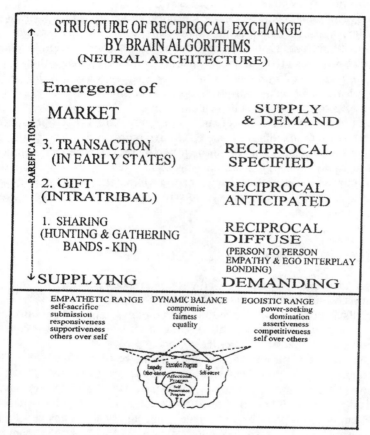

Figure 5. Evolution of the Market Shaped by Neural Architecture.

---

[17] The evolutionary sequence summarized here roughly conforms to the standard anthropological literature and follows the presentation in Chapter 8. Economic historian Karl Polanyi (1957) advanced the argument of a transformation from a gift economy to a market economy. Anthropologist Marshall Sahlins most fully developed this theory in his *Stone Age Economics* (1972). Sahlins made the important point that the difference between gift exchange and commodity exchange should be viewed as a continuum not as a bipolar opposition. Gift exchange, as indicated in Figure 5 and the supporting presentation, tends to be between people who are kin. As the kinship distance lengthens and the transactors become strangers, commodity exchange emerges (see Sahlins, 1972: 185–276). Commodity exchange is characterized by impersonal relationships, no desire for social bonding characteristic of kinship exchange, and specified or quantified reciprocals.

As we move to the transaction, however, the relationships become more impersonal, probably deliberately so. This brings us to the second difference. In the transaction economy the reciprocal is specified or quantified. You don't get the gift or object of exchange in the first place, if you can't produce the specified reciprocal. The exchange just doesn't take place. If you can meet the specified reciprocal, of course, then well and good. The exchange does takes place.

The third difference follows from the second. That is, the transaction involves no gain or loss of social prestige. It carries no residual obligation or behavioral tension. It's a clean deal with minimal social effects.

Gift economies and market economies to a great extent existed side by side over much of human history. The patron-client relations of the great feudal systems were primarily an extension of a gift-exchange economy. They were bound by residual obligations between patrons and clients underpinned by the behavioral tension of unequal exchange. In such a system when the patron could no longer provide, he/she lost the support and loyalty of the clients. Sometimes the breakdown of the social exchange relationship was marked by violence and bloodshed.

In the Middle Ages the emergence of the towns, merchant class, and the transactional market economy challenged the feudal patron-client power structure. And there were considerable tensions between the two. By the modern age the transactional, market economy had prevailed. Of course, the gift economy never went away. It still functions on a less visible scale among isolated social groupings, as well as among families and groups even in the most highly developed commercial economies.

THE INVISIBLE HAND IN THE STRUCTURE AND BEHAVIOR OF THE MARKETPLACE

As Figure 5 illustrates, in the transactional or commercial market, the dynamic tug and pull of ego and empathy becomes expressed as demand and supply. The behavioral tension driving toward a proper reciprocal balance between demand and supply in the marketplace accounts for the basic motive force for the invisible hand. Scholars have previously accounted for the hand's illusive dynamic in various ways. Early thinkers, beginning with Smith saw in it the workings of Deity or natural law. Later scholars, with more sophistication, appealed to Newtonian mechanics or other inappropriate physical processes. Some just gave up on the question, but still quoted it on faith. Such variables as history, culture, and institutions, of course, play their part. And they do so importantly. They give the market its unique expression in any social context. The hand can't do it all by itself.

To grasp the functioning of the invisible hand in the marketplace, it helps to keep a clear distinction between structure and behavior.

Structure

The invisible hand, as driven by our neural algorithms, tends to work despite the one dimensional overemphasis on self-interest in classical economics. This is because the *very structure* of the market itself is the *institutionalized product* of the ego/empathy dynamic of our evolved brain structure. Our basic self-survival ego demands are rooted ultimately in our ancestral protoreptilian or vertebrate neural complexes. Contrastingly, the act of providing or supplying, is fundamentally an act of mammalian nurturing. The market exchange system originated from this dynamic. The market could never have evolved or been maintained on the basis of ego or self-interest alone. Without empathy we would not know how or what to do to respond to the needs of others.

Behavior

Behavior, in individual choices and transactions within the above institutionalized structure, may vary considerably in the mix of ego and empathy motives on both the demand and supply sides. Nevertheless, even in the most ego-skewed (or self-interested) market behavior the overall tendency of the market will be toward a dynamic balance of ego and empathy. Individual and collective actors, whether seemingly motivated primarily by self-interest or not, will be compelled by the very market structure itself—to survive in the market—to perform the *structural equivalent* of *empathy*. That is, they will be required to provide (supply) a proper service or product to fill the needs (demand) of others. This is the source of the unintended consequences aspect of the invisible hand— referred to by Adam Smith himself as well as modern economists.

On a level playing field, left to its own dynamic, the invisible hand, stripped of its ghostly demeanor, will tend to come forth. The architecture of our social brain drives it. The dynamic equation of our social brain represents it.

The invisible hand largely expressed itself more fully in the small social units of primitive humankind. The interplay of ego and empathy in face to face groups led to a generally egalitarian sharing of resources and power.[18] Anthropologist, Mary Douglas (1990), writing in the foreword to Marcel Mauss's *The Gift*, makes the same point. She observes that the mandatory reciprocal nature of giving, present in pre-market societies, functioned as the equivalent to an invisible hand.

As the size of social units expanded, however, and the division of labor grew increasingly defined, the natural tendency could be obstructed in many ways. The very complexity and distances of the modern market block the natural tendency at many points. Such obstructions permit inequalities that would be unheard of in the small, largely kinship group environment of our evolutionary adaptation.

The concept of unintended consequences or the action of the invisible hand in early social exchange and in the evolved structure of the modern market is made possible by our evolved neural architecture. The idea comes to us intuitively and naturally based on the dynamic of our social brain—the ego/empathy dynamic playing out within each of our skulls as well as between us in social interaction.

The intuitive doctrine of unintended consequences or the invisible hand launched a determined research program to scientize it. This program called general equilibrium theory has been the core of modern economic theorizing from Adam Smith to the present day. The next chapter will take a closer look at the evolution and status of general equilibrium theory.

---

[18] Primatologist Christopher Boehm in his study of the origins of egalitarian behavior notes that all known foraging societies were egalitarian. He comments that one of the great mysteries of social evolution is the change from egalitarian to hierarchical society (1999: 88).

11

THE NEURAL BASIS OF
GENERAL EQUILIBRIUM THEORY

In the years following publication of Adam Smith's *Wealth of Nations* (1776), there was a movement to further refine his concepts. Additionally, scholars sought to move economics from the status of a moral science to that of a positive or objective science. The model chosen was, of course, physics. The monumental work of Isaac Newton (1642–1727) with his laws of gravity and the motion of heavenly bodies, was the natural inspiration. Economists sought to discover the natural clock-like laws of the universe that drove the market to equilibrium—like the forces of physical nature and the dramatically precise mathematical calculus that had been developed to describe them.

The prime challenge then was to account for the anticipated market equilibrium in terms of the equilibrium of natural force vectors. The invisible hand was, ambitiously, to be moved from the vague status of a divine intervention or intuited but ill-defined force of human nature or natural law into the status of a mathematically definable set of natural force vectors comparable to those of physics. This search for the underlying regularities of the invisible hand, seen as resulting from the interaction of demand and supply, became known as general equilibrium theory or GET.[19]

GET: OFF ON THE WRONG FOOT

Brain science was not yet born at this time and the model of the physical sciences was the only one available short of the prevailing philosophical speculation about human nature, natural law, or the mystical attributes of the Deity. Furthermore the Newtonian system and methodology were overwhelmingly venerated as the standard of true science in the intellectual circles of the day. This held true in England and also on the continent of Europe. It was impossible to know at that time that the foundation of the market was in the algorithms of our social brain—like brains interacting with like brains—not in the

---

[19] The most comprehensive historical analysis of the invisible hand and general equilibrium theory is contained in Ingrao and Israel (1990).

mechanical laws of physics. GET, thus, got off on the wrong foot to a long and tortuous history. But it couldn't be helped. There was no equivalent or acceptable alternative available.

The GET effort to find the universal physical laws driving the market to equilibrium occupied economists and mathematicians over the next 200 years. Almost every conceivable approach was tried without producing satisfactory results. The efforts continue to this date with at best some limited success but with mostly discouraging outcomes. The largely vain search has led some theorists to suggest that a new approach or paradigm may be needed. The proper model, the CSN model, based in neural architecture did not become available until the full emergence of evolutionary neuroscience in the closing years of the 20th century.

I will briefly trace the main developmental features of GET up to the present. In doing so I will omit much historical detail but hopefully still provide an appreciation of where GET came from and where it stands today.

LÉON WALRAS AND THE FULL ESTABLISHMENT OF GET

The effort to Newtonize the concept of the invisible hand shifted from Adam Smith's Scotland to continental France. The search for the laws of social equilibrium along the lines of Newtonian principles had a long history in France. Montesquieu (1689–1755), historically associated with the doctrine of the separation of powers so fully expressed in the American constitution, was early concerned with exploring the equilibrium of social forces in keeping with the Newtonian paradigm. Equilibrium thinking occupied the minds of many European scholars during the intervening period.

The French economist Léon Walras (1834–1910), however, is the one credited with putting GET effectively on the economic map. Drawing upon the partial work of a number of important predecessors, he put together a set of equations for all the markets of an economy. These equations were to be solved simultaneously to achieve an economy-wide equilibrium. It was an ambitious project, modeled after Newtonian mechanics, in the belief that the laws of economics, like the laws of physics, could be expressed precisely in mathematical form.[20]

Especially important in Walras's system was his development of the utility theory of value. Previous scholars like Ricardo and Karl Marx believed that the amount of labor put into a product determined the value. Walras held that not the labor but the utility or satisfaction that the product yielded to buyers in the market was the proper measure of value.

The prices, then, that people were willing to pay, marked the level of utility for buyers and these prices changed continuously as they groped for a stable equilibrium between

---

[20] Walras not only followed the model of Newtonian mechanics, he also followed Plato's concept of universals. Walras, citing Plato, held that the purpose of science is the study of universals; the only difference among the sciences is with the facts their practitioners select for their study (Walras, 1954: 61). Universals, of course, do not hold in evolved systems, because of the inherent variability we discussed in Chapter 7. Walras, as well as his followers in GET, was putting too great of a demand for precision upon a variable organic dynamic.

sellers and buyers in the market guided by natural underlying market forces. A stable equilibrium of price vectors became the aim of GET.

THE TOP DOWN FORMALIZATION OF GET

The bottom-up approach of Walras and his followers, attempting to match the success of physics, failed to produce the desired results. The mechanical model, then, later gave way to the top-down modeling of mathematician John von Neumann and mathematical economist Oskar Morgenstern. In 1944, they published their jointly authored *Theory of Games and Economic Behavior*. This work launched a new impulse toward axiomatization. This was matched by a somewhat parallel effort by economist Paul Samuelson of Harvard in his *Foundations of Economic Analysis* (1947).

Axiomatization involved the building up of a system or model economy by proposing, without necessity of proof, a set of principles that dictated the direction of movement within the model system. Such a system, then, may or may not have any connection with reality. It was primarily an effort to determine under what conditions a system *could* work.

The new approach was inspired mainly by developments of uncertainty in modern quantum physics. The uncertainty principle, articulated by German physicist, Werner Heisenberg, revealed at the quantum level—the particle-wave duality plus the fact that both the momentum and the position of a particle could not be determined simultaneously. The precise measurement of momentum and position was a process fundamental to the Newtonian system. The findings of quantum physics shook the previously unshakable foundations of straightforward Newtonian mechanics. With uncertainty produced at the foundations of physical science, it was plausible and justifiable to move to a top-down posture of formal modeling in economics. Formal modeling was an attempt to impose some certainty on what had now become an uncertain reality.

The new approach, in turn, led to the top-down axiomatic approach of French economist Gerard Debreu and American economist Kenneth Arrow. What the bottom-up approach failed to achieve, the top-down approach tried anew. The modeling and axiomatic approaches made little attempt to connect with real economic systems. Their purpose was to try to capture the illusive pattern of intuited market forces from the top-down by rigorously structured highly simplified models of possible economies.

The pursuit of the question of a market equilibrium produced by the intuited invisible hand became formally divided into the three categories of existence, uniqueness, and stability. Existence required a general equilibrium of sorts. Uniqueness required that the equilibrium settle at one overall set of prices. Stability required that the market forces themselves drive inevitably toward equilibrium—and not away from it into disequilibrium. All three aspects were considered to be essential to the proof of GET.

The axiomatic formalization of Arrow and Debreu, published jointly in the journal *Econometrica* in 1954, applied the new methodology to the earlier but recently updated GET theory of John Hicks. Hicks, who spent time at both the London School of Economics and Cambridge published his *Value and Capital* in 1939. These efforts, and some follow-on ones using the same approach, did achieve demonstration of the existence of GET under very general assumptions inherently fundamental to the basic Walrasian theory. On the additional problems of uniqueness and stability, the results have been disappointingly unsuccessful. Nevertheless, failure did not deter the committed. Formalization continued apace. In the continuing formalization process, however, form has taken precedent over content. Models have become more and more divorced from reality and equally from empirical verification.

THE FUTURE OF GET
AND THE ASSISTED FREE ENTERPRISE

The over-formalization of GET and the limited success at the end of the past century led Michio Morishima, a theorist at the London School of Economics, to judge the world of GET to be in fact a dream world not workable in the context of actual society (1992: 70–71). He stated that GET economists, including specialists in von Neumann mathematical modeling, had sunk into excessive mental estheticism. Morishima predicted a poor future for GET in the 21st century unless economists could forgo the delights of mathematical display and proceed to build models based on reality.

My own evaluation, based on the recent findings of the foundation of the market in the dynamics of evolved brain structure, is that the further pursuit of uniqueness and stability are probably exercises in futility. The neural algorithms, although providing the intuitive basis for the search for laws and patterns, are too weak and variable—too subject to blockage and frustration in the complexities and distances of the greater market—to ever assure us of getting to an unassisted equilibrium that is unique or stable.

Our challenge is, therefore, to pragmatically assist the market to reach these goals of meeting the needs of society with a minimum of inequalities and the accompanying social (behavioral) tensions. Of course, the motivation to do so is likewise an expression of the ego/empathy dynamic represented by the equation of our social brain.

We will achieve the sought after dynamic equilibrium in the society-wide market of the future only by an empathy/ego-motivated intentional, pragmatic assist to the market forces which themselves emerge from our neural architecture. Such assistance to the market will probably require wisely limited regulation to avoid stifling the incentives that challenge us to produce the societal wealth for the benefit of us all. The *assisted* free enterprise market can lead us into the future and serve the purpose of a global democratic society.

When the study of economics eventually shifts to its proper foundation in the dynamic of our neural architecture, it will have come nearly full circle from the days of Adam Smith. From its origins as a moral or normative science, through its failed transition to a purely positive science, the new economics will emerge as a mixed positive-normative science that will serve us into the future. When that happens the dynamic architecture of our social brain will provide the guiding framework.

12

FRIEDRICH HAYEK
AND WISHFUL THINKING

At the beginning of the 21st century, the legacy of Austrian born Friedrich Hayek (1899–1992) is one of the most influential among theoretical economists in the Western world. His 1944 classic, *The Road to Serfdom*, made the case against socialist command economies.[21] He argued that socialism, as collective or government ownership of the means of production, is not only unproductive, but also intrinsically not free. He felt that individual freedom could not exist under central planning and that private property is essential for both economic productivity and political freedom. In the years following the collapse of the Soviet Union, Hayek's position has become conventional wisdom.

Hayek spent many of his years in the United States, principally at the University of Chicago where he interacted with numerous prominent economic thinkers. He received the Nobel Prize for economics in 1974.

SPONTANEOUS ORDER VS. THE INVISIBLE HAND

Of interest here is Hayek's concept of spontaneous order. On the face of it, the concept sounds similar to Adam Smith's invisible hand. Hayek saw this similarity and acknowledged it. However, the two concepts are significantly different. Hayek's spontaneous order was an order based on the rule of law. Individuals could exchange and interact with each other freely, limited only by the rules of civil society. There was no place in his spontaneous order for the role of sympathy, fellow-feeling, or benevolence as

---

[21] Hayek's *Law, Legislation, and Liberty* (published in three volumes by the University of Chicago Press, 1973, 1976, and 1979) expanded on earlier works to develop his concept of spontaneous order. In *The Fatal Conceit* (1988), he attacks the assumption of socialism that the spontaneous institutions and practices of the market can be done away with in creating a command economy. The collected essays in *Economic Freedom* (1991) are a good source of Hayek's ideas. On moral instincts and social justice, see esp. pp 338–339. Good biographies of Hayek are: Butler (1985). *Hayek: His Contribution to the Political and Economic Thought of Our Time.* Ebenstein (2001). *Friedrich Hayek: A Biography.*

Adam Smith saw it. In fact, Hayek saw such moral feeling as injurious to the production of wealth and its equitable distribution. Hayek's spontaneous order was the invisible hand without the reciprocal of empathy.

Or was it? Let's take a closer look at Hayek's thinking, especially since it is widely accepted today.

HAYEK ON MORAL INSTINCTS
AS IMPEDIMENTS TO THE MARKET SYSTEM

Unlike Thomas Hobbes, Hayek acknowledges that we are not just self-interested but also have moral instincts. He sees these moral instincts, however, as unhelpful in the spontaneous order. In fact, he insists that the moral instincts that we inherited from the face-to-face societies of our primitive ancestors are the chief obstacle to the moral approval of the market system which creates our wealth. This somewhat counterintuitive contention by Hayek deserves some inspection.

According to Hayek, these moral instincts, driving concern for the visible needs of others, were necessary to the survival of the group in primitive times. Such moral instincts required that we consciously try to benefit others. The market system, on the other hand required that we concentrate on our own self-interested gain in order to achieve unknowingly and unintentionally, the best outcome for others. This market rule of conduct conflicts with our inherited moral instincts because we cannot see the benefit to others of our own self-interested efforts in the impersonal market.

The moral discomfort we feel, then, leads to the idea that we must consciously act to bring about social justice. This idea, in turn, interferes with the proper functioning of the market and is conversely destructive of the wealth necessary to provide benefits to all. From this Hayek concludes that the conscious pursuit of social justice is a mirage and destructive of the spontaneous order under which the unrestricted free market will take care of social justice automatically.

SPONTANEOUS ORDER OR WISHFUL THINKING

Hayek's is a hopeful case based, in part, upon wishful thinking. His motivation can be understood and appreciated as a reaction to the abuses if not horrors of national socialism in Germany and the failure of command, centrally planned economies under communism.

Nevertheless, it is, at best, a theoretical, if not an ideological position. There is very little evidence to support the positive and relatively balanced outcomes that he anticipates from a completely unrestricted market. And because of the harshness involved in establishing such a market no government has yet been able politically to implement such a system.

Although the evidence is clear that a relatively free market (there has never been a completely free market) does produce more wealth than centrally planned or centrally controlled ones, there is no evidence to show that the unfettered market achieves on its own anywhere near an equitable distribution or even the elimination of poverty. There are just too many obstructions that prevent the natural tendency from achieving its ideal equilibrium state.

However, the conflict Hayek sees between the market and our inherited moral instincts can be resolved with a proper understanding of the evolution and structure of the market as the institutionalized expression of our neural architecture. Just knowing that the productive, supplying side of the equation is fundamentally an expression of mammalian nurturing should relieve the moral discomfort somewhat. Moreover, paying close attention to one's productive enterprise—that is, insuring quality of product and service, being trustworthy and honest in business relationships, having concern for consumer safety and welfare—is not simply self-interest. It is, rather, the combined expression of self-interest and empathy necessary to a proper working of the free enterprise market system.

MARKET STRUCTURE AND MARKET COMPETITION

It is important here to keep in mind the real nature of market competition. Competition can be properly understood by holding in memory the distinction made in Chapter 10 between market structure and market behavior.

In the institutionalized market structure, expressing the dynamic of our neural architecture, behavior is different toward competitors than toward customers. This critical distinction is often forgotten or not grasped in the first place.

In the mammalian structure of the market, suppliers and producers *compete*—not with customers or buyers—but with each other to *serve* or *provide* for the needs of the *customers or buyers*. The very structure of the market requires or forces this as a fundamental posture. Providers or sellers don't *compete* with the customers to see if they can delude, outfox, or rip them off. Although this is a flawed posture that some seem to fall into. They compete with other providers.

To repeat—market competition, then, is not between providers and customers. It is between sellers and providers, to better serve the demands of customers—and, of course, to receive in reciprocity the reward or profit they well deserve for so doing.

STRUCTURAL EMPATHY VS. BEHAVIORAL EMPATHY

Empathy always plays its reciprocal role in the market. That role may be structural, behavioral, or both. In the face of market competition, suppliers—to survive in the market—*must* perform the *structural* equivalent of empathy. They must do so even if they do not feel empathy as a personal motivation. That is, in the face of competition from other suppliers, they must provide the best possible product or service to meet the needs of the customers.

On the other hand, however, if suppliers perform their services with concern for quality, care for the well-being of the customer, with a sense of social responsibility, and with a commitment to fair play, they express empathy in behavior. Empathy in market behavior builds trust and in the long run reduces the costs of market transactions.

Empathy in behavior may also act as a limiting influence on the runaway corporate greed we see so flagrantly practiced in the market. At least the acknowledgement of empathy's primary motive status would undercut the moral rationale for greed implicitly provided by the emphasis on self-interest as a sole primary motive. This faulty overemphasis on self-interest characterizes Hayek's spontaneous order as pervasively as it does mainstream economics.

The free enterprise market, when properly understood, then, does *not* conflict with what Hayek calls our inherited moral instincts (empathy), but provides the opportunity to consciously and intentionally satisfy them.

CREATIVITY, CREATIVE DESTRUCTION, AND THE FREE ENTERPRISE MARKET

A proper grasp of the dynamic nature of the competitive free enterprise market leads to a better understanding of one of its most important features—its remarkable creativity. As providers or suppliers seek, under terms of full and relatively free competition, to better respond empathetically to the needs, wants, and desires of the buyers, they each seek differential advantage in so doing. The natural outcome is a process of continuous innovation and creativity. The very institutionalized ego/empathy dynamic structure of the market not only forces but incents this posture. Those providers who fail to innovate fail to survive in a competitive market. Competition among suppliers and providers is essential to the innovative, creative process.

Economist Joseph Schumpeter coined the term *creative destruction* to characterize this constantly innovative aspect of the economy of capitalism (Schumpeter 1942).[22] Creative destruction and creative innovation are but two sides of the same coin. Without an understanding of the true nature of the market as the expression of our neural dynamic, Hayek was unable to grasp the essential structural role of empathy in the creativity of the competitive market.

Of course, as Schumpeter recognized, there are dangerous side effects to this unrestrained innovation and creativity. We face the rapid depletion of resources and the pollution of the environment—even international conflict. There is also the problem of inequalities. Such effects might provoke political intervention that stifles the productivity of the system. How to cope adequately with such side effects constitutes one of the greatest challenges facing the free enterprise system in the new century.

This takes us back to the problem of Hayek's spontaneous order.

RESPONSE TO MARKET FAILURE: PRAGMATISM VS. IDEOLOGY

Despite the wishful thinking of Hayek's poorly comprehended spontaneous order, the market fails. With the variability of the tug and pull of ego and empathy within the

---

[22] Schumpeter writing in 1942 saw the capitalist entrepreneur always seeking new commodities, new technologies, new sources of supply, and new organizational forms. This process brought large scale change if not upheaval. The great advances brought by computer and information technology seem to bear out Schumpeter's vision. Of course, Schumpeter saw an inevitable tendency toward socialism propelled by this dynamic aspect of capitalism. It remains to be seen if he eventually proves right on that score. Creativity and innovation continue to be at a premium in the competitive high tech environment. Rodan (2002) reports research indicating that innovation by managers is related to the diversity of knowledge to which they are exposed and depends also on sparse networks permitting the local autonomy required for the development and implementation of new ideas.

market structure, the market notably falls short of achieving its anticipated or predicted equilibrium states. In addition, factors with potential to obstruct the neural dynamic are simply too numerous and their interactions too complex. In the vast markets of today, there is more than ample room for market failure and the creation of undue suffering and inequality—even the persistent poverty we see existing among riches.

Such market failure permits the creation and accumulation of undesirable and destructive levels of behavioral tension. To cope with this I believe we must take a pragmatic approach, not an ideological one. In any countermeasures, however, we must keep the market sufficiently free to incent for production and the creative growth of wealth. At the same time we must assist the market where it fails to provide adequately or achieve an acceptable level of equitable distribution. Our responses to market failure should be pragmatic and situational, not ideological, or based upon wishful thinking with little evidence to back it

Hayek's naïve concept of spontaneous order, which excludes both the structural and behavioral role of empathy, fails before the new evidence from evolutionary neuroscience. The structure of the market, as the expression of the interplay between self-preservation and mammalian nurturing, provides the basic dynamic for the intuited invisible hand. The neural dynamic is the causal underpinning for the emergence of any spontaneous order. Empathy, or our moral instinct, properly understood, constitutes the necessary reciprocal for any market to exist.

Hayek's spontaneous order is, in the final analysis, no improvement on Adam Smith's intuitive concept of the invisible hand. It is, in effect, a step backwards to the earlier position of Mandeville in his *Fable of the Bees*.[23]

---

[23] See Bianchi (1992) for an interpretation of Hayek's debt to Mandeville.

13

NEURAL ARCHITECTURE
AND PRICE THEORY

It's time to take the analysis to greater depths. We've seen that the neural dynamic of the social brain captures the dynamic of market evolution, the interplay of supply and demand, and the motive power of the invisible hand. So far this is pretty impressive. But these are large scale generalities. How does the social brain dynamic stack up when we get down to the nitty-gritty of microanalysis? Let's take a look at price theory—one of the most well-worked and established branches of economics.

NEURAL ARCHITECTURE AND
THE SCHIZOPHRENIC DUALITY OF THE MARKET

Price theory is structured on the foundational premise that self-interest is the only primary motive of economic exchange. Theorists present and interpret demand curves, supply curves, and the combined form illustrating their intersection at the equilibrium price, from a self-interested viewpoint.

Two functions: demand and supply. One motive: self-interest. The presentation is fine. The interpretation is schizophrenic. The two functions, demand and supply, are themselves the motives of our social brain, ego and empathy, given new names from an economic vocabulary. In reality we have two primary motives disguised as functions with one disguised to the point of denial.

Like the disconnect from reality in the mental condition, the disconnect from reality in economics is not harmless. It creates problems. The denied motive of empathy asserts itself from under the covers as an amorphous irritant. Economists have to deal with its effects while denying its existence. I will return to this later on in the chapter. Right now let's take a look at the various single motive curves and see if the duality shines through.

The Demand Curve

Despite the fact that the demand curve claims to represent one economic function, two motives can be clearly distinguished with a little effort. The declining curve represents the quantity of something that will be demanded or purchased at different prices. At high prices a smaller amount will be demanded. As prices go down the amount demanded will go up. We see two elements, then, quantity on the x-axis, price on the y-axis.

Looking closely, we can easily see that this represents a give and take relationship. If this is my demand curve, for instance, it tells the world that if I must *give* $5 for a unit of a product, I will *take* only one. However, if I only have to *give* $1 for a unit, I will *take* five of them. Clearly, I both take and give in the possible transactions this curve represents. Take and give are just different words expressing the motives of ego and empathy, self-interest and other-interest. If I take something, I expect to reciprocate out of respect or empathy for the other guy's interest. That is, I am not going to steal it. If I were to cheat or steal—show no empathy for the other's interest—the demand curve would be meaningless.

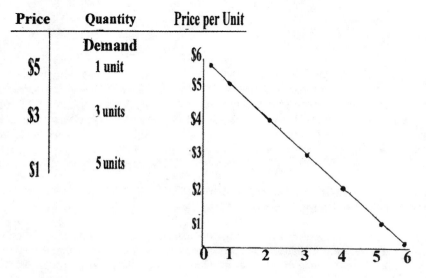

Price	Quantity	Price per Unit
	Demand	
$5	1 unit	
$3	3 units	
$1	5 units	

The demand curve, then, clearly shows the dual motives assumed in the transaction but denied in the theory and interpretation. There is not self-interest only, but also empathy or other-interest.

So much for the demand curve. But does the dual motive show up in the other economic curves? Let's take a look at the supply curve.

The Supply Curve

The supply curve represents the giver, provider, or supplier's viewpoint. I put all three words in—*giver, provider, supplier*—to show the continuity of meaning. Sometimes we loose this continuity when we shift words around. We get the impression we're talking about something new when we're really saying the same thing. This shifting and loss of continuity happens all the time when we cross the boundaries of academic disciplines.

I can also add another word to the list—*seller*. Of the now four word list, *seller* maintains the continuity but adds the special meaning of the transition in market evolution from the gift to the transaction. When we use the word *seller*, we clearly know for the first time that we have a transaction—an exchange with the reciprocal *specified*. We know that the giver, provider, or supplier—as a seller—expects to be paid a price for the product provided. The reciprocal is not diffuse but is now specified. The shift in market evolution, as discussed in earlier chapters, is clearly marked historically by the shift in words. History repeats itself every time we subliminally make this word choice.

The supply curve represents how much this giver or provider, now become seller (we know the historical shift has taken place because we see the prices on the y-axis) will provide at the prices indicated. The supply curve goes up because the seller is willing to provide or sell more as the price gets higher. That is, at $ 5 per unit, the supplier would be willing to provide five units. On the other hand, if the price were $1 per unit, the supplier would be willing to supply only one unit.

As in the demand curve the dual motive comes through clearly on close inspection. The provider-seller performs the empathetic structural role, the role of mammalian nurturing. His/her ego is reaffirmed by an expression of gratitude, a thank you, in the form of a payment specified by the price. Good job. Well done.

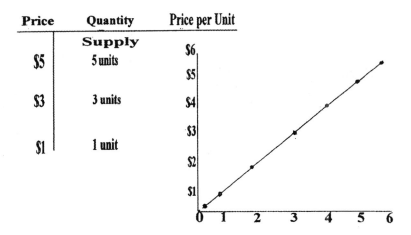

Price	Quantity
	Supply
$5	5 units
$3	3 units
$1	1 unit

The give and take, ego and empathy, of the supply curve are there for all to see. Not one primary motive of self-interest, but two primary motives working together.

Both the demand and supply curves, then, when we properly interpret them, confirm the hidden duality of the transaction. But what about the combined curve—that great artifice of price theory that brings supply and demand together? What does it say about duality?

Equilibrium in the Market

Piece of cake. Of the three, the combined curves show most clearly the duality of the market. Both supplier and demander, giver and taker, are overtly represented. True, they were always there in the demand and supply curves, but now they're out in the open. The driving motives of ego and empathy are revealed in all their splendid duality. To claim that self-interest is the only primary motive, as economic theory does, is clearly a flat denial of reality.

Price	Quantity	
	Supply	Demand
$5	5 units	1 unit
$3	3 units	3 units
$1	1 unit	5 units

The intersection of the two curves is said, in standard price theory, to represent the equilibrium price. Demand and supply equal each other and the market is said to clear.

On close inspection, however, the illustration says more. It represents the function of our dynamic neural architecture, the tug and pull of ego and empathy, in balance. The dynamic tug and pull has been pinned down, fixed artificially at a moment in time by price—the specified, impersonal reciprocal. On the grand scale of the market as a whole, the illustration can be said to represent the invisible hand as attested by such economist luminaries as Walras and Alfred Marshall among many others.

The entire process, then, at a microlevel of analysis, clearly shows the shaping power of our dynamic neural architecture. Let's crank in the expanded social equation to cover the dynamics of supply and demand as they reach equilibrium in price theory:

$$BT = EP \text{ (equilibrium price)} = \frac{Demand}{Supply} = \pm 1 \text{ (approx equilibrium, unity,)}[24]$$
$$\text{or dynamic balance}$$

---

[24] The plus or minus (±) 1 in this application of the equation not only represents the homeostatic, never stationary, tug and pull of the ego/empathy dynamic, it also captures the negotiating approach to equilibrium price traditionally see in small markets, such as flea markets or bazaars. In such markets buyers and sellers almost always haggle over prices and eventually narrow the range from which both may be satisfied and agree to consummate the transaction. Of course, in the larger markets prices are often artificially fixed within the normally anticipated "haggle" range of demand and supply. But even here, adjustments are often made by the device of sales and clearances. Another interesting point is that the homeostatic dynamic allows for the reversibility of numerator and denominator to keep the measures of magnitudes consistent and avoid unnecessary fractions. This reversibility is made possible because the convergence or divergence from unity is what is of interest. With reversibility the ratio between supply and demand can reveal in a single equation relationships of disequilibrium in prices as well as magnitudes of excess demand or excess supply.

Behavioral tension (BT) as it approaches dynamic balance is the same as or equal to equilibrium price (EP) as demand and supply reach equilibrium. Demanders and suppliers are experiencing minimal behavioral tension or, in other words, they are willing to deal, to complete the transaction at a common price.

Price theory is an expression of the social brain. The neural equation mathematically represents not only the dynamic of our neural architecture, of supply and demand, as well as the invisible hand—it is the foundational calculus for price theory.

Further, it cures the schizophrenic condition produced by the faulty interpretation of self-interest as the sole primary motive. The social equation allows us to see clearly the duality of the market. It heals the split between motives and functions in price and market theory.

THE BONUS EFFECT:
PRICE BECOMES AN ENDOGENOUS VARIABLE

As if the healing of schizophrenia were not enough, we get a bonus effect from the foregoing analysis.

In economics price is treated as exogenous. Exogenous means that price itself is outside the frame of analysis. Economists don't know where price comes from or why it changes. They just take it for granted—as given. That means that in standard economic theory, demand and supply curves are related *only* at the equilibrium price. Price, as an exogenous variable draws them together, but remains unaccounted for.

This lack of explanation is troubling to economic theorists and they often introduce an artificial device to make things sound sensible. Some use the French concept of *tâtonnement* or "groping" to characterize the indeterminate sourcing of price.[25] Others introduce the fiction of an auctioneer that calls the various prices across the span of the market and notifies both the suppliers and demanders when equilibrium is reached so that they can take advantage of it. Needless to say, it's a rather awkward if not humorous set of devices—not designed to inspire confidence except, perhaps, in the minds of the most committed devotee or true believer.

The neural equation, however, changes price from an exogenous to an endogenous variable. It connects the dynamic of neural architecture with price theory and demonstrates the continuing relationship between demand and supply that exists at all other points on the demand, supply, and combined curves.

BEHAVIORAL TENSION AS MOTIVATOR FOR PRICE CHANGE

We can now identify behavioral tension as the source of motivation for change that brings demand and supply into price equilibrium. At all points outside the equilibrium point demanders and suppliers are unable to get the reciprocity they expect and want.

Result? In keeping with our reciprocal neural algorithms, they experience behavioral tension. This behavioral tension is what motivates buyers and sellers to change their

---

[25] Walras used the *tâtonnement* or groping process to explain the upward and downward movement of prices which solved his set of equations bringing demand and supply into equilibrium (Walras, 1954: 170).

behavior to bring price into equilibrium. Therefore, all points on the demand and supply curves that do *not* match the equilibrium point are clear indicators of behavioral tension. This, again, effectively confirms the dynamic unity of neural architecture with economics.

Of course, this change brought by the social equation only explains the motivational source for price changes. The problem of communicating the changes to buyers and sellers across the greater market remains.

14

SELF-INTEREST AND
THE SELF-REFERENCE FALLACY

Before going further with the microanalysis started in Chapter 13, I want to make a short detour. I think the detour topic is timely and important. The topic concerns the well-known animal behavior or ethological phenomenon of defense of territory in the face of change. Both aspects—resistance to change and defense of territory are common among academicians as well as other higher primates. Economists are no exception.

In analyzing the fundamentals of price theory, we saw that there was an unacknowledged schizophrenic duality lurking in the shadows. It was resolved by the linkage with the dynamic of our social brain. The expansion of the social equation represented mathematically the linked relationship between neural architecture and the market dynamic.

$$BT \ = \ EP = \frac{Ego}{Empathy} \ = \ \frac{Demand}{Supply} = \pm 1$$

Despite the convincing demonstration, economists will likely be slow to accept it. I know. I have presented the material at several economic conferences. Economists, like other creatures, don't like change and they defend their territory. And, in this case, they have marked their territory meticulously.

SKEPTICISM IN THE AIR: IT'S IMPOSSIBLE!

On the return trip by air from one such academic conference, a fellow economist who had attended my presentation, was seated a couple of rows ahead. He looked back, saw me, and asked to look at my paper again. Obligingly I produced it. He studied it intently during a thirty minute leg of the flight. Finally, he handed it back to me saying, "I think it's accurate as far as the psychology or neuroscience, but it's not possible to apply it to economics."

The response was enlightening. It reminded me of when my mother and father took us kids to visit New York for the first time back in 1946. At that time the Empire State

Building was famously the tallest building in the city if not the world. My eleven-year-old younger brother, who was always the skeptic, stood with the family on the sidewalk in front of the building and gazed up at the towering structure almost disappearing into the low clouds. After a few studied moments, he muttered profoundly: "That's impossible!" Here was my first experience with the skeptic's denial of bare-faced reality.

TERRITORIAL DEFENSE AND *HOMO ECONOMICUS*

Economists, of course, are very human in their dislike of change and their defense of territory. Their pet concept *homo economicus*, or economic man, has been a proud icon of the discipline—of their territory. They rush to defend it when it appears threatened. The core of *homo economicus* is rational, self-interested man. Economists take considerable pride in the explanatory power of this venerable concept. Like true believers they try to extend its reach beyond economics into other social science disciplines. They even take pride in turning such venerated human institutions as marriage and child-rearing into the self-interest calculus of *homo economicus*.

In recent years, the evidence for empathy and cooperation among humans, has accumulated dramatically. This has caused some embarrassment for economists subscribing faithfully to *homo economicus*. Reacting to criticism of the exclusive emphasis on self-interest in the face of evidence for empathy, cooperation, and even altruism, economists have compromised. They grudgingly acknowledge the interlopers, but don't give them full status. Self-interest remains the only primary motive. The "softer" human qualities—soft-headed some might say—are called preferences or tastes. Let's take a look at the problems this half-hearted compromise creates.

SELF-INTEREST VIA SELF-REFERENCE

Economists maintain the primacy of self-interest while accommodating other motives by a shift in perspective. They do this by shifting from self-interest to self-reference. This is probably an unconscious defensive stratagem, but it amounts to a logical fallacy.

The confounding of *self-reference* with *self-interest* is, in fact, a fundamental fallacy of the entire traditional economic approach. The fallacy allows the subsuming of all motives under the rubric of self-interest and obscures the roughly equal role of empathy. Taking the individual as the starting point, microeconomic theory mistakenly *transforms* this individual or self-referential *perspective* into an all-inclusive *motive* of self-interest. From this logically unwarranted transformation any other motive is, thus, obscured or swallowed up in self-interest. Therefore empathy—and its derivatives of cooperation and altruism, even love—cannot be considered true motives. They must, therefore, be trivialized as tastes or preferences indistinguishable in significance from such banalities as coffee, tea, or milk.

But as we saw in Chapter 13, under the sweeping searchlight of the social brain dynamic, the hidden duality of ego and empathy is revealed in every demand curve and supply curve, especially when both are combined to show price equilibrium. The dual roles are always present implicitly if not explicitly. The supplier performs the empathetic role; the demander performs the egoistic role.

THE PROBLEMS WITH EMPATHY
AS A PREFERENCE OR TASTE

Economic theory has not yet come to terms with the new findings from evolved brain structure that I have been presenting so far. It's new stuff and many economists are probably still totally unaware of its existence. So mainstream economics currently proceeds happily on its way from the self-reference perspective to treat self-interest as the only primary motive. Empathy is treated as a taste or preference. The problems with such treatment are numerous. I have summarized the most important ones below:

1. Empathy becomes optional. You may have such a taste or preference or not. This is distorting because empathy is *not* optional. Empathy is a fundamental motive of our neural architecture roughly equal with self-interest or ego. It proceeds from the very large, very visible, and very identifiable mammalian neural structures.
2. It trivializes empathy. Empathy as a preference or taste is indistinguishable from a taste or preference for Fords or Mercedes or for tennis shoes or sandals.
3. It distortingly forces a rational self-interested perspective.
4. It misconstrues the real nature of the market.
5. It obscures the dynamic shaping effect of the ego/empathy interplay in all social exchange.
6. It is not consilient with evolutionary neuroscience—a more fundamental science.

Taken all together, the above six shortfalls add up to serious error. Any discipline devoted to the scientific method should manifest some uneasiness about such a gap between theory and fact. Perhaps it is time for economists to wake up to the new reality, forego their defensiveness and inertia to change, and meet the new challenges presented head-on.

I think the changes will do little damage to the discipline as a whole and will equip it to move more hopefully into the 21st century. Escaping the morally-challenged straitjacket of sole self-interest should be refreshing to economists as well as the rest of the world. Do we really need to continue educating our economists and business leaders in the fundamentals of self-interest? Do we really need a theory that provides subtle justification for corporate greed? Do we really need that a theory that presents our very valuable free enterprise system to the developing world, in the throes of globalization, as a heartless, materialistic expression of human selfishness? Especially, do we really need to hang on to a theory when that theory is no longer scientifically justifiable?

15

NEURAL ARCHITECTURE AND THE MARKET CALCULUS

Detour over. Back to analysis. In this chapter I take up some simple applications of calculus used in price theory. Calculus is loved by some, scary to many. I may be going back on my promise to keep the math simple. So I don't blame you if you choose to skip this chapter.

But if you hang in there I think it's worth doing. It allows me to demonstrate further the important linkage between our dynamic neural architecture and the market. It also lets me show you how clarifying that linkage brings new insights. That is, we can see relationships that were invisible before—hiding there in the shadows—like the duality of the market which was obscured from view by the faulty assumption of the sole self-interest motive.

I think you can follow the math with a little background in basic algebra. I will assume you are staying with me and plow right ahead.

CALCULUS IN PRICE THEORY

In standard texts on price theory, demand and supply are represented as *functions* that convert prices to quantities. But what are these things called functions?

Functions are mathematical devices that are defined by what they do. In this case, functions take numbers in one group and assign them to numbers in another group. Economists use the mathematical notation of functions to *represent* the relationship which they *perceive* to exist between demand and supply:

$$D(P) = \text{Quantity demanded at price P}$$

$$S(P) = \text{Quantity supplied at price P}$$

The notation D(P), when used to indicate a function, does *not* have the usual algebraic meaning of multiply D by P. And it is not read that way. As a function, it is read D of P or D at P. And D at P assigns a specific number demanded at P which amounts to a specific price. The number assigned is the quantity demanded at that price.

S(P) is read and treated the same way. S at P assigns a specific quantity supplied at a specific price.

From functions we can move to derivatives. Derivatives, simply put, are rates of change. They are indicated by placing a prime marker at the upper right of the symbol for function. The derivative, or rate of change, for the demand function D then is indicated by D'. It is read D prime. The same holds for the supply function. S' is read S prime. When expressed with the parenthetical P for price, they are read as follows: D'(P) reads D prime of P. S'(P) is read S prime of P.

Derivatives as used in price theory are expressed as follows:

The fact that the demand curve slopes downward is expressed by the inequality

$$D'(P) < 0$$

The above is read D prime of P is less than zero. A rate of change (derivative) less than zero means that the value of the rate of change is negative. Therefore price is declining (as reflected on the y-axis) and so the curve slopes downward. The curve also moves forward along the quantity demanded line (x-axis) marking the increase. The net effect is to illustrate or *represent* the standard relation believed to exist between price and quantity demanded—as price declines the quantity demanded increases.

The fact that the supply curve slopes upward is expressed by the inequality

$$S'(P) > 0$$

The above is read S prime of P is greater than zero. A rate of change (derivative) greater than zero means that the value of the rate of change is positive. Therefore price is rising (as reflected on the y-axis) and so the curve slopes upward. The curve also moves forward along the quantity supplied line (x-axis). The net effect is to illustrate or *represent* the standard relation believed to exist between price and the quantity supplied—as price increases the quantity supplied increases.

Equilibrium price is the price at which the functions D of P and S of P are equal to each other. This is *represented* by the notation

$$D(P) = S(P)$$

Equilibrium quantity is the common value which must be identified as the quantity both demanded and supplied at the equilibrium price or point on the graph. On the graph presented in Chapter 12, the common value is about 3 units at the equilibrium price of $3.

HIDDEN RELATIONSHIP REVEALED:
PRICE AS INDICATOR OF BEHAVIORAL TENSION

When treated in the standard manner above, demand and supply are related *only* at the point of equilibrium—the equilibrium price. As in Chapter 13 analyzing the demand, supply, and equilibrium curves, price is an exogenous (originating outside) variable that brings demand and supply together but remains essentially unexplained. In the calculus used above, demand and supply are treated separately prior to their intersection at the equilibrium point.

The calculus model used in standard price theory, then, does *not* represent the relationship that we discovered earlier in Chapter 13—the behavioral tension that *exists at all other points*. The equation of our social brain expressing the dynamic of neural architecture again reveals this hidden relationship. I repeat for effect:

$$BT = EP = \frac{DEMAND}{SUPPLY} = \pm 1 \text{ (unity, approx. equil.)}$$
$$\text{dynamic balance}$$

This extension of the neural social equation, applied also in Chapter 13, means, of course, that all other points (prices) on the demand and supply curves are indicators of behavioral tension. Behavioral tension, then, equates to price; or, said another way, price is an indicator of behavioral tension.

Price or behavioral tension *not* in equilibrium is what motivates demanders and suppliers to alter prices in the direction of equilibrium.

Price at equilibrium indicates minimal behavioral tension and so is acceptable to both demanders and suppliers.

The plus or minus (±) 1 indicating approximate or approaching equilibrium maintains the representation of the tug-and-pull homeostatic dynamic of the neural architecture. At the same time it represents the possible range of acceptable prices as buyer and seller haggle to reach agreement. In this case the equilibrium price can be the single price arrived at out of an equilibrating range of prices. Such is the essence of any negotiating process in the market, no matter how formalized. The give and take negotiating that leads to an acceptable price is seen clearly in domestic flea markets and in many similar institutions (e.g., bazaars) around the world. In our larger, impersonal markets, of course, the price may be arbitrarily fixed. But here, too, the price is often effectively negotiated within a range by such devices as sales or clearances.

Price, therefore, by linking with the dynamic of neural architecture now becomes an endogenous variable. That is, it becomes a variable that we can explain or account for within the now extended frame of analysis.

THE SOCIAL EQUATION AND
THE RELATIONSHIP BETWEEN DEMAND AND SUPPLY

I have now completed the excursion into mathematical analysis. This is as far into math as we'll go in this book. Even if the excursion was difficult for some, I think it was worth the effort because of the insights it afforded us.

We saw in Chapter 13 that the relationship between demand and supply represented by the demand, supply, and equilibrium curves was clarified by applying the social equation And by doing so we exposed and accounted for the hidden duality of ego and empathy, give and take, in every such curve. Also we were able to bring price into consideration as an endogenous variable. In this present chapter we saw that the standard use of the calculus in price theory also does not give the full story. The calculus model, customarily used, obscures the same dual relationship as well as the source of price. By applying the social equation to the market calculus, we further confirmed the insights of Chapter 13.

The outcome of our excursion into mathematical analysis, thus, provides confirmation that the dynamic of our neural architecture shapes the exchange process. And the application of the social equation, expressing that dynamic clarifies what has previously been obscure in the analysis of demand and supply in standard price theory or microeconomics.

16

THE NEURAL DYNAMIC IN EQUILIBRIUM MODELING

I will end this section on application of the neural dynamic to economics with a look at a more popular theme. We were captivated by the story of Nobel prize winner John Nash. We were fascinated, perhaps more by the human interest story than the mathematical achievements themselves. The book and the movie *A Beautiful Mind* played upon the mystique of mathematics as well as the popular fantasy that insanity and genius are closely related. We like to believe in the mysterious. And we also like to think that those who are different from us are a bit weird. Both mystique and weirdness played together to capture the popular imagination.

But mystique and weirdness contribute nothing to understanding. They, in fact, get in the way. Mystique emerges from superstition; weirdness from ignorance. Neither have a legitimate place in science. And neither help to clarify the nature of the so-called Nash equilibrium. Nash himself did not grasp the underlying dynamic necessary to such an equilibrium. In fact, the fundamental nature of the Nash equilibrium remains unclarified to this date.

As it stands the Nash equilibrium is simply a concocted mathematical structure without inherent roots. It dangles unanchored out in mathematical space tethered only tenuously to reality by the statement of arbitrary and not justified conditions, assumptions, and axioms, accepted as given and not subject to challenge—constraints called forth from the depths of a source unknown. Why then has it drawn so much attention in the social sciences?

THE MYSTIQUE OF MATHEMATICS

The answer is: Partly because of the mystique about mathematics. Partly because of its perceived utility. Math has been exceptionally useful in physics. What we require in physics is a good mathematical *representation* of a physical reality so that we can manipulate it and perhaps eventually control it. The key word here is representation. Mathematics *represents* the reality. It is not the reality itself and does not have the same authority. Anything that can be systematically discriminated—time, space, speed or change can be disassembled and reassembled tautologically, following the patterns of our neural network architecture, by clarifying, refining, and re-invoking the same relationships that held in the initial discriminations. In such cases math can be made to have application to the real world.

But then the mystique makers take it further. Captivated by the seeming ethereal uniformity of brain-discriminated and created units of representation—their so-called symbolic beauty—many have seen math as existing independently of the human brain that creates it. Such persons see the elements of math as platonic universals having an existence in the universe independent of humans or anything else. Perfect forms in themselves. Forms themselves existing without substance but strangely applicable to all substance.

It is quite a romance, this platonic math, this math of pure forms. But pure forms are one thing, utility in reality another. The success of math in representing, describing and quantifying the forces and processes of real life physics is quite impressive. It is also understandable.

There is, thus, an inherent duality in our perception of math. On the one hand, in applying math to physics as well as our daily lives, we are playing back and forth across the patterns of our neural architecture upon our own arbitrary units of discrimination. The fact that the units seem inherent in our neural architecture leads easily to the platonic illusion. On the other hand, math has proven of great heuristic tool for clarification of the relationships among matter-energy, time-space. This is an accomplishment of substance —not the speculative and highly dubious platonic math of pure and empty form. Math need not dangle, disembodied and unanchored, devoid of meaning but esthetically beautiful, in empty space. Math can lead us to something of value, some dynamic reality.

But the mystique of math combines the two, the empty speculation as well as the discovery and description of substance. The success of math in quantifying the discriminations of physics has inspired envy and mimicry by the social sciences. And the social sciences have imported not one but both aspects of the mystique indiscriminately.

MATHEMATICAL MYSTIQUE AND THE SOCIAL SCIENCES

The social sciences have thus become pervaded with mathematics. Not necessarily meaningful mathematics. But math for the sake of math. Entire journals are dedicated to such exercises. Almost all journals are infected by them. No matter how insignificant the research questions, if the math is presented in good form, the article is almost always judged on just that alone. The result is an outpouring, an overwhelming cascade of the trivial, transient, and ephemeral. Snapshots in time of shifting, amorphous, and dubious variables with no long term or generalizable significance. Mathematical manipulation of trivia almost totally lacking in social, economic, or political utility. Form without substance.

Why then has the Nash equilibrium captured the imagination of so many and been so widely called upon? Because it is expressed in terms of formal math, thus indulging our fascination with mystique? Probably. But also equally probably because it is innately, subjectively appealing. Why the subjective appeal? What social reality, if any, does the Nash equilibrium connect with that makes it intuitively appealing to us? If it does connect, we should be able to see its outcomes, its applications. We should also be able to discover the dynamic upon which it turns gropingly in the yet unpenetrated shadows of causality.

Consider this: we know the cause of the force of gravity. Before we knew the cause and properly described it, we just knew that things fell off other things in an earthward direction. They always fell down. They never fell up, except temporarily when impelled by an identifiable force.

We are still in the pre-causal-gravity-stage of understanding the Nash equilibrium. Nash's formalized artifice seemingly grasps at a social phenomenon—not as clear cut as gravity—but we think we see something like it occurring out there. We follow Nash through elaborate formal symbolism to try to frame the elusive dynamic—to prove our subjective intuition of its importance and reality. Yet we haven't the foggiest idea of why it does what it does. We have no grasp of the causal dynamic. Where should we look?

THE CLUES IN THE CONDITIONS, ASSUMPTIONS, AND AXIOMS

Perhaps we should look first at the triad upon which Nash's formalization is based: the conditions, assumptions, and axioms. These are the givens. They are not to be questioned. They are asserted—the framework that the dynamic must work within to achieve the equilibrium. But where do they come from?

Anybody's guess. The mathematician doesn't justify them or explain them. Like the first premises of the French renaissance philosopher, René Descartes, they come from intuition or common sense without having to be established or justified.

By postulating the triad, the mathematician, gropingly seeks to see if she or he can corral the intuitive, vaguely apprehended causal dynamics. This approach has heuristic or exploratory value. It can lead to eventual discovery and definition of the causal dynamics. But it is not a very scientific or objectively empirical beginning. Rather, it is a highly subjective one. Nevertheless, in the conditions, assumptions, and axioms may lay clues to the unarticulated, indeed not understood, dynamic. What are they saying or suggesting about the dynamic, which amorphous unspecified force they are trying to corral?

THE SOCIAL EQUATION AS THE CAUSAL DYNAMIC

Nash equilibriums as conceived by John Nash apply to human behavioral interactions. Nash's modeling proceeds like standard economic theory on the explicit assumption of rational, self-interest as the primary motive. Some game theorists have applied Nash's methodology to nonbehavioral situations in such areas as ecology, gene theory, and population biology. Such efforts draw on Nash's formalism, but they tap a different fundamental dynamic. They are at best analogous in form only. They are not and should not be called Nash equilibriums.

Nash equilibriums are always social and the social equation is the dynamic underlying the Nash equilibrium. Without the social dynamic the equilibrium—even the assumption of the equilibrium—would be impossible. Although entirely dependent on the social dynamic, the Nash equilibrium is not based on a conscious grasp or clearly stated articulation of that dynamic.

EMPATHY AS IMPLICIT IN THE NASH EQUILIBRIUM

The *essential* condition of a Nash equilibrium is a social exchange relationship—or a social game as implied and treated by the terminology of formal and mathematical game theory. And there could be no social exchange without empathy. Social exchange requires the ability to put oneself in the other's shoes, otherwise one would not be able to appreciate or evaluate the preferences of another. The understanding and evaluation of other's preferences are essential to a Nash equilibrium. The understanding and evaluation of other's preferences are also fundamental to any concept of empathy. Empathy, then, is foundational to any concept of a Nash equilibrium. It appears not to be only because it is obscured by the formal methodology. We should not be fooled by this.

Empathy, then, is a foundational, but unclarified assumption of any Nash equilibrium. But does it sometimes appear explicitly? Yes, it does. To see this we must go to the original statements by Nash himself, avoiding some later extensions of his work which in some cases have become so overly formalized as to be totally vacuous abstract exercises.

NONCOOPERATIVE VS. COOPERATIVE GAMES: IMPLICIT VS. EXPLICIT EMPATHY

First we have to look at Nash's distinction between noncooperative and cooperative games. In both games players reach an equilibrium in which no player may improve his/her position as long as other players maintain theirs.

In noncooperative games, no prior negotiation or agreement is assumed. Individual players just act on their own independently. But don't be fooled. The action inevitably takes place within a *social context*. Without the social context, there is no game. The social context, then, is crucial. Preferences of others must be understood and evaluated. And besides Nash lays on the requirement of "accepted ethics of fair play"(1951: 294). Fair play means we play by the rules and respect the rights of others. Such is the essence of empathy. Empathy is implicit but nevertheless clearly required.

In cooperative games, prior negotiation and agreement, take place. This is the only distinction between cooperative and noncooperative games. In the negotiation and agreement of cooperative games, the role of empathy becomes more obvious. To bargain and reach agreement *explicitly* requires the ability to understand, evaluate, and respect other's preferences, strengths, etc. Even when the additional condition of enforcement by a referee is added (1951: 295), this represents in itself just another agreement requiring empathy.

Without the agreements and ethics of fair play—the implicit and necessary empathy—the structure of both noncooperative and cooperative games, as conceived by Nash, simply collapses. The games become impossible, except perhaps in the most trivial, inconsequential form. Solutions become random.

Both noncooperative and cooperative games then involve the estimation and accommodation of self-and other-interest (empathy). In fact that's what the game is all about.

Let's take some further examples from Nash's own words. In an early paper (1950), titled *The Bargaining Problem*, Nash opens with the following statement: "A two person bargaining situation involves two individuals who have the opportunity to collaborate for mutual benefit"(1950: 155). "Mutual benefit" engages ego and empathy. It implies a chance to balance self- and other-interest. The game further requires equal bargaining skill, full knowledge of each other's preferences, the agreement of the two parties on what is a fair bargain, and both a give (empathy) and take (ego) between the two (1950: 159, 161). Empathy is clearly fundamental in this paper.

In a later paper (1953) called the *Two-Person Cooperative Game*, Nash expands on the bargaining problem. He writes:

The theory presented here was developed to treat economic (or other) situations involving two individuals whose interests are neither completely opposed nor completely coincident. The word cooperative is used because the two individuals are supposed to be able to discuss the situation and agree on a rational joint plan of action....

This statement clearly requires consideration of self- and other-interest and a consent to give and take within agreed rules.

The concept of a Nash equilibrium, as conceived by Nash, thus, rests clearly on the causal dynamic of the reciprocal algorithms of our evolved neural architecture. In terms of the social equation, a Nash equilibrium is an equilibrium that approaches dynamic balance as well as optimizing utilities.

THE SHORTFALLS OF THE GAME MODEL

There are several shortfalls of the game model set out by Nash. Most of these Nash himself acknowledged. Some of them characterize almost all mathematical and economic modeling. Some, but not all, of these shortfalls or limitations are:

1. The modeling is highly idealized. This is openly stated by Nash and is necessary to get where he wants to go with his modeling. Highly idealized means the modeling is divorced from the messy details of reality. It has none of the rich texture of real life situations.

2. It is totally dependent on the stated conditions, assumptions, and axioms. These are not justified but are asserted subjectively from intuition. They are all dubious in reality.

3. It doesn't deal with ongoing change. It fixes a transaction or situation artificially at a moment in time. It can't deal with change except at another artificially fixed moment in time. It can't and doesn't deal with shifting reality.

4. It draws on the causal social dynamic, but doesn't identify it. Further, it falls short of grasping the fullness or significance of the dynamic. Like most transactional analysis in economics, it is incomplete. It misses reality in truly important ways. Listed below are a few of these ways.

   a. It assumes the game is complete at the chosen moment in time. It allows for no after effects.

   b. It doesn't tell whether the players like their best solutions. The solutions are the best under the extensively stipulated conditions, assumptions, and axioms.

c. It obscures the effects of behavioral tension. If players are dissatisfied, feel cheated, have ambition to do better, and are motivated to change their outcomes, this means that, in reality, the game is not over! The game solution, then, just represents a snapshot in time of an ongoing process.

d. It obscures the cumulative effects of transactions. Given the human capacity for memory and the dynamic of behavioral tension, these cumulative effects are, in reality, potentially very significant. The modeling lacks any predictability for cumulative behavioral tension that might motivate change or even revolution to redress the progressive, less than equal or less than dynamically-balanced, so-called equilibrium solutions.

The obscuring of the behavioral tension inherent to the dynamic of social neural architecture is the most serious reality flaw in the modeling. The game of the moment is only over for the mathematician or economist who is doing the modeling. In reality—for the rest of us—the game goes on with cumulative, potentially momentous and dangerous effects. It may even blow up in our faces. The modeling blinds us to the cumulative dangers that may confront us, economically and politically.

PRACTICAL WISDOM VS. OBFUSCATION

In sum, Nash's modeling intuits and rides upon the causal dynamic of the social neural architecture. It rests upon the social equation. Nash, however, has no consciously articulated concept of such a dynamic. He tries gropingly to corral the intuited but undefined dynamic by a formal framework of conditions, assumptions, and axioms mediated by symbols—all largely subjectively based. As constructed, the entire edifice rests, not upon empirical reality, but upon intuition and subjectivity. Only the mathematical formality gives it unjustifiably the aura of objectivity. It is not objective, but only formal. By the time all the conditions, assumptions, and axioms are added in to force the solutions, the connection with reality is often very tenuous indeed.

There is, nevertheless, real utility in such modeling. It is useful to the extent that it helps us to focus attention, identify alternatives, and to facilitate systematic thinking. In other words it can be a helpful tool as long as we don't take it too seriously, or endow it and its practitioners with an unwarranted mystique of infallibility.

Of course, the mystique is facilitated and played upon for effect by the entertainment industry which regularly shows actors representing geniuses in front of chalkboards full of esoteric mathematical symbols designed to befuddle and awe-inspire the unsophisticated viewer.

PART III

NEURAL ARCHITECTURE
IN POLITICAL ECONOMY AND
INSTITUTIONAL ECONOMICS

17

POLITICAL ECONOMY:
THE NEURAL DYNAMIC AND SCARCITY

Human society is a product of the human brain. The aspects of society that we term political and economic are likewise products of the human brain. There is no other source for them. There are no political or economic essences or universals, independent of the human brain, existing out there in a positivist, mechanical world waiting to be discovered.

There are, however, environmental constraints. And the brain evolved in dynamic interaction with these constraints. Such constraints include not only the basic constraints of food, shelter, safety, but also the social constraints of the mammalian life form. The human brain functions, among other things, as a normative, evaluative, and environment-shaping organ based upon its evolved mechanisms to assure survival of the individual and the species within the existing constraints. This is accomplished by the dynamic programming for self-preservation and affection, ego and empathy, self- and other-interest.

All human politics and economics are manifestations of the normative, evaluative functioning of the human brain based upon this dynamic programming. There is no such thing as a positivist, value-free human politics, economics, or any other aspect of society.[26] There are only normative variants. Without referring to brain science, I take it that this is what Nobel laureate James M. Buchanan is saying when he writes about the inevitable normative aspects of economics:

And let us be sure to understand that there is no "is" that is "out there" to the observing eye, ear, or skin. We create our understanding of the "is" by imposing an abstract structure on observed events. And it is this understanding that defines for us the effective limits of the feasible. It is dangerous nonsense to think that we do or can do otherwise (1991: 41).

---

[26] The value-free claims of economics and economists are becoming more and more difficult to sustain. Appreciation of this difficulty has led to increased interest in ethics and economics (e.g., see Wilber, 1998: 2).

These normative variants are the range of possible expressions of the algorithms of reciprocal behavior of our evolved brain structure acting within and upon environmental constraints—many of them created by the brain itself, interacting of course with other like brains.

The environmental constraints, then, are the original ones constraining basic survival plus those modifications and additions created by the reciprocal dynamic itself as it shaped our social environment as well as altered our physical environment. Our social, political and economic traditions, institutions, and practices, to include the changes that we have made to our physical resources in the way of technology, are the products of our brain dynamic acting within and upon existing environmental constraints.

One of the greatest shortcomings of economic science to this date has been its failure to appreciate adequately the basic, prime moving, shaping power of the human brain in all things economic and political—as if there could be any other source for such phenomena. Thorstein Veblen, writing earlier, caught the essence of the problem in an eloquent and often quoted passage which described the self-interested or hedonistic conception of man as without antecedent or consequence, buffeted about by forces that push him mindlessly in one direction or another. He concluded that "Spiritually, *the hedonistic man is not a prime mover*" (emphasis mine) (Veblen, 1948: 232–233).

Although Veblen defined the problem of the passive economic man, he got caught up in the materialism and the emergent Pavlovian-Watsonian simplistic stimulus-response behaviorism of his day and merely substituted it for the Newtonian model of physical forces acting on the still passive economic man.

Despite the more recent addition of the concept of a more dynamic, wealth maximizing rational economic man, influenced even more recently by the addition of such neoclassically ignored factors as habit, convention, and institutions, which bring history to bear on the neoclassical isolated moment of economic decision, the economic man is still treated largely passively. This passivity is achieved by the imposition of narrow constraints that obscure the active, shaping dynamic of the brain and force the so-called rational economic actor into equally narrow pre-set options of behavior.

Even in the more process-oriented, evolutionary approach of the new institutional economics, the dynamic shaping power of the brain is not adequately appreciated (e.g., see Langlois, 1986a, b). Among the public choice and institutionalist economists, A. Allan Schmid gets close to a grasp of the reciprocal algorithms of behavior in his focus on the market as a set of interrelationships. He writes: "Rights and opportunity sets are seen as *reciprocal* (emphasis mine), where one person's freedom to act is another's limitation." (1987: xiv). There are important differences, however. In his psychological interpretation of the highly generalized concept of utility maximization, self-interest and altruism are seen as static or stable preferences rather than as the shaping dynamic proceeding from our evolved brain structure (1987: 197–206). This view of egoism, altruism, as well as all other behavioral attitudes, as nondynamic, stable preferences characterizes economic thinking and allows the broad economic approach to be seen as providing a comprehensive framework for understanding all human behavior (e.g., Becker, 1987; Frey, 1992).

The laws, principles, regularities, and the dynamics of politics, economics, and social life itself simply do not exist and cannot be understood independently of the human brain. Any presumed detachment from them is illusory. This holds even in the most rarefied applications of cliometrics and econometrics. Pull the human actors out and the dynamics and econometrics will simply disappear.

When researchers claim they are using positivist, objective approaches, they are simply deluding themselves. A positivist approach in politics or economics usually means that the researcher is implicitly accepting the pre-existing and undefined normative structure of whatever he/she is researching and then assuming that structure away. It is a fundamentally fallacious posture, although it may be assumed, with highly constrained plausibility, in the short term as an operational research position of convenience in order to reduce complexity. Nevertheless all findings or interpretation of findings above the level of triviality will inevitably fall back upon the denied normative foundations or an alternatively substituted set.

NATURAL ENVIRONMENTAL CONSTRAINTS
AND THE PROBLEM OF SCARCITY

The fundamental natural environmental constraint is scarcity. Life exists everywhere in a state of scarcity. The state of scarcity does not mean that the environment is hostile to life. And that life must struggle for survival against this fundamental hostility. The natural environment is, on the contrary, very supportive of life. Early fragile life forms would never have thrived and evolved the amazing variety and complexity of today if the natural physical environment were not extremely supportive.

Although the environment does have limits, much of this scarcity is created by the nature of the organism itself. In this rich, supportive physical environment, the organism, left to its own processes, tends relentlessly to increase to the carrying capacity of the environment. This is a fundamental biological principle. Life is resilient, relentless, blindly automatic, proliferating endlessly within the environment until it runs up against the limits of the environment's capacity to support it. Life inevitably, by its very nature, creates the constraint of scarcity.

We humans, like all other forms of life, create our own constraint of scarcity. This inevitable creation of scarcity by life is the most fundamental, shaping factor of what we call economics. The survival strategy of the human species, like any other organism, is the set of characteristics and behaviors the species evolves or develops for coping with the constraint of scarcity that it produces. This fundamental biological principle, followed also by the human species, that a species will expand to the carrying capacity of the environment, sets the Malthusian tone of economics as the dismal science.[27]

---

[27] Scarcity is seen by economists and presented in introductory texts as the basic economic problem (e.g., see Kohler, 1992: 3; 1968: 5; Allsopp, 1995: 11–29). Economist and Nobel laureate Gary Becker sees the definition of economics in its broadest and most general terms as concerned with scarce means and competing ends (1987). This reflects the influential definition given by Robbins first in 1932. Robbins defined economics as "The science which studies human behavior as a relationship between ends and scarce means which have alternative uses" (1952: 16). Arndt, however, calls scarcity the Cinderella of economic theory because while recognized as basic to economics, it is excluded from effective consideration in economic theory through a series of assumptions including that of equilibria and the more dubious assumption that all scarcity can be overcome by exertion of human industry—in other words, that there are no limits to productivity (1984: 17–36). On the latter theme according to Simon (1981) modern resource economics treats limits as a short-term constraint that a dynamic economy will overcome. In this view neither resources nor any other form of limit is seen to ultimately constrain what the competitive economy can do. Schmid sees scarcity as a function of nature and human tastes (1987: 8).

The human brain evolved as a scarcity coping organ in a primarily kinship based foraging society where sharing or reciprocity was essential to survival and which reinforced the adaptive evolution of the mammalian characteristics of self-preservation and affection (e.g., see Cummins, 1998; Erdal & Whiten, 1996; Isaac, 1978; Humphrey, 1976). The algorithms of reciprocal behavior of our brain structure are, likewise, a scarcity-coping dynamic. They are the dynamic by which human society manages, to the extent that it does, the constraint of its self-produced scarcity.

TECHNOLOGY—COPING WITH NATURAL CONSTRAINTS

The tools, skills, and knowledge which humans create for coping with the natural constraints of the physical environment, as well as later devised social constraints, constitute technology. The evolution of the more recent neocortex gives us the capacity, unlike other species, to alter many of the constraints imposed by nature. Most significantly, we can and have altered the carrying capacity of the environment. For example, we have increased food production and distribution and we have increased living space by erecting buildings skyward. The fundamental thrust of the technology of production is to increase the carrying capacity of the environment, to overcome the constraint of scarcity that we ourselves produce in the first place. Productivity itself has a circular, self-reinforcing effect. The logic of productivity carried to its logical extreme as a limitless end in itself plays upon the scarcity-coping dynamic of our brain structure and turns it, further, into a scarcity-generating dynamic. I will return to this thought later on.

Technology allows us to alter the carrying capacity of the environment. It does not, however, eliminate the inevitable self-generated constraint of scarcity. Instead, it sets up an arms race with an uncertain outcome. As our technology increases the carrying capacity of the environment, we have the inevitable biological tendency to increase in numbers inexorably to reach the limit of that capacity. Ultimately, we will either control by the rational power of our evolved brain this previously inevitable biological principle, or we will continue to increase the carrying capacity of the environment infinitely, or we will exhaust the resources available to us even for additional technology. In the end we will either overcome, control, or become victim to our self-generating constraint of scarcity.

DERIVED ENVIRONMENTAL CONSTRAINTS—INSTITUTIONS

Within this self-produced scarcity-constrained natural environment, humans devise additional constraints. Such devised constraints are called institutions in the economic literature (e.g., North, 1990). These institutions are constraining rules or principles for dealing ultimately with the natural and fundamental constraint of scarcity. Since our three-level brain mechanism is our fundamental evolved social mechanism for dealing with scarcity, these institutions, rules, or devised constraints invariably regulate or order our evolved dynamic of reciprocity.

BETWEEN ECONOMICS AND POLITICS

In recent years the new field of positive political economy has emerged from advances in interdisciplinary research in economics and politics. It is explicitly theoretical seeking to discover principles and propositions by which to compare, explain, and understand actual economic and political experience. It is microeconomic in its focus and is grounded in the rational actor methodology, applying the assumption of constrained maximizing and strategic behavior by self-interested agents to explain the origins and persistence of political institutions as well as public policy (Alt and Shepsle, 1990: 1). Its claim to be "positive", however, is suspect because it rests on the acknowledged evaluative, normative assumption of self-interested, wealth-maximizing individuals. In its failure to recognize the reciprocal nature of exchange as primary, its findings will always be distorted by its underlying assumption of exclusive self-interest. Reciprocity, in the absence of its recognition as the proper basis for microeconomics, will nevertheless be dealt with pervasively and implicitly. Only the fundamental, shaping dynamic of movement and change will be obscured—as it has and continues to be in microeconomics.

The irony and contradiction of the emphasis on self-interested, wealth maximizing behavior by the new positive political economy, which denies empathy or benevolence its place in the reciprocal dynamic, is clearly reflected in the survey introduction to the new subject by Alt and Shepsle (1990). Whereas in the introduction the editors unequivocally claim, as pointed out above, that the theory and methodology is based on the wealth maximizing self-interested rational actor, in a later included article economist Gordon Tullock begins by telling a story about the first time he saw famed Nobel prize winner, Milton Friedman, at a public debate of free enterprise versus socialism. According to Tullock, in that debate Friedman based his entire lecture on what a *benevolent* (emphasis mine) dictator would do. Tullock explains that Friedman intended this simply as a rhetorical device to argue for a free economy and was doing what all economists of that time did—"investigated optimal policies and considered what *well-intentioned* (emphasis mine) people would do if they had control of the government" (Tullock, 1990: 195). At the conclusion of the same article Tullock again acknowledges inadvertently the pervasive factor of empathy when he writes: "Almost all economists, whatever they say, are actually reformers who would like to improve the world."(1990: 210).

In other words, as indicated plainly by Tullock, the finest and foremost in the field of economics are always motivated by and act on empathy, benevolence, and good-intentions rather than the wealth maximizing self-interested motive ascribed to all actors by their theory and methods. These economic theorists are either seeing themselves with implicit arrogance as possessing morality superior to the motives of the lessor rational economic man that they deign to study. Or else, caught up in the rhetoric of self-interest, they implicitly acknowledge, but are overtly and explicitly blind, to the pervasive function of empathy in the socio-economic-politico process of exchange.

COST/BENEFIT ANALYSIS AND HUMAN RECIPROCITY

At this point it is useful to reemphasize that every human relationship or interpersonal act is a social exchange relationship or act. Every such relationship or act can be analyzed in economic terms on a cost/benefit basis or rather in cost/benefit terms.

Cost/benefit is the economic vocabulary for the give and take, the empathy and ego of human reciprocity. Cost/benefit carries the positivist illusion of objectivity because of the association with mathematics, things that can be counted, quantified.

Cost and benefit, what we give and what we take (or get), are just alternative ways of talking about reciprocity, the tug and pull of ego and empathy. We demand and take for our ego, we provide (supply) and give through the vehicle of our empathy. Without empathy we could not engage in a social exchange, economic or otherwise. We would lack the basis for recognizing, responding, and supplying to the needs or demands of others.

In fact, the social equation can be expressed in cost/benefit terms as follows:

$$BT = \frac{Cost}{Benefit} = \pm 1$$

Viewing reciprocity in the artificially detached, quantified cost/benefit terms of current economics may be useful in the counting house. And there need be no overly compelling objection to such as view, held temporarily as an operational convenience, as long as it has some utility and it doesn't claim or substitute itself, explicitly or implicitly, as a full and complete representation of human reciprocity. Unfortunately, such a view inevitably gravitates to that latter position—which is expressed best in the simplistic, reductionist, dehumanizing assumption that pervades economics—the assumption of a solely wealth maximizing self-interested individual economic man. This pervasive assumption obscures or denies the true nature of human reciprocity and has the effect of distorting and dehumanizing social, economic, and political exchange at all levels of the process.

POLITICAL ECONOMY AND
THE MANAGEMENT OF BEHAVIORAL TENSION

The new emphasis on the unity of economics and politics, however, is appropriate and welcome. Broadly speaking it may be considered that institutions concerned with order are political and those concerned with reciprocity and exchange are economic. There is, however, no clear separation between the two. Where they merge into each other, we have institutions of political economy.

To the extent that institutions provide order (regulate)—and they invariably do—they are inherently political. To the extent that they are social—and they invariably are—they impact reciprocity and are therefore economic. Most institutions, whether in the form of principles or whether expressed in concrete organizations reflect this duality. They are concerned with ordering reciprocity in some way. And in that sense they are politico-economic.

The institution of private property, or individual property rights, for instance, has this dual function. It is political in that it provides for the maintenance of a personal and protected resource base for the economic purposes of survival and reciprocal exchange. According to the algorithms of reciprocal behavior, to the extent that unequal holdings of private property or property rights are permitted in any society, the institution of private property produces unbalanced reciprocity among members of the society. Unbalanced reciprocity, potential or actual, leads invariably to inequalities of power. Schmid, for instance, bases virtually his entire concept of power on the presence or absence of property rights.

One's right is another's cost. One person's property right is the ability to coerce another by withholding what the other wants...To own is to have the right to coerce (1987: 9).

And further on he writes:

Power is inevitable if interests conflict. If everyone cannot have what they want simultaneously, the choice is not power or no power, but who has the power (1987: 9).[28]

Power is another way of speaking of hierarchy or relationships of dominance or submission. The algorithms of reciprocal behavior dictate that such relationships invariably carry a degree of behavioral tension to the extent of the imbalance.

Unbalanced reciprocity, hierarchy, power, inequality, dominance and submission are all aspects of the same phenomenon, the dynamic of the reciprocal algorithms of our evolved brain structure. And wherever and whenever any of these aspects are manifest, there will be an accompanying proportion of behavioral tension.

This is not to argue against private property. Private property rights are the basis of the free enterprise economy which is essential to our democratic political processes. The purpose here is to acknowledge the behavioral tension of inequalities in the holding of property rights. Such behavioral tension, such inequalities, constitute one of the major management problems of political economy.

---

[28] See Bartlett (1989) for the development and application of an economic theory of power which accepts scarcity as a given and maximizing utility as the driving assumption.

18

INSTITUTIONS, ORGANIZATIONS, AND RECIPROCITY

In primitive societies, or in the more natural state of humankind, unbalanced reciprocity may result from natural differentials in strength, talent, ability, or intelligence. In simple societies the hierarchies created by such natural differentials will be inherently unstable because of behavioral tension and will shift as the differentials become less so. Underlying all inequalities or unbalanced transactions is a measure of restless behavioral tension. As a matter of historical record, people act to change them as circumstances will permit—sometimes quietly, sometimes violently.

INSTITUTIONS AND TRANSACTION COSTS
THE MARKET IS SOCIAL; ITS MECHANISM IS RECIPROCITY

Primitive societies reveal the evolution of the market based upon the reciprocal algorithms of our neural architecture. The market, then, evolved out of social interaction (see Slater & Tonkiss, 2001 for a review of alternative perspectives).

The market is by nature a social institution. Its essence is social; its mechanism is reciprocity. Economic analysis excerpted from the social context tends to triviality since it misses the essence of the market. Nowhere is the social context more important than in institutional economics. And nowhere is the essential mechanism—reciprocity—more poorly understood than in the literature on institutions and transaction costs.

In more complex societies, economic or political institutions, whether expressed as principles or concrete organizations, order or regulate reciprocity to some degree. In doing so they enter into the behavioral conflict of the tug and pull of ego and empathy, self- and other-interest, the give and take among the members of society. All such institutions and organizations, then, carry an inherent load of behavioral tension. They also add additional costs to the exchange process. Such costs are referred to in economics as transaction costs. Such transaction costs are an index of the behavioral tension added by the institutions.

Consider for instance the institution of private property. As noted, that institution attempts to order (regulate and systematize) reciprocity by providing for the maintenance of a personal and protected resource base for survival and for reciprocal exchange. Such an institution may serve to mitigate natural differentials. It may also, however, ceteris paribus, have the effect of interfering with the free flow of reciprocity, the natural give and take among members. To the extent that it interferes with the free flow of reciprocity, it creates behavioral tension, which is reflected in increased transaction costs.

In other words, as the cost or value of my gift to you, or your gift to me, is increased by imposed or added transaction costs, greater empathy is required to offer the gift. The greater the empathy, the greater the behavioral tension. And according to the reciprocal algorithms of behavior, the greater the reciprocal required in payment to ego to offset or balance out the tension. In pure economic terms it may be said that the expressions of empathy vis à vis ego are, in acknowledgment to the increased behavioral tension or costs, responsive to price.[29]

In addition, to the extent that the institution in implementation allows for the accumulation of differentials in the personal, protected resource base for survival and exchange, it further creates and perpetuates behavioral tension in the society. Whenever there are differentials of resource base, there are inequalities. Inequalities that are institutionalized constitute institutionalized or structured behavioral tension. Such structured behavioral tension equates to structured and unbalanced transaction costs. In terms of transaction costs the individual on the inferior side of the inequality is unable to meet the transaction costs reciprocally and therefore is disadvantaged or subordinated to the superior by the short fall. This, then, is the origin and nature of hierarchy, dominance and submission expressed in term of transaction costs.

This structured behavioral tension, then, constitutes the framework within which the everyday reciprocal behavioral dynamic goes on.[30] The degree to which the framework, then, is unequal sets the institutional outer limit to which the ongoing daily give and take can approximate a dynamic balance. If the institutional framework is significantly unequal, it blocks achievement of an approximate dynamic balance of reciprocity within such framework. Therefore such a society will always be confronted with the management of internal tension.

---

[29] See, for example, Eckel and Grossman (1997). Without making any connection with brain science or the reciprocal algorithms of behavior, the authors use a typology of fairness (for me, for you, for us) which expresses the conflict systems model and the reciprocal algorithms of behavior. Although their research design is quite contrived and limited, they find evidence from their bargaining experiments that fairness for you (empathy in my terms) is responsive to price.

[30] What I have called institutional or structured behavioral tension, which sets the framework for the daily ongoing reciprocity of behavior, is covered essentially in economic terms by Carl J. Dahlman. He writes that the economic system must make two related decisions concerning property rights. First, it must decide on the distribution of wealth. That is, who shall have the rights to ownership of the scarce resources even before trading and contracting begin. Secondly, it must determine the allocative function of property rights. That is, their use in the process of exchange. Clearly transaction costs involved in the defining of a social contract that sets the preconditions for the ensuing economic trading game, must be taken into account (1980: 85). Daniel W. Bromley (1989) deals extensively with what he sees as the two levels of transactions in a society. The first level concerns negotiations and agreements over the structure of choice sets or in other words the rules of the game. The second level concerns the ongoing market transactions that take place within the agreed or structured choice sets or rules of the game. Neither Dahlman nor Bromley has a concept of the reciprocal algorithms of behavior and the behavioral tension bound by unbalanced choice sets and/or unbalanced exchanges. But obviously some behavioral dynamic must be assumed to lie beneath the economic phenomena. The subfield of constitutional economics, represented by Buchanan, et al., focuses primarily upon the first level (e.g., see Buchanan, 1991).

Institutions, whether manifested as principles or as concrete organizations, inevitably carry a load of behavioral tension. The load varies greatly with the inequalities permitted and the manner of implementation. The unbalanced transaction costs and the amount of hierarchy index both the differential and the behavioral tension. The linkage between transaction costs and behavioral tension provides the motive dynamic for adjustments in the transactional market. And transaction costs are an index of the behavioral tension added by the institutions.

The current focus on transaction costs in the economic theory of institutions derives from two articles by Ronald H. Coase on the nature of the firm or business organization and on social cost (1937, 1960). The interest in transaction costs was also abetted by the work of George J. Stigler (1961) and Friedrich A. Hayek (1945, 1937). The work of Oliver E. Williamson (1996, 1991, 1985, 1975) led to the full development of transaction cost economics treated more fully in Chapter 19 of the present work. Institutions are seen by Williamson as created to *reduce* transaction costs. But such a view assumes the preexistence of a market. The market and associated transaction costs develop in a mutually reinforcing feedback relationship. Once the market is established, the question becomes which among the institutional alternatives carries the lower transaction costs. Or can we create institutions that carry lower transaction costs? My point here is that all institutions inherently carry transaction costs. Those that carry the lesser costs can be said to reduce costs within an existing state of the market.

IS ALL BEHAVIORAL TENSION BAD FOR A SOCIETY?

Utopias generally aim intuitively for the elimination of behavioral tension, a peaceful, conflict-free, idyllic society. But is all behavioral tension necessarily bad for a society?

Actually, as an ongoing dynamic of our neural architecture, which evolved under constraints of scarcity, it would probably be impossible to eliminate all conflict from human social life. The process of exchange is the vehicle that expresses this conflict. And reciprocity within the process of exchange keeps it within safe, if not healthy bounds, when allowed to operate reasonably freely. Dynamically and approximately balanced reciprocity expresses and dissipates the behavioral tension as it functions to maintain society in a process of social and economic exchange. Unbalanced reciprocity accumulates behavioral tension to the approximate extent of the imbalance and creates conditions of dominance and submission or hierarchy within a society.

PRODUCTIVITY, INCENTIVES, AND BEHAVIORAL TENSION

In a society that aims at a constantly increasing production of goods and services, the behavioral tension resulting from unbalanced exchange serves as an engine to drive the process of production. It incents each individual to strive to alter the unbalanced reciprocity or hierarchy in her/his own favor. This can lead to an escalating productivity for the sake of productivity logic. The more open the society is to change or shifting of the hierarchy, dominance-submission, or inequality, the better the engine works for production. Empathy, as noted earlier, is what allows each person to settle without undue stress for a minimum position of equity (balanced reciprocity) instead of a reversal of the hierarchical relationship in his/her own favor that would be inevitably required under a maximizing of self-interest.

Given the dynamic of our evolved brain structure, some degree of tension is inevitable in any human society. It need not necessarily be harmful and may, indeed, be used productively.

From the standpoint of managing the behavioral tension within the society, among the key variables to watch would be: 1) the nature and extent of the institutionalized differentials; 2) the extent of ongoing differentials permitted (i.e., differentials in short term income and wealth); 3) openness to equalization, if not reversal, of institutionalized as well as ongoing differentials; 4) excessive or cumulative behavioral tension.

From the standpoint of the survivability of the society, however, we must consider more long-term effects. As noted earlier, the logic of productivity carried to its logical extreme as a limitless end in itself draws upon and reinforces the scarcity-coping dynamic of our brain structure and turns it into a scarcity-generating dynamic. The capitalist system as an institution or set of institutions is designed to do just exactly this.

For example, the generation of scarcity under capitalism is captured in the ever popular phrase, *the creation of demand*. The major thrust of the advertising industry, which supports that logic, is unabashedly the creation of demand. The created demand is, of course, to be responded to by a reciprocal of newly created supply. The engine of reciprocity based upon our reciprocal algorithms of behavior, primed and reinforced, grinds away relentlessly—creating demand, generating scarcity. Escalating increase of productivity becomes an end in itself.[31] This, in fact, has been the thrust of western and, particularly, Anglo-American economic theory. It underpins all economically-based theories of growth and development. And it is underpinned by the normative assumption that *all* productivity is good. The more of it the better. Standard economic theory assumes no negatives to what is produced and no limits to the growth of productivity. It is an amazingly naive and simplistic normative paradigm.

DESIRABLE VS. SUSTAINABLE LEVELS OF PRODUCTIVITY

A dilemma, intruding to some degree these days in all societal level thinking about productivity, and looming ominously on the horizon, is the question of desirable versus sustainable levels of productivity. A major question facing us ultimately—if and when we have achieved the maximum desirable or sustainable productive state or equilibrium— is: what will be the fate of capitalism or the nature of the economy at that time? The reciprocal dynamic of our evolved brain structure will still be with us. We may need to find other ways to express our social reciprocity than the endless and mindless production of goods and services. Will we find other effective and satisfying ways of expressing our reciprocal sociality in more balanced and humane forms of community? Will we shift more to reciprocity in esthetics, morality, intellectual expression, or even spirituality?

---

[31] Compare the discussion in Power (1996: 211–213). Without reference to the dynamics of brain structure, Power captures the social effects descriptively in his section on the treadmill of competitive consumption.

But we are not there yet, from either the standpoint of desirability or sustainability. Most clearly, we have certainly not reached the maximum desirable level of productivity. From a world viewpoint, we still have considerable deficits in survival essentials (e.g., food, shelter, and health care) and even greater differentials in their balanced reciprocity throughout the world. This is the major source of behavioral tension within and among nations.

From the standpoint of sustainability—the other side of the question we must confront—the answer is not so clearly cut. There are, however, warning signs aplenty in the environment. When confronted with the threat of a limit to maximum sustainability, under the existing assumptions of our economic theory, we will depend upon the further evolution and development of our technology to move the threat further toward the distant horizon—to increase and extend the carrying capacity of the environment as we continue to generate the constraints of scarcity. The concern over the question of sustainability has produced a new subdiscipline of economics, called ecological (or sometimes, living) economics (e.g., see Daly, 1980; Daly & Cobb, 1989; Ekins, 1986; Ekins & Max-Neef, 1992).

It is urgent in any case to understand the dynamic of our brain structure. And develop the ability and the sense of urgency and responsibility to manage it. The logic of the present *relentless and endless production as an end in itself* economic system is spreading now to all corners of the globe. If it cannot be managed wisely, or if it spins out of control, it may lead us to the brink of extinction as a species by exhausting the carrying capacity of the environment. We are not there yet, but it is time to take very seriously the responsibility for management and to consider modifications and alternatives.

Our brain structure has endowed us with a two-horned dilemma. When we crank up the productivity engine, at the same time we inevitably crank up the scarcity-generating engine. When we full throttle the engine under the governing logic of relentless and endless production as an end in itself, we also full throttle the relentless and endless generation of scarcity.

There are three possible outcomes:

1. We will exhaust the ultimate carrying capacity of the environment and go extinct.

2. We will reach a compelled, but managed, equilibrium and survive by recognizing and accommodating the limits of sustainability.

3. We will continue to develop new technologies that will infinitely extend the carrying capacity of the environment, perhaps extending it into the reaches of space, which we will then colonize.

The final answer concerning each of these possible outcome scenarios is uncertain and, at our current state of knowledge, is impossible to predict. The one out of the three that we as individuals choose to consider to be most likely depends on whether we are disposed to be pessimistic or optimistic. The pessimistic position on the issue of sustainability is eloquently covered in the literature on population and ecology (e.g., Ehrlich & Ehrlich, 1996, 1990; Ehrlich, 1969; Mazur, 1994; and somewhat more hopefully, Chertow & Esty, 1996). Crispin Tickell, longtime advisor to successive British prime ministers and former president of the Royal Geographical Society presents an elegant overview of the issues in an article titled provocatively, "The Human Species: A Suicidal Success?" which appeared first in *Geographical Journal* (1993) and is repeated as the concluding chapter in *The Human Impact Reader* (Goudie, 1997). The optimistic position is mindlessly fueled,[32] implicitly if not explicitly, by the several varieties of mainstream economics which assume away the basic economic problem of scarcity or limitations (e.g., see the criticism in Arndt, 1984: 17–36) and seek endlessly increasing productivity based upon unbalanced appeal to the wealth maximizing self-interested side of human nature—the so-called "rational" economic man. Wealth-maximizing self-interest may be anything but rational in the scenarios that are developing before us in the not-to-distant future.

In the interim, however, while we grope for a better balance between self-interested, egoistic consumerism and other-interested, empathetic social responsibility, we must manage politically the inevitable behavioral tension that exists and develops within and among nations—so that we do not destroy ourselves prematurely, along the way to one outcome or the other. This is the short- to mid-range challenge of both economics and politics.

---

[32] Economist Julian Simon argues the most straightforward and unabashed case for our ability to overcome any scarcity problem by full throttling our productive economy (Simon, 1981). See also his debate with Norman Myers, who argues the opposite case (Myers & Simon, 1994, especially, p. xv).

19

THE NEW INSTITUTIONAL ECONOMICS: WILLIAMSON AND TRANSACTION COST ECONOMICS

The emerging study of new institutional economics aims at the integration of the neoclassical economic theory with institutional theory.

Neoclassical economic theory broke from the somewhat ad hoc economic history of the eighteenth and nineteenth centuries and applied to that history a systematic body of theory buttressed by sophisticated quantitative methods. The motivation for neoclassical theory was the search for principles and regularities that could apply generally to economic analysis independent of history. Of course, once you find universal or general principles and regularities that operate independently of history, history becomes unnecessary or irrelevant—except perhaps, as an absorbingly interesting human social record. Much of this has been covered, in part, in earlier chapters.

Neoclassical theory, with its history-independent principles and regularities is further ahistorical in that it focuses on the allocation of resources at a moment in time, rather than such allocation over more extended periods of time. In that sense, then, ahistorical neoclassical economic theory effectively killed its historical subject matter. The methodical application of price theory to economic history was, however, undoubtedly a major contribution producing important insights. Nevertheless, it was the application of an ahistorical theory and methodology to a historical subject matter and it therefore obscured as much as it elucidated.

But neoclassical theory obscured even more than history. In its focus on principles and regularities the effects of institutions were also assumed away. This allowed the principles and regularities to operate in what is called a frictionless or socially cost-free environment. In effect, then, the theory assumed away both history and social context.

This assuming away of both history and social context left neoclassical theory with no effective way to explain change, differential performance, or the decay of economic societies over time.

But there was even a third limiting factor—one that has never been effectively resolved. That factor is the assumption of an exclusively self-interested, wealth maximizing human nature. This assumption made accounting for the pervasive factor of human cooperation, so fundamental to the maintenance and function of any society, difficult and awkward to explain. The new institutional economics attempts to deal with the problem of cooperation. Leading thinkers Oliver Williamson and Douglass North approach the problem from different perspectives. This chapter deals with the new institutional economics from Williamson's perspective. The next chapter looks at the same subject from the perspective of Douglass North.

WILLIAMSON'S NEW INSTITUTIONAL ECONOMICS

The new institutional economics, popularized as a term by Williamson (1975), harks back to the former ad hoc, more broadly based institutional analysis and aims at overcoming the shortfalls of neoclassical analysis by bringing back in the historical perspective plus the constraining and shaping effect of institutions. Nevertheless, as Langlois (1986: 2–5) points out the new version, although sharing the concern for institutions with the earlier American institutionalists, is not historically or conceptually continuous with that tradition, but rather may owe more to their opponents, especially the Austrian economist, Carl Menger. Williamson's study focused on markets and hierarchies. Hierarchies refer to institutions and organizations. Williamson, in this work, never makes a clear distinction between the two.[33]

In his pioneering study of the new institutional approach to markets and hierarchies, Williamson maintains the economic assumption of wealth maximizing self-interested individuals. To this he adds the further emphasis of opportunism, which means "self-interest practiced with guile"(1975: 26) or deceit. He sees the control function of hierarchies aimed partly at restraining this more blatant aspect of self-interest—opportunism. Since hierarchies also have transaction costs, this can be seen as increasing on set of transaction costs to control a second set.

However, one must look very closely to grasp the implicit, pervasive ground of Williamson's analysis. This is because he spends the greater part of his time on exceptions, or barriers, to effective cooperation that he wishes to control or overcome. This implicit ground is, nevertheless, identifiable as the reciprocity of ego and empathy. This is revealed in the statement on what Williamson considers "attitudinal considerations." He explains that the problem is to determine when such considerations are strong enough to be dealt with and when they can be safely ignored. He conjectures that transactions which influence "conceptions of *self-esteem*" (emphasis mine; read ego) or "conceptions of *collective well-being*" (emphasis mine; read empathy) are especially important. He further relates that those who bring such attitudes into the workplace do not regard transactions to be settled one for one but rather look for a favorable overall balance (1975: 256–257).

---

[33] Bromley sees the failure to distinguish between institutions as rules of organizations and as the organizations themselves as the source of considerable confusion in the new institutional literature. The term institution is variously used to refer to organizations; e.g., banks as financial institutions; to a person or position; e.g., the presidency; and to the rules defining economic relations between individuals; e.g., private property (1989: 27–28). A somewhat cleaner distinction is offered by Davis and North who define the institutional environment as the set of political, social, and legal ground rules that govern economic and political activity (1970: 133). Schotter (1981: 11) defines an institution as follows: "A social institution is a regularity in social behavior that is agreed to by all members of society, specifies behavior in specific, recurrent situations, and is either self-policed or policed by some external authority." See also North (1990).

The above qualifying passage in the concluding pages of Williamson's analysis reveals clearly the assumed reciprocal dynamic of ego and empathy, self- and other-interest, that plays implicitly at the foundation of Williamson's analysis of organizational market hierarchies.

The underlying reciprocal ground of Williamson's study comes out most clearly in his chapters on peer groups, simple hierarchy, and the employment relation (1975: 41–81). In assessing the worth of worker peer groups, he writes:

Associatiohal benefits can accrue to peer groups through increased productivity among members of the group who feel a *sense of responsibility* (emphasis mine) to do their *fair share* (emphasis mine) as members of a group but, left to their own devices, would slack off. Also, and more important, a *transformation of "involvement" relations* (quotes in original, emphasis mine), from a *calculative* (emphasis mine) to a more nearly *quasimoral* (emphasis mine) mode, obtains (1975: 44).[34]

The use of the terms *sense of responsibility* and *fair share* are judgmental statements incompatible with the assumption of an exclusively self-interested, wealth maximizing individual, but fully compatible with an individual experiencing the tug and pull of ego and empathy, the reciprocal algorithms of behavior. Followed in the next sentence by the transforming effect of *involvement relations*, which term clearly refers to empathetic social relations, and the movement from a self-interested *calculative* to a more empathetic *quasimoral* mode, these statements confirm the implicit and unclarified assumption of reciprocity in contradiction to the stated one of self-interested wealth maximizing economic man.

Further on, after discussing why hierarchical organization can overcome the shortfalls of peer groups by controlling opportunism and accomplishing more efficient decision-making, Williamson ponders the question of what prevents the peer group from displacement by simple hierarchy. He concludes that the chief reason is because peer groups offer "valued involvement relations" that hierarchy tends to upset. He further advises us that "inequality of rank" as well as "auditing and experience-rating may offend their sense of individual and collective well-being" (1975: 55).

This passage, like the previous one, not only confirms the implicit dynamic of reciprocity, but it also implicitly acknowledges the role of behavioral tension accompanying the tug and pull between ego and empathy, self- and other-interest. It does so by describing involvement relations as being upset by hierarchy. inequality of rank, and auditing—all of which offend the sense of individual as well as collective well-being. Why on earth should exclusively self-interested, wealth maximizing humans be upset by the effects of hierarchy and inequality on collective well-being? Only people who equally experience empathy for others would have such empathic responses.

In discussing the efficiency challenges of collective organization, Williamson tells us at one point that:

...Self-enforcement is tantamount to denying that human agents are prone to be opportunists, and *fails for want of reality testing* (emphasis mine)... 1975: 69).

---

[34] In his later work, Williamson observes that when managers stop playing—that is, behave ethically (empathically, morally)—it reduces transaction costs. For example, he refers to the Japanese case, writing that transaction costs are reduced in Japan because Japan has institutional and cultural checks on opportunism (1985: 122).

At another point he notes that the pursuit of individual interests sometimes leads to faulty collective outcomes. He finds the solution in an enforceable social contract to impose a "cooperative solution." At the same time he calls upon "norms of cooperation" as devices for "realizing cooperative solutions." (1975: 73).

And in a following paragraph, he adds that although it is in the self-interest of the worker "to acquire and exploit monopoly positions, it is plainly not in the interest of the *system.*" As a solution he suggests that "employment relations be transformed" in such a way to assure that system objectives prevail. He tells us that "consummate rather than perfunctory cooperation" is to be encouraged (1975: 73).

When Williamson claims that self-enforcement fails for want of reality testing, going on to say that *cooperation* must be *imposed* by an *enforceable social contract* or perhaps by *norms of cooperation,* he is vacillating between assumptions of self-interest and reciprocity. When he refers to the conflict between system and worker interests, he is fully within the self-interested, wealth maximizing framework. When he aims at *transforming employment relations* so that workers *consummately* (wholeheartedly and empathetically, because it's the right moral thing to do) suppress their own self-interested maximizing rather than *perfunctorily* (minimally to keep from getting fired) so cooperating, he is either engaging in wishful speculation, attempting to transform human nature as understood by economics, or grasping implicitly and hopefully at the intuited but unarticulated dynamic of reciprocity.

WILLIAMSON'S ANALYSIS:
AMBIGUITY, CONTRADICTION, AND IMPLICIT PREMISE

Ambiguity and Contradiction

Williamson's analysis may be viewed, contrary to his explicit stance, as largely an analysis of exceptions. It is focused upon exceptions and the control of deviations that disrupt this implicitly hoped for reciprocity and add transaction costs to the process of exchange—to the desired and implicitly expected identity and commitment to the collective welfare. His definition of opportunism (which hierarchy is designed to control) as self-interest with guile or deceit is a loaded term which carries the unspoken, unclarified fundamental assumption that self-interest must have its limits. In other words, the definition contradicts the individual wealth maximizing self-interested assumption of microeconomics. It implies that when self-interest reaches the border of those tolerable limits, something (may I suggest *empathy*) must set in or be called upon to restore balance in the form of commitment to collective welfare.

The emphasis on self-interest and its deceitful extreme, opportunism, has become a fundamental of Williamson's theory as it has continued to develop along the lines of the earlier work (e.g., 1985; 1991; 1996). The focus on the transaction as the basic unit of analysis and the increased transaction costs associated with the assumption of ever-present opportunistic behavior has stamped the mainstream of the new institutional economics, which is now more frequently referred to as transaction cost economics (TCE) (e.g., Groenewegen, 1997).

Implicit Premise

The truth is that Williamson (as well as other transactional researchers), despite his negative emphasis on the control of opportunism, operates on the *implicit premise* which I would state as follows:

The basic purpose of business organization and organizational behavior is to achieve the collective welfare of the firm by *rewarding the self-interest of individual members* and, in return, *capturing the empathetic behavioral reciprocal of the same individuals* in the form of *identity with the firm* and *commitment to the firm's market objectives and collective welfare.*

In another context not directly related to TCE, Hampden-Turner and Trompenaars make essentially this same point when they write

Another vital requirement of all work organizations is the provision of care, attention, information, and support to each of its individual members...It is an underlying condition of the success of an enterprise that the individual's initiative, drive, and energy be harnessed to the purposes of the organization (1993: 8).

THE CONTRADICTORY PARADIGM OF WILLIAMSON'S TCE: ONE FOR THE FIRM; ANOTHER FOR THE WORKER

The reciprocal algorithms of behavior, then, are clearly present and fundamental. They are obscured by positivistic assumptions and the vocabulary of received microeconomics.

But more important than that, the analysis is obscured by the contradictory nature of the paradigm. Under a socio-economic system that has as its fundamental goal the profit-maximizing collective organization or firm—backed by the equally fundamental assumption of the wealth maximizing, exclusively self-interested individual—it becomes glaringly obvious, in fact, that Williamson's analysis applies one set of framework and rules to the system and presses another contrary set upon the individual worker as a part of the system.

There are in fact two different paradigms being applied, one to system or firm, another to worker or individual. The firm is seen as maximizing self-interest. The employee is called upon, not to self-maximize, but to submit empathetically to the firm's collective good. The faulty and contradictory paradigms, as applied, obscure and frustrate the necessary reciprocity and generate high levels of transaction costs/behavioral tension that impede effective management.

Thus we have high-lighted some of the frustrating and embarrassing Ptolemaic epicyclic-like exceptions that spin off from the assumption of the exclusively self-interested, wealth maximizing economic man that underpins and pervades the paradigm of our current economic science. Simply acknowledging the reciprocal algorithms of human exchange behavior would go a long way toward eliminating the exceptions as well as understanding and properly accounting for the dynamics of economic exchange.

THE TRANSACTION AS THE BASIC UNIT OF ANALYSIS

There is a further problem with current transaction cost economics (TCE). TCE fails to grasp the true nature of its self-proclaimed basic unit of analysis, the transaction. According to Williamson, emphasis on the basic transactional unit is seen to be a distinguishing feature of TCE vis-à-vis more traditional approaches (1996: 6). Part of the confusion in current TCE thinking is to be found in the failure to properly grasp the nature of the basic atom of transaction. This failure is likely brought on by having proceeded from within the long-standing, exclusively self-interested behavioral assumption of classical economic theory. This faulty assumption has long obscured and distorted the true nature of the market, causing self-interest rather than reciprocity and cooperation to be seen as central to market function. It is a complete misplacement or misstatement of the reality of the market.

The *basic unit of analysis*, the *transaction*, is itself fundamentally a *unit of reciprocity*, of cooperation, of the tug and pull of ego and empathy. We see this clearly in the anthropological literature examined in earlier chapters. The transactional atom when opened up or unpacked consists of the two elements, ego and empathy in a state of negotiated tension or cooperation. Reciprocity, or cooperation, then is the over-arching, all-bracing essence of the transaction. Opportunism, or the unbalancing tug toward self-interest, then, is *deviancy* within the *centrality of cooperation and reciprocity*.

As illustrated in Chapter 8 the transaction evolved from the gift. The transaction, like the gift, is an expression of our mammalian legacy, an act of providing reciprocated by a return act of affirmation with the reciprocal specified to head off the residual tension that produces the added unwanted effect of excessive residual obligation or bonding. TCE's failure to properly define the transaction is in lock step with the failure of received economic theory to properly define the true nature of the market. The exaggerated and inaccurate emphasis on self-interest, opportunism, and greed as the driving forces of the market—rather than cooperation and reciprocity—has served to reinforce and encourage deviancy and give the very valuable institution of free enterprise exchange an undeservedly very bad press.

THE COSTLY PARADOX OF TRANSACTION COST ECONOMICS

One is further led to wonder at the logic of the transaction cost version of the new institutional economics. Since the normative concern of the discipline is, in the name of efficiency, to control and reduce transaction costs caused by self-interested opportunism, why would one want to emphasize self-interested opportunism as the central characteristic of what Williamson comes to call contractual man? The constant self-interested, opportunistic rhetoric fed into the business world through the standard economic literature and in the education and training of economists and managers serves, by well-established principles of behavioral psychology, to perpetuate and reinforce such behavior as central and fundamental.[35]

---

[35] Frank, Gilovich, and Regan (1993) in their article, "Does Studying Economics Inhibit Cooperation," report empirical evidence that exposure to the self-interested model of economics encourages self-interested behavior. See also Maxwell and Ames (1981) and Etzioni (1988).

By emphasizing such behavior as central, it becomes the expected, the natural, and, in effect, the encouraged behavior. Cooperative, empathetic, trustworthy behavior then becomes by definition the difficult to be achieved, exceptional behavior that goes against the grain of human nature. This is amazing since cooperative behavior is absolutely pervasive in society and no social organization would be possible without it. The fact that opportunism need not be central to the firm is further evidenced by the Japanese alternative (which Williamson acknowledges), and also the German and French (see Hampden-Turner and Trompenaars, 1993).

One could as easily and as accurately emphasize empathy, ethics, and moral commitment. Controls could easily be seen as encouraging and reinforcing our natural, pervasive empathetic, cooperative behavior, rather than as limiting pervasive opportunistic behavior.

The reality is that the centrality of self-interested opportunism is not the necessary reality of human nature or Williamson's so-called contractual man, but the self-confirming artifact of the particular paradigm of received economic theory made more extreme by the current, and primarily, American version of transaction cost economics. It is, in fact, a self-defeating, counterproductive artifact because it unnecessarily legitimizes, reinforces, and perpetuates the very transaction-costly behavior that it wishes to control and reduce.

If current transaction cost economics should shift to a more accurate central concept of reciprocity, the tug and pull of self- and other-interest, it would treat opportunism, not as central, but as deviancy or extreme behavior (which it really is). It would propagate and encourage empathy (trust) to counter that deviancy. By doing so, it would thereby contribute to a normative theoretical position that would reduce the transaction costs rather than adding to them. There is little to lose and much to gain by such a shift.

Niels Noorderhaven (1996), an economist at the Catholic University, Brabant, The Netherlands, has taken a strong step in this direction by arguing for what he calls a split-core model of human nature that includes opportunism and trustworthiness. Although it lacks the flexibility, dynamic and the derivation from neuroscience of the conflict systems neurobehavioral model presented as the foundation of this book and gives too much emphasis to self-interest with deceit (opportunism), the split-core model gets much closer to the underlying reciprocal algorithms of behavior.

20

THE NEW INSTITUTIONAL ECONOMICS:
THE PERSPECTIVE OF DOUGLASS NORTH

In the most complete statement of his position, new institutional economist, Douglass North, who sees the problem or question of cooperation more clearly as central, tells us that we must look to two aspects of human behavior to get at the deficiencies of rational choice (wealth maximizing self-interested) theory as it relates to institutional economics. These aspects are motivation and deciphering the environment (1990: 20).

In dealing with the motivational issue, North, in contrast to Williamson, tries to integrate altruism into the calculus. In doing so he draws upon and stays within the externalized, gene-centered work of such sociobiologists as Richard Dawkins of selfish gene fame. His attempted integration of altruism is somewhat forced and unsatisfactory since his externalized perspective does not allow him to enter into the dynamic of motivation. In effect, beyond acknowledging the importance of such behaviors as altruism, he doesn't give us much more in the way of enlightenment on the subject.

In moving on to the question of deciphering the environment, which is the cognitive (as opposed to motivational) issue, North acknowledges the limited capacity of individuals to process adequately all environmental signals and data. In what appears to be an interim or stopgap effort to explain variance in motivation from the perspective of wealth maximizing behavior, he makes the following statement

The complexity of the environment, given the limited processing ability of the actor, can explain the *subjective perceptions* (emphasis mine) of reality that characterize human understanding and even the *sense of fairness or unfairness* (emphasis mine) that the individual feels about the institutional environment....(North, 1990: 25).

How "the complexity of the environment" could fully and ultimately explain subjective perceptions and even the sense of fairness or unfairness is very difficult to see. At best such externalities can only partially explain such subjective states. To get a complete explanation one must assume or identify some other motivating sources internal to the human than wealth maximizing acted upon by, or responding to, the said complexities of the environmental factors. For a sense of justice or fairness one must have, in addition to self-interest, the capability to identify or empathize with the situation of others—or else the statement is meaningless. To see that just one's self-interested, maximizing self is shortchanged in an economic transaction or situation scarcely constitutes what we consider a sense of fairness or unfairness. One must add to that a capacity for empathizing with others who are shortchanged and perceive that shortchanging of either self or others in the economic transaction or situation is unfair—an instance of unbalanced reciprocity—that offends our human nature.

North acknowledges that his explanation is inadequate to account for a broad range of human behavior (e.g., anonymous free donation of blood, dedication to ideological causes, commitment to religious precepts, self-sacrifice for abstract causes) and that our understanding of motivation is therefore very incomplete (1990: 26). After giving this acknowledgment to motivation, he, then, dodges the essential question of motivation and moves on, for further insight, to focus on the study of institutions.

Undoubtedly the examination of institutions needs to be done. And equally undoubtedly, such study will further elucidate the issues of motivation. Nevertheless the project will eventually and inevitably take us back to the more fundamental question of human nature itself. The question which was sidestepped because of inadequate knowledge and behavioral concepts.

THE RECIPROCAL DYNAMIC AND
THE STUDY OF ECONOMIC INSTITUTIONS

The reciprocal dynamic of our evolved brain structure—the tug and pull of ego and empathy, of self-interested, wealth maximizing behavior counterpoised and complemented by empathetic, other-interested, other-maintaining behavior—provides a more accurate view of the motivational dynamics of the individual upon which any satisfactory explanation and understanding of microeconomics must ultimately rest.

As defining central tendencies, the reciprocal algorithms of behavior can account for the motivational dynamic of exchange. This does not mean that they can explain *all* aspects of motivation. And, of course, they cannot explain or give much guidance on the cognitive issues of deciphering the environment. They can, however, take us further in the clarification of the fundamentals of social and economic exchange and they provide a superior underpinning to the study of institutions than the univariate assumption of a solely wealth maximizing individual.

As noted in previous chapters, institutions are both political and economic in that they give order to and regulate reciprocity. The manner in which they do so is, in large part, a function of the history, traditions, ideology, and indeed the entire context, past and present, of the society. History, tradition, and ideology as conservative factors will tend to preserve whatever imbalances that exist and have existed in a society. The structured behavioral tension bound by these conservative unbalanced constraints is the ultimate motive power for the changes in hierarchy, inequality, and power—when the opportunity for change presents itself as a realizable alternative.

In addition, the social or institutional incentive structure, which is consensually acknowledged to be one of the most important factors in assessing the efficiency of institutions, will be based upon or designed consciously or implicitly to exploit or manage this innate reciprocal dynamic within the permissible constraints supported by the society, its institutions, and its ideology. In this way institutions may block, mitigate, or facilitate the increased production of goods and services in the society. Empirical research into the specific aspects of institutions that impact and channel the reciprocal dynamic should prove useful to achieving a deeper understanding of the role of institutions in the growth, stagnation, and decay of societies.

PARADIGMS AND SELF-CONFIRMING INVESTIGATIONS

The new institutional economics broadens the narrow normative paradigm of neoclassical microeconomics. In that sense it offers opportunities for a much more comprehensive and socially relevant grasp of the total question of economic exchange. The second critical point (the first being reciprocity) that has not yet been adequately grasped, however, is that new institutional economics accepts the normative desirability of the current paradigm of relentless and endless increase of productivity as an end in itself. And like the neoclassical economic approach, it operates entirely within the paradigm, without questioning the paradigm itself.

In our current and prevailing paradigm, we have created a set of institutions and an ideology that overemphasize one side of our nature—the wealth maximizing, self-interested. In our so-called "value-free", "positivistic", "objective" economic investigations within this blatantly normative framework, we confirm what the framework already dictates. That is: within a wealth maximizing, self-interested framework, individuals are rewarded for doing so and therefore tend to demonstrate such wealth maximizing, self-interested behavior. And when we constantly emphasize and promote the results produced within this normative framework as "objective"—as the way things really and necessarily are—we further reinforce the framework as well as the same pre-directed, predictable outcomes. It's simple and straightforward: in a wealth maximizing, self-interested institutional framework, people do exactly that. With cooperative, altruistic exceptions, of course, that are difficult to account for.

In an alternative paradigm, we *could* create a set of institutions and ideology that emphasizes the other side of our nature—the empathy maximizing, other-interested. Within that framework we could account for all exchange as empathy maximizing, other-interested. And most of the behavior we observe in our investigations could be interpreted to fit within that motive. Of course we would then have self-interested exceptions that would be difficult or embarrassing to account for.

But the alternative paradigm would also be a distortion of our nature. Each of the two alternatives would produce behavioral tension owing to the overemphasis on one side of human nature rather than the other. In other words we would have side-effects, spillover empathetic or egoistic behaviors, that deviated from the expected and would have to be explained away—like Ptolemaic epicycles which accumulated to explain deviations in astronomy prior to the Copernican revolution.

An institutional framework—which appropriately recognizes and encourages both ego and empathy, self- and other-interest, reciprocity in dynamic balance, however imperfectly it functions—moves us further in the direction of not only wealth maximizing, but also wealth sharing and social responsibility.

An important principle to keep in mind in any so-called scientific inquiry, but especially so in social science, is that an investigation conducted within a paradigm will inevitably tend to confirm the paradigm. Only when the discrepancies accumulate sufficiently to be glaring will an alternative paradigm begin to emerge—as in the Copernican revolution and in the move from Newtonian mechanics to relativity and quantum theory.

SOCIAL MALLEABILITY VS. FRIEDMAN'S ERRONEOUS AXIOM

In the social sciences the raw materials are much more malleable than in the physical sciences. They do not represent a fixed and immutable reality. This is because we create the whole of the social sciences out of what we are. And herein lies the reason why it is so foolish and misleading to speak of "objective" social science. Society is not a given like the physical world (e.g., the laws of gravity) to be discovered essentially the same everywhere. Society has been structured, created by us, mostly unconsciously and incrementally, sometimes more self-consciously.

All research within the existing, created structure tends to confirm that structure since behavior operates within the constraints imposed by that structure.[36] To take the results gleaned from research within a particular *created* socio-institutional structure, accepted and interpreted as necessary, objective reality, does not inform us about alternatives and may limit our choices. This factor of creation indicates the limitations of Milton Friedman's axiom that—"the only relevant test of the validity of a hypothesis is comparison of its predictions with experience." (1953: 9). Adhering to such an axiom will almost certainly cause us to miss alternatives.

This does not mean that, within the created institutional frameworks, we must abandon the tools and methodologies developed under the positivist pretense, but rather that we should use them with a clearer understanding of their limitations. In other words, we may use the observational and measuring tools to gather data and assess whether the institutional framework which we created is doing the job—generating the behaviors and results—that we intended or hoped that it would do.

The basic materials that we have to work with in modifying any existing social paradigm, or in creating any alternative one, are our inherited protoreptilian-mammalian brain structure topped with a massive generalizing/analyzing cortex. Out of this structure emerges the reciprocal algorithms of behavior. These algorithmic rules are the basic shaping dynamic of our social, economic, and political lives, and the institutions and ideologies that we create, incrementally and unconsciously, or intentionally and thoughtfully, greatly channel their expression and the degree of behavioral tension that exists within our society.

It is perhaps incumbent upon us, in keeping with the focus of constitutional economics (e.g., see Buchanan, 1991), to fully understand these algorithms of reciprocity and consciously design our institutions to facilitate their expression, to manage the inevitable behavioral tension of their tug and pull at all levels of social exchange, and to accomplish our normatively chosen and desired objectives—rather than leaving our institutions to fortuitous formation that may take us in directions we do not really want to go because we erroneously believe that the dynamics and features of our social world have the same inexorable objective reality as those of the physical universe.

---

[36] Paul Feyerabend, a leading philosopher of science, for instance, takes the cautionary position that the meanings of both observational and theoretical terms are dependent upon the theory in which they are imbedded (1975: 320–321). Robert Heilbroner (1997) suggests that economics, as conceived today may well be a product of the capitalist system and have no applicability outside such a system. Miller goes much further when she writes: that orthodox economics "conceives a world consonant with cherished prejudice, irrespective of brute force, irreducible facts." She concludes that "orthodox economics seems to be in a permanent and unyielding state of cognitive dissonance." (1996: 7).

RECIPROCITY AND THE NEW INSTITUTIONAL ECONOMICS:
A CONCLUDING OBSERVATION

As noted the new institutional economics uses the same methodology of received marginalist economic theory. It adds, however, four important changes to the theory of production and exchange to accomplish the analysis of institutions. They are: methodological individualism, utility maximization, opportunistic behavior, and bounded rationality.[37]

1) Methodological individualism. The focus of analysis is changed from organizations or other collective entities (e.g., the state, society, the firm, etc.) to the individual human actor. That is, the theory of the larger social unit must, contrary to orthodox theory, now begin with and base its explanations not upon the behaving social unit, but rather on the behaving individuals within that unit.

2) Utility maximization. The individual members are assumed to seek and maximize their own self interests within the constraints established by the existing, self-interest seeking and maximizing organizational structure.

3) Opportunistic behavior. Williamson's concept of opportunistic behavior (1975) adds a further complication to self-interested utility maximization. It assumes that individuals (either principals or agents) are likely to be dishonest in the sense that they may disguise preferences, distort data, deliberately confuse issues, and so on. Williamson refers to such behavior as "self-seeking with guile"or deceit.

4) Bounded rationality. In keeping with the conceptual term "bounded rationality" coined by Simon (1948; 1972), individual members do not have the perfect knowledge assumed by the orthodox theory, but have only limited ability to acquire and process information. The limitations imposed by imperfect knowledge mean in effect that not all economic exchange can be organized by contract and market but is impacted by unknown and unforeseen contingencies.

How would the acknowledgment of the algorithms of reciprocity affect these assumptions?

Let's consider the case of the free enterprise business firm. Under the new institutional economics, the self-interested, utility maximization assumption, combined with the added assumption of opportunistic behavior or the seeking of self-interest with deceit or guile, seemingly sets up a unifying, consistent behavioral assumption applicable both to the firm and its individual members. Actually, in effect, the seemingly unifying assumptions pit the firm and its members against each other in an almost inevitable conflict of interests. This is because, externally, the firm is viewed basically as a self-interested and opportunistically utility maximizing entity in the market and, internally, the positions of the individual members are, likewise, fundamentally viewed as self-interested utility maximizing made worse by opportunistic behavior.

Nevertheless, contrary to these fundamental assumptions, the other-interested, empathetic qualities of cooperation and trustworthiness are deemed essential on the part of members to the successful and efficient workings of the firm. Cooperation and trustworthiness are the firm's necessary and desired member attributes. To overcome the assumed self-interested, maximizing behavior of the individual members in favor of cooperation and trustworthiness, which by presumption goes against the grain, imposes

---

[37] For example, compare the summary in Furubotn and Richter (1991: 4–5).

major production and transaction costs upon the firm. Nevertheless, the establishment of such empathetic behavior is the object of intense management concern.

Management, thus, wants cooperative, trustworthy behavior, in spite of the very paradigm that contradicts and militates against such empathetic behaviors. So management incurs great costs in attempting to overcome the implications of the paradigm by efforts to impose a standard different from the firm's market behavior on the individual members. Against the grain of the self maximizing assumption, then, management wishes to impose a contrasting standard of empathetic cooperation and trust on the individual members. Given the overall maximizing assumption, this can only be done by rigid control, deception, or assuming that the individual members are fools. The attempt to do so, therefore, not only involves huge production and transaction costs expended on either controls or the deceptive effort, but must also contribute enormously to cynicism and alienation on the part of individual members.

The problem of double standard and conflicting messages can be avoided or mitigated by acknowledging the algorithms of reciprocal behavior based on the tug-and-pull of ego and empathy. Under these algorithms the firm offers compensation and benefits, an act of providing or empathy which acknowledges and affirms the ego demands of the individual member. Based upon the affirmation of ego (value, dignity), the individual reciprocates empathy in the form of cooperation and trust toward the firm and a commitment to the firm's utility maximizing behavior in the marketplace. Empathy would thus be a reciprocal factor mitigating purely self-interested, individual maximization and making more effective, less costly organization itself possible.

Under the paradigm of reciprocity, the firm could also harmonize its internal with its external operating assumptions reducing both cynicism and alienation. Under the paradigm of reciprocity, the firm would see itself as maximizing not just self-interested profit, but also empathetic provisioning done with quality and social responsibility. Of course, in keeping with the dynamics of our brain structure, the tension between ego and empathy is carried inevitably into firm's market activities in the form of tension or the tug-and-pull between egoistic self-interested, profit maximizing and empathetic, other-interested social responsibility. A measure of the firm's success would be how well it achieves a dynamic balance of the two.

By shifting to acknowledgment of the reciprocal algorithms of behavior, the double standard would not only be eliminated, but the market relationship would be more accurately defined—as the reciprocal relationship of exchange that it truly is—based upon our evolved brain structure.

Additionally, opportunistic behavior, especially the costly opportunism with guile, would be viewed as the exception and not as the expected behavior assumed and reinforced by the very paradigm of competitively self-interested maximization. Opportunistic behavior, as a result, would be seen not as central, but rather as deviant behavior. And it could be dealt with as such.

The problem of bounded rationality, of course, would remain.

INSTITUTIONALISTS NEED HAVE NO FEAR

The new institutionalist literature, following Williamson (1975), recognizes that, in the absence of bounded rationality and opportunistic behavior, all economic contracting problems would be trivial. Indeed there would be no need to study economic institutions.

There need be no fear, however, in accepting the paradigm of reciprocity. Doing so will, in fact, better define the task of the new institutional economics. It may also be expected to contribute to the reduction of production and transaction costs. It would not, on the other hand, given the persistence of bounded rationality and the need to cope with opportunistic behavior as deviancy, eliminate the need for institutional analysis or put the practitioners out of work.

As a final word of caution, even fully acknowledging and taking into account the reciprocal algorithms of behavior will not eliminate, but only help to mitigate, the costly integrative and transaction cost problems of the firm. This is because behavioral tension is inherent in any hierarchy. Accordingly, despite the clearest understanding of the dynamics and best efforts of all involved, there will be an inevitable tendency to adjust the imbalances or inequities of the hierarchy, whatever specific form they take (e.g., power inequities, status inequities, economic inequities, etc.). Given the dynamic of our evolved brain structure such is the nature of the beast. It applies not only to firms but also to the administrative hierarchies of any type, economic, social, or political.[38]

---

[38] The inherent instability of hierarchies is indicated by the analysis of the breakdown of the Soviet administrative hierarchies (Solnick, 1998).

PART IV

NEURAL ARCHITECTURE
IN SOCIAL STRUCTURE AND
GLOBAL POLITICS

21

EVOLUTION, SCIENCE, AND SOCIETY

This will be a transitional chapter. In this section I shift from a primary focus on the market and economics to the concerns of sociology and politics. There is, of course, no real separating of the subject matter. Our academic disciplines, our departmented university systems, force artificial divides upon the indivisible texture of society.

Often they introduce confusion and distortion into an otherwise seamless fabric—splitting it by alternative language, definitions, and concepts that in many cases only say the same things in different ways. So I will almost inevitably continue to draw upon the themes of economics as I make the transition into the issues of social structure and politics.

In Chapter 9 I blamed the misrepresentation of Adam Smith on merchants eager to escape the intrusive micromanagement of the mercantilistic bureaucracy. Like all one dimensional explanations, this was a partial explanation of a more complicated subject.

For a more complete understanding we must look to the larger social and intellectual context. This context was colored by centuries of the Judeo-Christian tradition with its emphasis on the struggle between good and evil. In that tradition, which dominated the Western world across the centuries from the fall of the Roman Empire to the Renaissance, good and evil were seen as cosmic forces personified as the Deity versus Satan. Central to this dichotomous tradition was the doctrine of original sin. Humans fell to the temptations of evil Satan to be ultimately redeemed by the Deity of goodness.

As England emerged from the tradition-bound Middle Ages into the Enlightenment, the religious dichotomy took on a secular form. The struggle between good and evil was shifted into human nature itself. The big question became: Was human nature good or evil?

As is customary in human affairs scholars split on this issue. One stream of thought, in keeping with the Judeo-Christian tradition and the doctrine of original sin, saw humans as evil. This group was represented in part by the English philosopher Thomas Hobbes (1588–1679) who held forth in his *Leviathan* that men must submit to an absolute ruler in order to control their conflicting, self-interested motives and assure their safety in an orderly society. Hobbes saw humans as motivated by two forces: self-preservation and the desire for conquest. On this belief, in the absence of an absolute sovereign, Hobbes saw the natural state of humans as a war of all against all.

An alternative group centering around the thought of John Locke (1632–1704) saw humans as having a strong sense of moral obligation as well as self-interest. Based upon his perception of human nature, Locke argued for a limited rather than absolute form of government. Adam Smith, with his dual concept of self-interest and fellow feeling, fell closer to the position of Locke. But the essential dichotomy prevailed in discussion. Evil was replaced with selfishness; good with morality and altruism.

Into the midst of this controversy was injected the momentous advent of Darwinian theory.

CHARLES DARWIN: SURVIVAL, SELF-INTEREST AND ALTRUISM

With the publication of Charles Darwin's *The Origin of Species* (1859) seventy years after Adam Smith's death, the one-sided emphasis on self-interest, already running strong, was powerfully reinforced as the dominant view of humankind in the world of capitalism and capitalist economic thought.

Darwin's classic work created an intellectual revolution with its demonstration of evolution based on natural selection interpreted as the bloody struggle of the fittest to survive. His theory influenced almost every area of serious thought and stirred controversy throughout society.

Like Adam Smith, Darwin suffered from misinterpretation. "Fittest to survive," in Darwin's view, referred to reproductive success or fitness. However, the more dramatic connotations of terms like "struggle" and "fittest" were seized upon by some zealous enthusiasts to evoke, in the words of the poet Alfred Lord Tennyson, "nature red with tooth and claw"—the personal struggle to the death for survival among nature's creatures. This was selfishness and self-interest to the extreme.[39]

The bloody tooth and claw interpretation certainly reinforced the already prevalent Hobbesian position. It led to a philosophy called Social Darwinism, which excused all forms of economic exploitation and inequality as the natural and inevitable expression of the law of evolution—"the fittest to survive." The wealthy were judged as more biologically fit than the poorer classes. Social Darwinism thrived in the latter part of the 19th century as a justification for such excesses of industrial capitalism as sweat shops, slums, and child labor. It was abandoned as an overtly influential school of thought because of its conspicuously negative social effects.

THE MAKING OF "SCIENTIFIC" ECONOMICS

Parallel to the rise of the tooth and claw interpretation of Darwin, the nineteenth century launched the movement to a "scientific" economics. The academic or intellectual study of economics had previously been a moral enterprise. It was pursued primarily by moral philosophers of the type of Frances Hutcheson, the mentor of Adam Smith, David Hume, Lord Shaftesbury, and Smith himself.

---

[39] Loye has written significantly on the misinterpretation of Darwin (see Loye 2002a, b).

Economic thinkers, however, who were inclined toward science, as noted in earlier chapters, had always taken as ideal the model of Isaac Newton's physics and mathematics. Newton represented the epitome of science with his model of a clockwork universe working on immutable laws of physics. The well-known "physics envy" of the social sciences which prevails even today began here.

To model their scientific version of economics on physics and math, the "scientific" economists sought to be objective in the manner of physics and quantitative in the manner of math. The normative issue of morals had no place in an objective, positivistic economics bent on aping the success of physics. Science was considered to be value-free or value neutral. Morals, underpinned by the motives of Adam Smith and other's fellow-feeling and sympathy, were declared unscientific and eliminated from the newly evolving economic calculus.

The effort to move to a positivist economics involved the marriage of both inductive and deductive approaches. These were the two essential components. The inductive component required the collection and analysis of sufficient economic data. The deductive component required identifying the mathematical equations that represented the law-like relations of economic behavior.

On the inductive side the emerging discipline of statistics provided the main empirical thrust. British scholars Thomas Tooke (1774–1858) and William Newmarch 1820–1882) set statistics firmly on course by publishing a six volume work titled *History of Prices and the State of the Circulation from 1792 to 1856.*[40] This work constituted an extensive compilation and systematic ordering of empirical data for the period covered. In 1861 Newmarch commented in an address to the British Association of for the Advancement of Science that economics, by drawing upon empirical, statistical data, had ceased to be an abstract science. He noted that the only safe basis on which we could establish economic laws was not hypothetical deduction but careful collection and analysis of empirical facts.[41]

On the deductive side William Stanley Jevons (1835–1892) stands out. He is, in fact, considered the father of "scientific" utilitarian economics. The utilitarian approach of the Britisher Jevons is to be distinguished from the French grand Cartesian deductive approach of GET (general equilibrium theory). GET, as represented by Walras, was discussed earlier in Chapter 11. Jevons, as appropriate to his utilitarian perspective, focused not on the grand design of GET but rather on the troublesome, but fundamental issue of defining the concept of utility.

---

[40] Tooke was technically the author of all six volumes assisted by research assistants. Newmarch was mainly responsible for the last two volumes. Tooke and Newmarch, of course, drew on a long tradition of data collection in Britain going back to the famous "Domesday Book" of 1086 which recorded the lands under control of William the Conqueror for purposes of taxation and revenue collection. Figures such as John Graunt (1620–1674), William Petty (1623–1687), Gregory King (1648–1712), and Charles Davenant (1656–1714) developed statistical and income accounting systems useful to the mercantilistic system. For information on statistics as related to the development of economics see, Schumpeter 1954: 519–526; Porter 1986; Stigler 1986; Mazlish 1998: 237–239; Perlman & McCann 1998: 137–156.

[41] Newmarch, from the standpoint of statistics, was aware of the difference between that inductive approach and the deductive one of mathematics. He stated that in statistics there was no body of general laws such as found in the mathematical and physical sciences. He viewed statistics as a useful tool for investigating recurring phenomena (1861: 457). This suggests, of course, that some deductive methodology must be applied to make sense of the inductively obtained data.

JEVONS AND THE CHOICE TO IGNORE, NOT DENY MORALS IN "SCIENTIFIC" ECONOMICS

As an accomplished mathematician, Jevons sought to develop the deductive framework that could handle the statistical data produced by the likes of Tooke and Newmarch. In doing so he made a conscious decision to ignore moral values in his economic analysis. It is important to note that Jevons did *not* deny the existence of caring, moral motives. He simply chose to eliminate them from consideration. Jevons admittedly felt that the calculus of economics could best be built on the baser or self-interested motives of humans. He chose to give the fellow-feeling and sympathy of earlier thinkers no role in his calculus and focused on self-interest as the sole primary motive.[42]

Jevons' deductive value choice, combined with the inductive emphasis on empirical data, resonated well with others who wished to model economics after physics. Scientific economics, thus, moved away from the position held by Adam Smith and adopted, for scientific purposes, a position more consistent with Hobbes. The development of the scientific school of economics, then, contrary to economic lore still passed on in the standard texts, was based on Hobbes' view of human nature, not the view of Adam Smith. It was clearly a choice made, not on the basis of science, but on the basis of values, convenience, and the desire to look like physics—to capture part of the reflected glory of that esteemed science.

FROM CHOICE TO IGNORE MORALS TO DENIAL-IN-FACT IN "SCIENTIFIC" ECONOMICS

As frequently happens in the social sciences, what is deliberately excluded from examination comes eventually to be denied in reality. "Scientific" economists, who followed in the 19th and 20th centuries, seemingly forgot that Jevons did *not* deny the existence of empathy or higher motives, but rather specifically chose to exclude them to concentrate on what he personally acknowledged to be the baser motive of self-interest. This post-Jevons transition constitutes, in effect, an instance of the naturalistic fallacy by economists. That is, they made the forbidden leap from value to fact. Jevons had made a value choice to ignore empathy and morals in "scientific" economics. His followers

---

[42] Jevons' position is stated in several of his publications. For his justification to exclude the higher motives and concentrate on the lower ones in economics as well as for his case for economics as a mathematical science, see the introduction in his work on political economy (1988). The introduction to his *Essays on Economics* (1905) is also interesting. Jevons includes all subjective economic forces under the utilitarian doctrine of maximizing pleasure and minimizing pain. This is called the hedonic approach which is later developed by Kahneman and associates (1999). The very high level of integration or generalization of the hedonic approach, although defensible and virtually unarguable at that high level, has the unfortunate effect of obscuring the tug-and-pull of ego and empathy which would require dropping to a lower level of integration. This is one of the problems inherent in levels of reduction and integration. When the level is too high it loses power to discriminate. In the case of economics the effect has been profound. The level of integration adopted does not permit a proper understanding of the evolution or dynamic of the market.

moved from that value choice to a denial-in-fact of the existence of empathy as a primary motive in the exchange process.

The effects of Jevons' choice and the associated "forgetting" were to be profound. Scientific economics chose to ignore half of human nature in building the foundations of its edifice. The inadequate foundations were thus faulty and unstable. As the discipline moved into the 20th century, it began showing cracks in the faulty foundations. These cracks had to be pasted over—much like the epicycles created to explain "deviant" planetary motions by the Ptolemaic geocentric theorists prior to being swept away by the Copernican Revolution in the early Renaissance.

There are two conspicuous examples of epicyclic patchwork work of the faulty foundations of modern economics. The first includes the treatment of fundamental empathic motives such as altruism, love, and caring as tastes or preferences. The second egregious epicycle is the extended conceptual fabrication called *enlightened self-interest*. Such examples were created in a vain attempt to hang on to the erroneous sole self-interest motive. The epicycles conceal only poorly the flaws in the self-interest centric perspective of economics.

The negative social side effects of the mistaken perspective are, of course, considerable. They include the encouragement of greed and the promotion of cynicism in society. When everything is at bottom self-interest, such primary empathic motives as caring, love, and altruism—the precious foundational motives of the family, the gift, and the market itself—cannot be admitted to be the genuine motives that they are. They are dehumanized. Such motives must then be the result of fakery, or otherwise trivialized and turned to self-interested purposes. On the other hand, when the duality of the market, the tug and pull of self-interested and other-interested (empathic) circuitry is recognized, the flaws in the foundation disappear taking the bad side effects and the epicycles with them.

LOGICAL POSITIVISM AND RADICAL BEHAVIORISM

The focus on self-interest gained additional allies from two related perspectives that emerged in the early 20th century—logical positivism[43] in philosophy and radical behaviorism[44] in psychology. Both denied consciousness and subjectivity as valid for investigation by science. The entire focus was to be on externals—primarily on

---

[43] Positivism is seen to have begun with the inductive method of Francis Bacon (1561–1626) and continued to develop in the centuries following. Logical positivism or logical empiricism is associated with the emergence of the Vienna Circle in the 1920s. Moritz Schlick, a professor of inductive science at the University of Vienna, organized a Thursday evening discussion group of like-minded thinkers in 1925. Over the years members included Rudolf Carnap, Herbert Feigl, Kurt Gödel, Otto Neurath, and others. Although not participating directly in the Circle itself, thinkers such as Ernst Mach, Bertrand Russell, and Ludwig Wittgenstein had significant influence on the development of logical positivism. Good introductions to logical positivism are Ayer (1959) and Hempel (1966). Also see Caldwell (1982) who discussed positivism as well as other methodologies in economics. Mazlish (1998: 37–66) provides a brief history.

[44] B. F. Skinner is the central figure in radical behaviorism during the middle quarters of the 20th century. In his *Beyond Freedom and Dignity* (1971), he tries to extend the narrow premises of behaviorism into an explanation of everything that denies the essential human motives of freedom and dignity, seeing such notions as hindering our proper use of behavior technology.

experimental methods applied to such externals that could be repeated in the laboratory. Although good as far as it went, this focus became much more than just a useful methodology. Again, as in the case of "scientific" economics, researchers came to deny the very existence of what they declined to study.

The externalized objective perspective fed into the original sin, tough-minded, stiff upper lipped mainstream of Anglo-American thinking. Science bought it hook, line, and sinker. Behavioristic psychology, which denied the existence of consciousness or inner mental states, went in lock-step with scientific economics, logical positivism, and original sin. The result was an externalized, so-called objective concept of science that denied and tried to divest itself of all things subjective and soft-headed.

Being hard-headed, tough-minded, and stiff upper lipped meant one must focus on such human attributes as selfishness, fear, aggression, and nastiness in general. And 19th and 20th century science did just that. With a vengeance. Altruism, cooperation, affection, love were softheaded and few stiff-upper-lippers would dare consider them seriously.

THE SELFISH GENE AND ORIGINAL SIN IN BIOLOGY

All the foregoing contributed mightily to a parallel trend in biological approaches, particularly the Anglo-American approach, toward a form of objective negativism. The approach has a detached, self-deprecating, long-suffering quality about it. As previously in this chapter, I have chosen to call it the stiff upper lip approach in acknowledgment of its characteristic Anglo-Saxon ambience. It bespeaks the "too painful to be endured, but I will do so nevertheless." It carries the "I can stoutly confront the difficult truth with head painfully, but resolutely unbowed" demeanor.

The practitioners of this approach were largely attracted to the cold disciplines of mathematics and game theory. They seem to utterly lack warmth in their presentations. They suggest autistic-like savants unable to connect with any emotion except the negatives of fear and aggression. Their pessimistic calculus sees little good in human nature.

An example? Without necessarily ascribing the above attributes to him, British mathematical ethologist Richard Dawkins comes readily to mind. In his negatively titled *The Selfish Gene*, widely read and admired by the hard nosed mathematical game theory community, Dawkins identifies himself enthusiastically with the bloody tooth and claw perspective on evolution (1976: 2). Early on in *The Selfish Gene*, he writes with true stiff upper lippedness:

Be warned that if you wish as I do, to build a society in which individuals cooperate generously and unselfishly toward the common good, you can expect little help from biological nature. Let us try to teach generosity and altruism, because we are born selfish (1976: 3).

Original Sin! The biology version. We are born sinners. Shades of medieval monastic spiritual masochism! But don't despair totally. We are redeemable, at least in theory, by training and education.

But by whom are we redeemable? And where do their credentials and expertise come from? Following Dawkin's logic, certainly not from the detached-from-human-warmth mathematical scientific community. After all, according to them, we lack the emotional neural substrate from which a sense of morality can be derived.

Who then is to save us? To be the teachers?—the fundamentalist religious bigots who easily reject the cold logic of the scientific community. Certainly they are eager candidates. Is Dawkins suggesting this indirectly? If so—surely, he can't be serious.

We have a dilemma. How can we achieve what "science" denies we have the capacity for by nature?

WARMTH, EMPATHY, AND THE SOCIAL BRAIN

Fortunately, we can all relax. The dilemma is a false one. Dawkins is simply wrong. Whatever the advantages of such dramatic, socially-misleading titles as *selfish gene*, we will, hopefully, see less of such fallacious and inaccurate science in this new century.

Other than being simply wrong on his science, Dawkins commits a glaring fallacy of reasoning in the quoted passage. He reasons fallaciously from gene to gene-created mechanism. The selfishness he attributes to the gene, he totally inappropriately extends to the motivated behavior of the phenotype or the individual. There is no logical basis for making this jump. And the empirics contradict him. The contradictory empirical science comes from evolutionary neuroscience, about which mathematical game theorists and likely Dawkins himself, seem appallingly uninformed.

NEURAL ARCHITECTURE AND BEHAVIOR

In the emerging discipline of evolutionary neuroscience we to go to the physical source—the evolved circuitry of our neural architecture. Here we look at what evolution *has* produced, not what we *think* it should have or could have produced.

We study the structure of the brain through actual physical examination. We code its responses through experiment and observation. The anatomical structure of the human brain can be and has been studied extensively and compared with the brain structures of other mammals and vertebrates.

Evidence shows clearly that certain behaviors first appeared in fully articulated, integrated form with mammals and still exist in the mammals we study today. These behaviors are nurturing: nursing, seeking contact comfort, clinging, using vocal and visual signals—a set of behaviors that have been called affectional. Different brain structures developed with the full appearance of these behaviors and are experimentally as well as logically held to be responsible for them. We still have a lot to learn about the interactive detail of brain structure and behavior, but the general features of the wiring diagram are well-established and indisputable.

Brain circuitry and behavior show, above all, that mammals are social animals. Humans, as the most highly evolved mammals, are the most social—and the most dependent on social life. We humans are born in social groups, live in society, and reproduce in society. And it is obvious that we must have the behavioral equipment to make this possible—that is, our contending behavioral circuits of self-preservation and affection, ego and empathy, along with the homeostatic rules that govern their operation. This is the dynamic expressed so elegantly by the CSN model and the equation of our social brain.

CONVERGING TRENDS

Parallel to the emergence of evolutionary neuroscience, but running on a separate track, were changes in the perspective of psychology. Such changes included a shift in focus from the externalized perspective of radical behaviorism to the inner workings of the mind. Also significant was the rise of an approach called evolutionary psychology.

Because these are important to the emerging insights into the social and political aspects of society, I will cover them briefly in the next chapter.

22

INCLUSIVE SOCIAL FITNESS AND EVOLUTIONARY NEUROSCIENCE

The last quarter of the 20th century saw a major shift of scientific interest in human behavior. The previously forbidden domain of human cognition and consciousness was opened up to scientific study. The intrepid few who breached the gates did so at first very cautiously. Emboldened by the newly spectacular success of computers, the new researchers adopted the model of information-processing. It was a timid first step, anchored in the safe haven of cold, nonhuman mechanical analogy.

In their view we humans would now become reducible to a mechanical information-processing device. From this perspective the brain was nothing but a computer, an information processor. And information processing was all that was studied. Emotions, human warmth, and caring, were excluded from the researchable. It was an essentially barren effort that soon exhausted its useful research programs, but it did open the gates to the more adventurous.

ETHOLOGY OR THE STUDY OF ANIMAL BEHAVIOR

Parallel to the behavioristic tradition, popular principally in the U.S. and the Soviet Union, the study of animal behavior, called ethology, had been progressing largely in continental Europe. European ethologists Konrad Lorenz, Niko Tinbergen, and Karl von Frisch won Nobel prizes in 1973 for their pioneering work in the new field. These ethologists did across species comparisons and proceeded from an evolutionary perspective. They observed and described behavior. They did not, however, look into the black box of the brain and attempt to speculate on neural mechanisms.

EVOLUTIONARY BIOLOGY TO EVOLUTIONARY PSYCHOLOGY

At the same time evolutionary biology powered by the engine of Darwin's insights proceeded on a track largely isolated from mainstream psychology, whether behaviorism or the more recent cognitive information-processing endeavor. Despite a few heroic efforts at integration of the biological with the psychological and social sciences, the isolation remained essentially in tact.

In the last two decades of the century, the evolutionary perspective and psychology finally hesitatingly married up in what became known as evolutionary psychology. Like the behavioristic psychology before it, evolutionary psychology viewed the black box of the human brain largely from the outside. It began speculating upon what could be within—that is, what could be there that was passed on in the evolutionary process through our genes.

Evolutionary psychology paid little attention to actual brain structure, but sometimes made elaborate speculations about presumed isolated and dedicated processing modules which dealt with specific environmental challenges that had arisen. Such modules were likened to a Swiss knife, each blade put neatly in place with imaginary precision in the manner of an equally imaginary professional engineer represented by the process of natural selection.

Such improbable speculation proceeded largely unchecked. It was, at times, reminiscent of the pseudoscientific phrenology of the previous century. Phrenology had notoriously sought to identify human characteristics through external examination of lumps on the cranium. The unwritten command driving evolutionary psychology seemed to be "find a behavior, posit a dedicated brain module." The approach was considerably naïve and open to endless proliferation of imaginary neural components.[45]

EVOLUTIONARY NEUROETHOLOGY

In the broad panorama of science many tracks proceeded independently at varying levels of reduction and integration—and in isolation because of our departmented university system. One of these tracks that moved outside the mainstream of emerging research on neuroscience was the evolutionary neuroethology of Paul MacLean discussed in the opening chapters (see also, Cory & Gardner, 2002).

In a sheltered laboratory of the National Institutes of Health, MacLean, a medical doctor, began a research program in the 1950s aimed at understanding evolved behavior through a study of the substrate neural circuitry at various stages of evolution. His emphasis was on certain lizards and lower mammals.

MacLean chose lizards because they resembled most closely the ancestral bridge between ancient vertebrates and mammals. His research program focused upon the neural circuitry underlying behavior with emphasis on emotion—especially those nurturing emotions and motivations that lay at the foundation of mammalian family life and that were apparently lacking in ancestral vertebrates.

---

[45] Considerable criticism has been written on the tendency to over-modularize in evolutionary psychology. Evolution simply doesn't work that way. Rather than creating new modules evolution seems rather to co-opt existing circuits and perhaps elaborate them for new adaptations. Often seemingly new behaviors are only slightly nuanced expressions of pre-existing adaptations. Also the somewhat general purpose six-layered structure of the neocortex is considerably plastic and may be modified to produce new behavioral patterns of response. See Panksepp and Panksepp, 2000; also de Waal; 2002 for critiques of evolutionary psychology's tendency to over modularization.

MacLean's emphasis on the evolution of emotion was ahead of its time and out of step with the mainstream research in the emergent area of behavioral neuroscience. In keeping with the superficial behavioristic tradition, mainstream neuroscience lacked an evolutionary perspective and focused only on the mechanics of information-processing.

It called itself cognitive neuroscience, acknowledging, in its name, the exclusion of emotion. When emotion was occasionally studied it was under the limited, coldly formal information-processing aspect of "learning." When actual emotion was admitted into the chill halls of such science, it was the usual faire of fear, aggression, and human nastiness in general. Original sin, in sublimated guise, still dominated the paradigm. Stiff-upper-lippers, real he-men, tough guys of science—with some very rare exceptions—didn't study love, nurturing, warmth, caring.

At the close of the twentieth century, the study of emotion, based in part on the long-neglected pioneering work of MacLean, combined with the dramatic efforts of a few dispersed, but bold researchers, seemed at last to gain attention.

The big challenge now seemed to be how the externalized, essentially cold-blooded, gene-centered perspective of evolutionary biology and evolutionary psychology could be reconciled with evolutionary neuroscience and the study of warmblooded, nurturing side of humanity.

HAMILTON AND INCLUSIVE FITNESS

The conceptual bridge came principally from the work of British scholar W. D. Hamilton. In his kin selection model, Hamilton (1964) formalized the issue of how genes for cooperation and altruism could evolve and be etched into the human ancestral genome.

The core of this inclusive fitness model is that it weighed the effect of genes not only on the individual that carried them but also on kin individuals who shared the same genes. According to what has come to be called Hamilton's rule, genes coding for cooperation, reciprocity or altruism could evolve if the costs of cooperative behavior to the individual were outweighed by the benefits to related individuals carrying the same genes. Hamilton's rule is expressed varyingly as

$$rb - c > 0 \quad \text{or} \quad c < rb$$

In this formula r is the coefficient or degree of relatedness or kin, b is the benefit of the cooperative or altruistic behavior to the kin, and c is the cost of the behavior to the individual. The equation predicts that as r increases, benefits will exceed costs and cooperation, reciprocity, or altruism would be favored by natural selection. Hamilton's rule gives the basic formula for inclusive fitness from the external gene's eye view. It shows mathematically how it is possible for such traits as altruism and reciprocity to get into the genome.

Neither the concept of inclusive fitness nor the formula, however, can predict the mechanism created by the genes to sustain altruism and reciprocity. And, accordingly, Hamilton, displaying no knowledge of neural architecture, did not speculate on the actual nature of such neural mechanisms.

The formula of our social neural architecture derived from the CSN model, however, expresses this motivating mechanism and establishes linkage with Hamilton's formula. In other words, the equation deriving from the CSN model expresses the function of the neural architecture that the genes actually *did* produce under the terms of Hamilton's rule.

The social brain formula can, in fact, be expressed in the same cost/benefit terms that Hamilton uses. Empathy can be considered the cost to the behaving individual, ego can be benefit to the survival requirements of the recipient. Substituting cost and benefit into the formula, we get the gene-based operational mechanism for Hamilton's rule (see Cory 1999: 97–100).

$$BT = \frac{Benefit}{Cost} = \pm 1$$

According to the algorithms of our social neural architecture, *any* empathetic, cooperative, or altruistic behavior will serve to improve the odds of survival of self *plus* others *inclusively* over purely egoistic or self-interested behavior. This is compatible with Hamilton's rule which says that as long as the benefit to related individuals exceeds the cost to the behaving individual, the genes supporting such behavior can be favored by natural selection.

Of course, once the neural mechanism, the social architecture, is in place, as it has been for thousands of years, the empathetic or altruistic behavior may be extended to non-kin—even the universe itself—by appropriate education and socialization through the medium of language that draws upon, modifies, and elaborates the existing neural substrate.[46]

The concept of inclusive fitness, combined with the findings of evolutionary neuroscience of the homeostatic circuitry of the social brain, established the motivated foundations for society as an expression of social exchange. This dynamic is, of course, represented by the CSN model and its related equation of our social brain.

---

[46] The fact that the altruism or other modules or circuits, once in place, can be extended by our higher brain architecture to others, perhaps even to the universe itself has been acknowledged by a number of writers (e.g., see Buss, 1999).

23

THE NEURAL DYNAMIC, EXCHANGE, AND SOCIAL STRUCTURE

All societies are societies of social exchange—from the give-and-take of the family to the give-and-take of one-to-one friendships, groups, communities, up to nations and beyond. Wherever and whenever individuals are in social contact there is give-and-take or social exchange. The neural substrate for such exchange is the ego/empathy dynamic expressed by the CSN model and the equation of the social brain.

To the extent that these exchanges are out of balance we have behavioral tension and inequality. To the extent they approach dynamic balance behavioral tension is reduced and inequalities are likewise. The following form of the social equation mathematically represents such social exchange relationships as they approach dynamic balance:

$$BT = \frac{Ego}{Empathy} = \frac{Dominance}{Submission} = \pm 1$$

As the ratio diverges from ± 1 or dynamic balance, the equation indexes the behavioral tension in the society. The equation also allows us to conceptualize mathematically the relationship between equality and inequality. It gives us a framework for estimating the magnitude of inequality and ultimately to quantify it ever more precisely.[47]

---

[47] The equation of the social brain does for social stratification exactly what the calculus was expected to do for economics by the founders of mathematical economics. The French mathematician and economist, Antoine Augustin Cournot (1801–1877), a predecessor of Walras, is considered by some scholars to be the first to successfully apply mathematics to the study of economics. Mathematics—the calculus—was seen as a framework for understanding rather than for simple calculation. Cournot emphasized that the simple numerical calculation of magnitudes was not the point of mathematization. It was to provide a tool for the demonstration of functional relationships leading to the understanding and elaboration of form and structure. Numerical precision was difficult, if not impossible, to obtain because the relationships among the variables were too complex for our analytical powers (1963 [1838]: see especially pp. 2–3).

SOCIAL STRATIFICATION AS
STRUCTURED BEHAVIORAL TENSION

Social stratification is a major concern of sociologists. A truly vast literature expresses the extent of that concern. In terms of our neural dynamic such institutionalized inequalities represent structured behavioral tension. Apparently intuiting the tension through the dynamic of their own neural architecture, most sociologists see social stratification as a problem. Some see it as a necessary evil proceeding from the inevitable division of labor in any society of any size. Others see it as an *un*necessary evil based on exploitation of one group by another.

Almost all will agree that it is a source of tension even when it appears to contribute to stability. Almost all will also agree that those on the lower levels envy or resent those above and would change the situation given the chance. Likewise those above seemingly empathetically sense this tension and react to defend or rationalize their upper position in the inequalities.

On the one hand this is common sense. No one, given the choice, would willingly and knowingly choose to be on the short end of a significant or meaningful inequality. This is intuitive—any fool knows it. Nevertheless, we have never been able to explain it coherently or scientifically by linking it to neural architecture. We have previously intuited or postulated a sense of justice in human nature without a grasp of the dynamic. And we have justified and qualified "what is just" almost beyond recognition based on accommodation to the existing social context.

The CSN model and the social equation change that. We now have a dynamic framework that explains the fundamental tension behind the motivation, the associated dislike of inequality, and the desire for social justice. That dynamic framework is our neural architecture driven by behavioral tension. The rest is contextual and situational. When social justice is defined contextually, it accepts, reinforces, and justifies the existing social system. When social justice is defined ideally it foresees or calls for change in the existing system.

SELF CORRECTIVE TENDENCY VS. SOCIAL STRATIFICATION

Our neural architecture evolved in small family units where the interpersonal interactions resolved the tension of inequalities. The logic of the neural architecture tells us that while most of us will willingly accept some inequality in favor of ourselves, none of us will willingly and knowingly accept *less* than a position of rough equality on all matters of significance.

The interactive, negotiating exchange process that goes on in small face to face family groups driven by behavioral tension tends to come to dynamic balance or rough equality. Even within the family, members will tend to ally with each other to overcome or moderate efforts at domination by one member. For example, the average dad of today's democratic societies is no match for an alliance of mom and the kids. Lesser developed societies still, however, block such natural corrective tendencies by restrictive tradition and institutions.

In larger groups this self-corrective tendency, historically, became increasingly blocked by the lack of close interaction. Both the distance of interaction and the division of labor contributed to blocking the self-correcting action demanded by the evolved neural architecture. This blockage built behavioral tension in the societies. The resulting inequalities and behavioral tension, then, had to be rationalized or made minimally palatable by institutions or ideology—or, ultimately, maintained by force.

The somewhat steady movement toward democracy in the overall social exchange system today is propelled by this self-correcting tendency of our neural architecture. In the United States, as well as other countries around the world, we have seen this tendency expressed in the movements toward equal socio-political participation. In the United States, we saw the emergence and successes of first the civil rights movement and, then, the women's movement. These have been followed by the call for equal rights by gays, lesbians, and other minorities.

Such minorities have been held in unequal states of behavioral tension by institutions, ideologies, or outright force. Their movements emerge, motivated by the pent up tension, as change becomes possible—that is, as institutions, ideologies, and force become weakened, tolerant, or otherwise subject to challenge. A recent social thinker, Francis Fukuyama, has even gone so far to say that with the failure of communism and the breakup of the Soviet Union, Western-style democracy has become the end system of human political history.[48]

The blockages to the natural corrective tendency, then, will tend to be overcome if the relations among the components of the total social exchange system are permitted to operate freely. For further insight into why this is so, we can look to the evolutionary process of species closely related to our own.

THE INSTABILITY OF SOCIAL STRATIFICATION AMONG PRIMATES AND HUMANS

The emergence of evolutionary neuroethology permits new insights into social stratification. Evolutionary neuroethology combines the study of evolutionary neuroscience with the perspective of evolutionary ethology or the study of behavior across the range of animal species. Like others it is a Darwinian perspective.

An emphasis on the pervasive presence of social hierarchy or dominance/submissive relationships is a hallmark of the ethological approach in animal studies. Paul MacLean pioneered the study of brain circuitry substrating such behaviors. The term neuroethology, which encompasses the study of both brain and behavior from an evolutionary perspective, captures this combined focus well.

An important insight emerged from these conjoined efforts. The earlier vertebrate circuitry common to fishes, amniotes, and reptiles (MacLean's reptilian brain or R-complex) which scripted self-preserving, often life and death contests for dominance, became integrated with the attachment or affectional circuitry of mammals. This combined circuitry permitted the emergence of social competition—the tug and pull of ego and empathy that is captured in the CSN model. Dominance modified by affection

---

[48] Fukuyama's article first came out in 1989. It was followed by a book expanding the topic (1992).

leading to cognitively emergent empathy became possible among higher primates and humans.[49]

Although dominance, without engagement of affectional mechanisms, could still be a life and death all or nothing contest, hierarchy could now be achieved through alliances, serving and preserving others by engaging affectional circuitry. Submission could be accepted and integrated into the social fabric. Conflict resolution, as we currently practice it in our behavioral, social, and management sciences, thus, became possible.

Of course, the behavioral tension, motivating the contests remained. The tug-and-pull of self-preservation and affection, ego and empathy, persisted latently or covertly to drive later changes in the hierarchy when the supporting contingencies and/or relative prowess of the contestants changed. Thus, human hierarchies, like those of other mammals and primates, are inherently unstable because of the latent or potential behavioral tension. Depending on the degree of social, economic, or political inequalities, they must be held in place by institutions, ideologies, and/or police or military power. In other words social stratification is inherently unstable based upon the dynamic of our neural architecture.

SOCIAL EXCHANGE AS SOCIAL COMPETITION GOES CLINICAL

Over the past decades there has been a growing, research, theoretical, and clinical literature that proceeds from this neuroethological perspective. Social exchange relationships, intensified by the social imbalances, get out of whack. They cause behaviors and emotional states that bring us to clinics for help. The reciprocal algorithms and the equation developed from them provide a useful organizing concept for current thinking on hierarchy or dominance/submissive relationships in psychotherapeutic theory.

British psychiatrist John Price (1967) initiated the present effort to incorporate the concept of hierarchy into human psychotherapy from the ethological perspective by introducing his theory of the dominance hierarchy and the evolution of mental illness. American psychiatrist Russell Gardner (1982) carried the effort forward in his ethological approach to the mechanism of manic-depressive disorder. Other scholars took up the call and contributed to more fully developing the social competition hypothesis of clinical depression.[50]

---

[49] There is a substantial literature on hierarchy among primates. The following works may serve to give the interested reader an introduction. Primatologist Frans de Waal (1988, 1996) has observed such behavior in chimpanzees. Christopher Boehm (1999) devotes a whole volume to the instability of hierarchy in primates and humans and the tendency to a democratic society. See also Sapolsky (1999, 1992: 315–319).

[50] There is a growing literature on social competition and other evolutionary approaches to psychotherapy (e.g., see Price, Sloman, Gardner, Gilbert, and Rohde, 1994; Paul Gilbert and Kent Bailey, 2000; Harris, 2002; Price, 2002; Sloman, 2002; Bailey, 2002; Wilson, 2002, 1993).

FROM PSYCHOTHERAPY TO SOCIAL STRATIFICATION

More recently a British clinical theorist and practioneer, John Birtchnell (1993, 1999) has developed a neuroethological approach to psychotherapy which, in his own words, "grew out of a preoccupation with the concept of psychological dependence." (1999: xi). He went on to tell us that:

The breakthrough came when I realized that dependence had two parts, one to do with getting close and one to do with being lower. Once that became clear, I could see that there had to be other kinds of relating that involved becoming distant and being upper. It occurred to me that being close, distant, upper, and lower must be the only possible ways we could relate. So that was it—everything we do has to involve becoming either close or distant, or upper or lower (1999: ix).

The hierarchical aspect of Birtchnell's theory is easily captured by the basic formula or equation of reciprocal interaction. Since, as a therapist, he focused on dependence in relating, he can be forgiven for not clearly seeing a fifth possibility in relating; that of dynamic equality—although he does allude to it later in his text (e.g., 1999: 14).

Significantly, the research committee of the Group for the Advancement of Psychiatry (GAP) has recently affirmed the essential nature of the human brain as an organ that evolved to mediate our social interactions. The committee, which addressed psychiatry's need for a unifying foundation, concluded that the relevant physiological focus for psychiatry is the social brain. The committee noted that conversation, feeling, and thinking can happen only from brain-actions in the involved individuals. Therefore, non-biological and non-social psychiatry cannot exist (Gardner, 2002: 100–102).

What should be suspect from the social brain equation and the algorithms of reciprocity is that all relating other than dynamic balance or rough equality carries a potentially significant load of behavioral tension. Any equilibrium of such unbalanced or unequal relationships should always be seen as a temporary adjustment on the way to maturity or psychological independence rather than dependence of any variety. This should be important to a therapist who assists clients to achieve more satisfying, less tension-filled, interpersonal relationships.

The clinical issues are of interest here because they capture in microcosm the issues inherent in social stratification. The clinical syndromes not only reflect the behavioral and emotional tensions of the neural dynamic in interpersonal relationships, they mirror the tensions in society at large.

SOCIETY AS AN OVER-ARCHING SOCIAL EXCHANGE SYSTEM

Our neural architecture evolved in the extended nuclear family. For millions of years of hominid evolution before we reached our final species level of homo sapiens sapiens some 100,000 years ago, we survived and evolved as small, kinship or family groups or bands. The deeply binding interactive dynamic of self-preservation and affection, ego and empathy, preserved us from one precarious generation to the other. All aspects of our economic and political lives were bound into the family unit, driven and maintained by the social architecture. Motivated by deeply felt and powerful affectional reward circuits, we shared with each other and cared for the young, the weak, the handicapped, and the aged. There is growing evidence that higher primates who trace back with us to a common ancestor do the same. The kinship groups were essentially egalitarian. All shared in the power and the economic necessities for survival.

This leads us to a fundamental fact of social organization. In the larger units of modern social organization the power and economic functions of the primitive family have been split. All social units, from the modern family on up, are social exchange units. Society, at the very top, then, can be viewed as an overarching social exchange system (Figure 6). It occupies the place of the extended family and combines its functions. A large scale society like a nation-state has two essential societal level components previously combined in the primitive family unit: an economic exchange system and a politico-legal exchange system. In keeping with the literature on economic sociology, these systems are imbedded within the larger social exchange system (see, Granovetter & Swedberg, 2001).

Although the two systems have different jobs or functions, they work together to form the essential character of the society. Both are needed. One can't do the job of the other. The dynamic of our social brain helps us to make the distinction as well as recognize the necessity for both. Let's look at the different jobs they do. The market exchange system first.

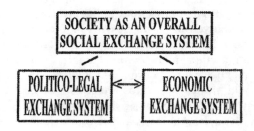

Figure 6. Society as an Overall Social Exchange System.

THE MARKET OR ECONOMIC EXCHANGE SYSTEM

The free enterprise market exchange system operates according to the so-called laws of supply and demand. Supply and demand, as we have seen repeatedly, are not really laws but an expression of our neural dynamic. In the market exchange system, however, the neural dynamic or equation is constrained by the definitions of economics.

Economic Demand and Supply

In economics, *demand* consists of two elements: (1) *taste* and (2) *ability to buy*. To be counted among demanders in the market exchange system, then, an individual must have a taste for a certain commodity and must also have enough money to pay for it. The economic definition, thus, excludes all those who may need commodities of necessity, like food, clothing, shelter or health care, but who lack the money to buy them.

The poor or needy, then, whether they desperately need essential commodities, or even clamor vociferously for them in street demonstrations, are excluded from the economic concept of demand. That is, economists simply don't count them anymore. They drop out of the equation.

The concept of supply is similarly constrained in the market exchange system. Suppliers, likewise, must meet two requirements: (1) they must be *able to sell* and (2) they must be *willing to sell*. The ability to sell means, of course, the suppliers must be able to cover their costs of production and supplying or else they would soon go out of business. They also must be willing to provide at the prices available. Sometimes they may be willing to sell at a loss for short periods to avoid further losses, but they can't go on doing so forever because they will be forced out of business by the very structure and definitions of the market system.

The constraints of the economic definitions of demand and supply place limits on what the free enterprise market exchange system can do. It may produce a vast number of commodities—more than not-free systems—but it may still fail to meet the actual needs of the society. By its very structure and definitions, then, the market historically may fail to meet all the needs of the society. In fact, historically speaking, there has never been a free market system that has, without assistance, met all the needs of society. Even the best free market system, operating on its own defined principles, has failed to eliminate poverty and social deprivation. This takes us to role of the politico-legal exchange system.

THE POLITICO-LEGAL EXCHANGE SYSTEM

The political exchange system requires a different set of definitions. It must respond to the overall social exchange system. In response to behavioral or social tension, it must act to counter failures or limits of the market system. It must balance out the social brain dynamic over the entire overarching social exchange system—like the primitive family did over evolutionary history.

Social Demand and Political Exchange

Demand in the politico-legal system may appropriately be called *social demand* as opposed to *economic demand*. And the definition is different. Social demand contrasts with economic demand on the two elements of its definition. In social demand *taste* becomes *need*. The second element *ability to buy* is dropped. It is replaced by *willingness and ability/inability to work*.

The politico-legal system, then, complements the market exchange system and balances out its failures and limitations. It fulfills the charter of the primitive family in which the neural dynamic evolved. It cares for the unemployed, the handicapped, the aged, and others who lack the ability to qualify in the demand definition of the market exchange system. The politico-legal exchange system must readjust, by taxation, subsidy, or other method, the imbalance or failure which is an inevitable outcome of the market exchange system as defined.

Civilized democracies, responding to the interactive dynamic of ego and empathy, can not afford to allow their citizens to lack the necessities of life. The behavioral tension created by the market failures drives this corrective action. Of course, for its part the political system must exercise great care not to stifle the creative energy of the market system while correcting the inevitable failures, distortions, or imbalances.

Let's take a look at the equilibrium curve of Chapter 13 to illustrate what this means. For instance, take the equilibrium graph to represent the total social demand for an item of necessity. This means, as a simple example, that there are six (billion, if we include the world population) items of necessity and six (billion, if world) persons comprising the society.

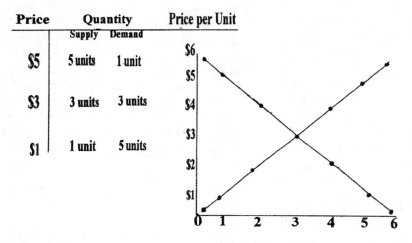

Price	Quantity		Price per Unit
	Supply	Demand	
$5	5 units	1 unit	
$3	3 units	3 units	
$1	1 unit	5 units	

Under the concept of economic supply and demand the three items above the equilibrium point as well as the three items below the point are dropped out of the picture. The market is said to clear. All those who have the taste and ability to buy have been supplied by those able and willing to supply. That is, we have a perfect market! It sounds great, but it is misleading.

Social Demand and Excess Price

Looked at from the perspective of social demand, things are not so good. In fact, we have a serious problem. Assuming the excess supply will go away or simply not be produced may get us out of difficulty on the supply side. But what about the three, or three billion, items which represent items of necessity to three or three billion social demanders or citizens?

Their essential needs go unmet. As a result we have substantial failure or inequity in the market and substantial behavioral tension. Will these three, or three billion, persons demonstrate in the streets, commit crimes, initiate an insurrection expressing this tension? Or will they instead appeal to the political exchange system for redress to this imbalance in necessities of life? And will the political system respond?

Whatever happens, we have socio-behavioral tension to deal with because of the market failure. The social equation indexes this tension. The ratio between what is supplied in the market and social demand is 6/3 or a behavioral tension magnitude of 2. The market in this case has met just half of the social demand. From the perspective of the overall social exchange system, we have to deal with the behavioral tension magnitude of 2, which translates numerically into half of its citizens going without a necessity.

To further clarify things, we may introduce the term *excess price* to describe the difference between the market equilibrium price and the price we must reach to fulfill the social demand of 6. According to the graph, a price of about $0.25 would satisfy the social demand. Anything above that, then, would be excess price.

So how do we get the price to that point? As a civilized society we cannot tolerate the behavioral tension in the situation—that is, we cannot allow half or, for that matter, any of our citizens to go without necessities. But we can't ask suppliers in the market system to lower the price below their ability to recover costs. The suppliers would go broke. In effect we would destroy the market.

So what do we ask of our political system? Essentially we have two options. We may subsidize the supplier or give aid to the demander. That is, for example, we have the choice of such things as industry subsidies or welfare payments and food stamps. Our politico-legal exchange system has been known to use both.

The dynamic equation of our social brain quickly reveals the problem as we shift from necessities to non-necessities under the contrasting definitions or constraints of the market and the overall social exchange system.

MARKET STANDARD FOR NON-NECESSITIES
SOCIAL STANDARD FOR NECESSITIES?

To satisfy the discrepancy or behavioral tension that exists between the market exchange system and social exchange system, we must act politically. So, what should we do? Should we adopt a two-tiered overarching social exchange system? Should we apply the market standard or set of definitions to non-necessities and the social standard or set of definitions to necessities? We already do this in a fuzzy sort of way in the United States. Some of the European free enterprise democracies do it much more self-consciously.

THE PREDICTIONS OF THE SOCIAL DYNAMIC

The dynamic of our neural architecture predicts that to the extent that the two subsystems—the market system and the politico-legal system—interact freely, behavioral tension and inequalities within the society will tend to dynamic balance. This condition of freely interacting can only be met in a democratic society with a free enterprise market exchange system.

In a freely functioning democratic society the limitations or failures of the market exchange system will tend to be corrected in the politico-legal system. That is: when the market fails to produce or distribute adequately, or when businesses show excessive greed, corruption, or monopolistic tendencies, citizens will demand counteraction through legal or political processes. We see this on almost a daily basis in developed democratic countries.

The major challenge facing a free society is to keep the interactions between the two key systems free of undue interference or obstruction. This is what intuitively drives most government regulation of business. It clearly drives anti-trust legislation and enforcement. It conspicuously drives such movements as campaign finance reform— which aim is to correct attempts to interfere with the normal self-corrective tendency via the political system by those holding greater power in the market system.

In sum, the inequalities generated in the market exchange system will tend, driven by behavioral tension, to be corrected in the political-legal system if allowed to work without interference. In the overarching social exchange system, then, driven by the behavioral tension of our neural architecture, things will tend to balance out.

INCENTIVES, PRODUCTIVITY, AND BEHAVIORAL TENSION

If there is one thing we learned from the experiments in socialism in the twentieth century, it is that incentives are required for a highly productive economy. Varying incentives, of course, mean the creating of inequalities. This exploits the fundamental expression of our neural architecture. We don't like inequalities. And we will strive to alter or overcome them in our own favor or at least to the point of rough equity. Such is the engine of social competition in both the market and political sub-arenas. It is the engine that drives our free market system. It works for us.

But there are dangers to the system when the tensions or inequalities permitted for production become excessively cumulative and extreme. Our society becomes unstable. The economically or politically disenfranchised, or excluded, become motivated to change—through crime, riots, and other forms of disobedience and violence.

Ideally, to avoid excessive behavioral tension which translates into social unrest, the inequalities necessary to incent a free market economy should be held within the range approaching dynamic balance. Also, like the moment-by-moment, day-by-day tug and pull of the ego and empathy circuitries, the inequalities should be temporary and shifting. If both conditions hold, the behavioral tension or inequality will be neither extreme nor cumulative in its effects. And if the market exchange system and the politico-legal exchange system are allowed to interact and self-correct freely, the overall system driven by behavioral tension will tend to dynamic balance.

Social institutions and practices which impede this self-corrective tendency, like undue influence by powerful special interest groups, will skew the dynamic to the extremes and create behavioral tension and inequalities in the society. This, of course, translates into social discontent and unrest. The behavioral tension underlying the discontent motivates efforts toward social change in the direction of a better balance.

24

THE NEURAL DYNAMIC AND
OUR POLITICAL CHOICES

In recent decades the studies of political science and economics have largely gone their separate ways. The emerging new emphasis on political economy reflects a change in that state of separation. It is based upon the perceived underlying unity of the political and economic sides of social life. Political economy emerges at the point on a spectrum at which the disciplines of political science and economics, coming from differing perspectives on social life, flow into each other or converge. At this point there is occurring an exchange or blending of theory and methodology.

Indicative of this convergence is the importing of self-interested rational choice theory into political science under the rubric of public choice. Despite the advantages of uniform theory and methods bridging the two disciplines, there is also a downside. The preexisting problems and distortions are carried from economics into the public choice literature based upon the self-interest emphasis and the failure to recognize the reciprocal nature of all exchange and choice. An excerpt from an introductory text on public choice is sufficient to illustrate this claim.

...chaos and anarchy do not exist in the economy. The daily...tasks of feeding, clothing, housing, transporting, and entertaining the population are accomplished without fanfare or centralized control. The source of this order is individual *self interest* (emphasis mine) channeled by competitive supply and demand incentives (Johnson 1991: 53–54).

This excerpt (and similar ones can be selected from almost any text or monograph), with its emphasis on self-interest, obscures the fact that the market operates in a pervasive social context and the ordering principle is not self-interest but is, instead, reciprocity. There is an entire community, nation, or world out there stating its egoistic demands or wants, which are indexed by the price mechanism. A supplier or businessperson looks at this egoistic demand or want indicator of price and decides how much or what empathetic services or products she/he will produce or perform for provisioning or responding to this demand. The businessperson then fulfills the empathetic, nurturing, or provisioning side of the economic equation, meeting the egoistic demands of the individuals grouped into the concept of market. She/he then receives payment in reciprocal acknowledgment to his/her own egoistic demands or needs—and the reciprocity is complete. The ubiquitous equivalent reciprocals of *thank you* and *you're welcome* are always there. The mechanism is reciprocal because if the community, nation, or world were not out there, the businessperson would simply not provide.

True, the market as described is impersonal and rarefied. Therefore subjective feelings of ego and empathy may be weak to almost nonexistent. Nevertheless, the reciprocal algorithms of behavior, as shown in earlier chapters, are clearly the driving 'source of the market mechanism—not self interest alone as claimed by the prevailing market theory and set out as gospel by economic, rational choice, and public choice texts. Market or exchange theory, as it exists today is inaccurate, distorted, and has the unfortunate side effect of promoting self-interested egoism, Social Darwinistic propensities, and cynicism throughout the society, by failing to understand and grasp the empathetic nature of the provisioning required to fulfill the equation.

In political science one of the most important issues is that of legitimacy—the question of how people are bound into a political community—a local, national, or even worldwide identity. Patriotism and loyalty illustrate that empathy, with its roots in affection, accompanies identification with the political unit, community, nation, or perhaps world, as kin, as benefactor, as provider of safety and services. When the political unit provides, the citizens reciprocate empathy, attachment, identity, loyalty. It would be easy to obscure these essential issues of politics within a self-interested, rational choice model.

FROM CONFLICT TO RECIPROCITY: THE IMPLICATIONS FOR NEW INSTITUTIONS FOR A NEW MILLENNIUM

The reciprocal algorithms of behavior prescribed by our evolved brain structure show us how to get from conflict to reciprocity by the balancing of our self-interested and empathetic programming. These algorithms of reciprocity have been shown to be the guiding dynamic of social organization and exchange. What then do they require of us in building new institutions and behaviors to accommodate self-consciously, in a more enlightened manner appropriate to the new millennium, their inevitable dynamic?

First, I would point out the implications for orienting the discipline of political science. Although it has stirred controversy and cleavages, there is no question that the rational choice model of economics and exchange theory is becoming the dominant model in political science (Bates, 1997; Johnson, 1997; Lusick, 1997). By adopting, instead, the alternative model presented here, political science connects with evolutionary neuroscience, as well as avoiding the negatives, the moral discomfort and criticism that have plagued the overly self-interested economic and exchange theory models. It also gains a heuristic that can better account for such important political phenomena as loyalty, commitment, and the shifting involvements of private interest and public action (e.g., Hirschman, 1982). Finally the model shows the moral basis of exchange and choice which is increasingly important to our society, and avoids the implicit and troubling academic endorsement and propagation of a one-sided self-interested egoism in public affairs. And hopefully, with the dethroning of unmitigated self-interest by the appropriate acknowledgment of the balancing role of empathy, the last vestiges of Social Darwinism will begin to fade from our social, economic, and political thought.

Even economist Kenneth Arrow, Nobel prize recipient and the acknowledged creator of social choice theory, has commented in an oral history interview:

People just do not maximize on a selfish basis every minute. In fact, the system would not work if they did. A consequence of that hypothesis would be the end of organized society as we know it (Arrow in Feiwel, 1987: 233)[51]

And economist Thrainn Eggertsson of the University of Iceland refreshingly and candidly puts it in terms that match those used here when he writes: "A society where everybody behaves solely in an *egotistical* and *cold-blooded* (emphasis mine) fashion is not viable" (1990: 75). It is further interesting that Eggertsson, intuitively, as most of us do since we all share similar brain structures, associates egotistical with cold-bloodedness—our protoreptilian or premammalian heritage. Our mammalian heritage gives us warm-bloodedness, nurturing, the capacity for cooperation, trust—and the warmth and comfort of friendship.

Now that we can more clearly see the natural state of humankind, proceeding from our evolved brain structure, we can proceed to more self-consciously and intentionally construct our institutions and conduct our behaviors within these institutions to exploit these insights.

Concerning our domestic institutions and behavior, the reciprocal algorithms of behavior driven by behavioral tension, as the foundation of all social organization, prescribe that such institutions in their structure and methods of operation should facilitate the give-and-take, the reciprocity, among the citizenry, that allows the expression of the tension between self- and other-interest as it tends toward balance.[52] Such facilitation should begin early, especially in our socially critical educational institutions, and it should permeate the socializing curricula throughout the education process.

This means such institutions must respect and facilitate both dynamic aspects of our makeup. They must preserve and facilitate the freedom to express our ego, our self-interest, our individuality, in the form of self-expression, productivity, and creativity. And they must also facilitate and cultivate our expressions of empathy, relatedness, and social responsibility. The proper balance of the two means that individual self-interested creativity and productivity is performed empathetically in the process of social exchange as a gift or contribution to society. Creativity and productivity in fact make no sense except as a gift or contribution to be shared with others—with society. Said another way individual creativity and productivity invariably have a social context.

---

[51] This is increasingly recognized in the new institutional economic literature although no effective model to account for it has yet been devised. For other examples, see also Plant's article on the moral limits of markets (1992) and Lars Udehn (1996: esp., pp. 60–114).

[52] The findings from brain structure, gene-theory, and ethology reported in this book support the new emphasis on empathy, cooperation, and altruism by scholars in economics, business, social and political science (e.g., Lawrence & Nohria, 2002; Mansbridge, 1990; Lynne, 1999, 2000; Frederick, 1995; Etzioni, 1988; Frank, 1988; Hirschman, 1982; Margolis, 1982).

This tug and pull between ego and empathy, self-preservation and affection, is the biological source of the tensions between our values of liberty vs. equality that so pervade our modern thinking. The innate dynamic, that we all share and strive to articulate, divides well-intentioned scholars into opposing camps depending on which derived value, liberty or equality, we feel most strongly about, and our assessment of the means by which we can best achieve the most socially desirable balance between the two.

Although liberty and equality need not theoretically be in conflict, this is an issue with deep divisions in current thinking. Total liberty would seem inevitably, even on an ideal level playing field, to involve some inequality, because of innate individual differences in intelligence, skills, talents, energy, and/or developmental factors of health, age. Total equality would likewise, seem inevitably to involve some suppression of liberty, because it would, inhibit or redistribute the advantages gained through the same innate and developmental factors. As radical institutionalist William Dugger, who exhibits a frank, emotionally-charged, and clearly normative position on inequality, remarks: "We can pretend to be value neutral about inequality, but we never are." (1996: 21). On the other hand, Friedrich Hayek worries normatively, and with evident emotion, about social or distributive justice when he writes:

I am not sure that the concept has a definite meaning even in a centrally directed economy, or that in such a system people would ever agree on what distribution is just. I am certain, however, that nothing has done so much to destroy the juridical safeguards of individual freedom as the striving after the mirage of social justice. (1991: 388–389).

Such are the normative variants that our reciprocal brain structure pushes upon us, as ego and empathy, self- and other-interest tug-and-pull against each other within our skulls and between us in society. And such clearly normative, value-bound variants are not dispassionate, but are emotionally-charged as is equally clearly displayed in the rhetoric of both Dugger and Hayek. The value as well as the emotional charge reflects the behavioral tension that drives the dynamic of the reciprocal brain.

OUR NEURAL ARCHITECTURE
SHAPES OUR POLITICAL CHOICES

The dynamic, shaping forces of our neural architecture structure expressed as the reciprocal algorithms and the related equation set the fundamental power or political options open to each of us as individuals as well as to all humankind.

First, is the *egoistic* option by which we pursue self-interest relentlessly, with all our physical and psychological energies. To the extent that we pursue this option, according to our reciprocal algorithms, the ultimate product would be a physical as well as a psychological world filled with the tension and conflict of our contending behavioral forces, internally within each of us and externally as inequities in society. Only force would prevail to control the conflict.

This world would require an imposed authoritarianism in the nature of Hobbes' *Leviathan* to which we surrender power in the face of coercion—whether in fascism or some other form of totalitarian statism.

Second, is the path of *self-sacrifice* along which we surrender our selves to the primacy of others in the form of a subordinated collectivism. The ultimate result would be an absorption of self, a loss of identity, in the identity of others. This, too, according to the reciprocal algorithms of our behavior, produces a physical and psychological world of tension and conflict in which some dominate and some submit. This, too, would be a path toward a collective form of oppression.

The third option is the pursuit of *dynamic balance* of self with others. Physically and psychologically, this path leads to a partnership in unity. Here tension and conflict may be limited and managed, if not fully resolved, in a free and full interplay of ego and empathy, self-preservation and affection, acceptance of self and others—a unity in diversity inclusive of all humankind.

We do not yet have a full and proper definition or concept of such a system, but it would surely include the essentials of free choice (freedom) and fundamental equality. What we currently call *democracy*—at its best—would be an essential component.

Our brain was structured for such choices. And the possible range of socio-political choices is set by our evolved brain structure. These choices, again, can be expressed by the conflict systems neurobehavioral model of our neural architecture.

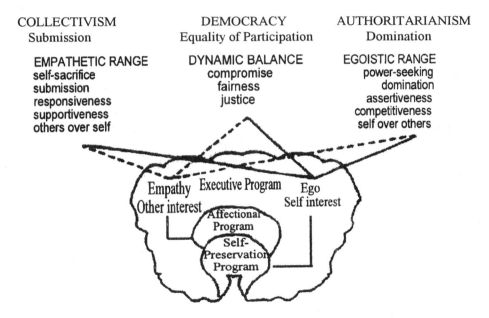

COLLECTIVISM   DEMOCRACY   AUTHORITARIANISM
Submission   Equality of Participation   Domination

EMPATHETIC RANGE   DYNAMIC BALANCE   EGOISTIC RANGE
self-sacrifice   compromise   power-seeking
submission   fairness   domination
responsiveness   justice   assertiveness
supportiveness   competitiveness
others over self   self over others

Empathy   Executive Program   Ego
Other interest   Self interest
Affectional Program
Self-Preservation Program

Figure 7. Socio-political options set by the reciprocal algorithms of our triune modular brain structure.

Falteringly, the innate dynamic seems to be moving us generally in the direction of the center option. Academia sometimes leads, sometimes obscures this process.

For example, concerning the world situation, Kurt Steiner, emeritus professor of political science at Stanford University, in discussing his study on the Tokyo war crimes trial, points out that the overwhelmingly predominant paradigm in international relations theory today is the so-called realist theory. This theory has a Hobbesian concept of conflict and power at its core. As a result of this paradigm the study of international law has all but disappeared from the political science curriculum in America.

This myopic focus on power alone obscures the considerable progress made since World War I in limiting sovereignty in cases of human rights and crimes against peace and in the growing significance of international organizations. At the turn of the 21st century, we have a former head of state, Slobodan Milosevich, brought before the international court at The Hague. The movement has become so strong that the United States, in its role as principal international peacekeeper, has insisted upon exemption of its military personnel from the court's jurisdiction. Leaders of other non-democratic rogue states also face the possibility or threat of being brought before the court of international justice.

The continued expansion of these academically neglected phenomena in international relations, despite the prevalent "realist" paradigm, indicates that the tug-and-pull of empathy vis-à-vis ego (power) is alive and well and that empathy and cooperation invariably are invoked as counters to excesses of power.

An ordered society, to include international society, must, of course, have a framework of power and authority.

That is why the *type* of power structure (Figure 7) is so important. The type of power *structure formalizes* the behavioral tension (inequalities) of the system. Within that structure the tug-and-pull of the reciprocal architecture goes on within and among individuals, groups, and organizations. The power structure either suppresses, distorts, or allows the relatively free venting or expression of this tension.

As we absorb the horror and the threat to human life of a total reliance on power, we are perhaps, stumblingly, but relentlessly, moving in the direction of choosing a more balanced, reciprocal path between ego and empathy, not only in our domestic society, but also in our international social and political relations.

The equation of our social brain provides us with a mathematically expressed index whereby we can estimate our progress toward a dynamically-balanced political system. Such as system can be no less that an increasingly participative and freely functioning democracy. As the ratio between dominance and submission increases to the extremes, we approach one of the fascist or collectivist alternatives fraught with behavioral tension. As we move progressively toward dynamic balance or approximate equilibrium we become increasingly democratic.

$$BT = \frac{Dominance}{Submission} = \pm 1$$

Our institutions of democratic participation and economic upward mobility, although until now lacking a satisfactory scientific foundation, implicitly recognize the instability of imbalance between ego and empathy, dominance and submission. At a minimum they allow institutional vents for the behavioral tension, promoting social stability amidst social change. At best they lead us toward a minimizing of social and political inequality.

THE LONG VIEW FROM HISTORY

The entire story of human society, economics, and politics can be seen as the expression of the tug and pull of the alternatives presented us by our brain structure. At this point in history it seems to have a circular or returning quality about it—shall we say a de jà vu?

Scholars mostly agree that our species began in small egalitarian foraging bands some probable 100,000 years ago. We continued to live in such generally equal conditions until sometime about 10–12,000 years ago (e.g., see Knauft 1991, 1994).[53]

Human political life begins with the nuclear family. But what we usually think of as the political aspect becomes more clearly expressed in the increasingly larger social units of bands, tribes, chiefdoms, and ultimately nations. In the larger social units with their increasing division of labor, small, normally self-correcting differences become amplified into significant wealth and power inequalities. The naturally self-corrective tendency of our neural architecture becomes blocked or stymied by multiple contingencies and at multiple levels. The dynamic and the associated tension do not go away, however. They remain locked in states of varying tension by customs, ideology, institutions, and coercive power (e.g., see White, 2001).

In the Western world we emerged through the theocratic absolutism of Egypt and Mesopotamia to the early return to relative egalitarianism or democracy in Greece. Then we passed from republican Rome through the imposing hierarchical, yet all-inclusive power of Imperial Rome. With the fall of Rome we entered the somewhat chaotic Middle Ages dominated by the contesting powers of theocratic church and emerging new states.

Entering the Renaissance we saw the self-conscious rebirth of egalitarian ideals from the Greek world. Society opened, institutions loosened, power relaxed sufficiently to permit the self-corrective tendency of social architecture to emerge into open discussion. In America, especially, these ideals expressive of our dynamically-balanced neural architecture burst forth in fullest political expression.

Driven from their homelands by the social tensions of hierarchy and inequality, the early European settlers spread out into a sparsely populated continental expanse with no all-pervasive pre-existing customs, institutions, or ideologies to block the natural expression of human brain structure. In some cases the bands and tribes of the Native

---

[53] Boehm (1999) argues for what he calls an "ambivalence model" of human nature grounded in highly contradictory behavioral tendencies, which we share with other primates (1999: 3). The capacity for subordinates to make alliances to overcome the domination of leaders is seen as an important component. This, of course, is also supported in the psychiatric literature on social competition cited in Chapter 23. In fact, Boehm speaks of a typology of hierarchies and antihierarchies (pp. 9–10) to explain much of egalitarianism. I suggest that the CSN model, deriving from the self-preservational and affectional circuitry provides the neural substrate that can account for this. In their interactive social context the dynamic interplay of ego and empathy can account for both perspectives. Boehm, of course, makes no use of evolutionary neuroscience, but proceeds from the perspective of cultural anthropology. The variances in social structures that Boehm sees can probably all be accounted for by the flexibility of the dynamic neural architecture. Patterns of domination and reverse domination are probably not hard-wired in our species but reflect the neural dynamic responding to difference conditions. And, of course, for the estimated 5 million or so years since our first hominid ancestor, the neural architecture based on the conflicting circuitry was progressively refined as the neocortex or higher brain centers evolved to manage the conflictual dynamic and affirm its homeostatic regulating features in small kinship-based groups.

Americans provided reinforcing examples of egalitarian lifestyles.[54] The last century especially has marked the dramatic struggle between the dynamically-balanced democratic ideals and the extremes of authoritarianism and collectivism.

The extremes simply don't work in an open human society. They suppress one or both of the primary dynamics of our social brain. In doing so, they create the behavioral and social tensions that lead to their own ultimate demise.

As a young person, I pondered in awe the seemingly vast history of human civilization. A 5000 plus years of recorded human history! It seemed an eternity. Now, as I enter my seventies, I marvel at the exceedingly brief span.

How young we still are. Hardly, my own age multiplied by itself! That is, my own age squared—to the second power. The length of our recorded history is captured by a most elementary of mathematical operations—seventy-plus times my own age of seventy-plus. And our brain has not changed much in the past 100,000 years. For over 90 percent of this time we lived—driven by our evolved neural architecture—as essential egalitarians.

Now, after a brief 5000 year interlude, we face planet-wide globalization, with our new technologies bringing virtual face-to-face communication and powers of mutual destruction. We now replicate on a large scale the conditions of our overwhelmingly predominant history. In the virtual face-to-face interactions, as in the earlier nuclear family and kinship bands, the interactive dynamic of our brains drives us toward resolution of our relative differences in essential equality or dynamic balance.

TO THE FUTURE

The same choices face us as before. This time, however, in the self-conscious maturity of our species. As now customary, thinkers emerge to express the variable options provided by our neural architecture.

On one side, as I review much of the so-called leftist literature, I see increasingly detailed prescriptions offered to achieve the essential equality we desire. Such detailed prescriptions—well-intended though they may be—would require bureaucratic invasion of privacy and freedom on a massive scale. The dynamic of our neural architecture will never tolerate the ultimate collectivist authoritarianism such invasiveness would lead to. The cumulative behavioral tension would lead to repression, then resistance and probable social upheaval.

On the other hand, the radical "hands off" idealizations of free market and political libertarians would lead us ultimately to a society of increasing inequality as the self-corrective tendency of our social architecture is blocked and frustrated by the exercise of cumulative differentials of wealth and power.

The trick, of course, is in the dynamic balance—the ever illusive, never quite satisfactory state of shifting homeostatic equilibrium. In the frustratingly indeterminate, groping democratic process by which we self-correct, pragmatics not ideology must be

---

[54] Among the Native American tribes, the influence of the Iroquois Confederation is often cited (Morgan, 1877; Weatherford, 1988).

the rule. Pragmatically and situationally, we may place shifting and variable limits on the market and on the politico-legal system as well—to correct the inevitable instances of failure in both. We must also prevent one from overwhelming or swallowing up the other, lest the corrective balance be lost.

There will be no final answers in a process that, by its nature, takes us back and forth between conflict and reciprocity as it gropes for a dynamic balance of our inner motivations as well as their expression in our socio-political institutions.

25

GLOBAL POLITICS, RECIPROCITY, AND THE CSN MODEL

The dynamic, shaping forces of our neural architecture having global impact? Can it truly be? The very thought sounds far-fetched. Nevertheless, the case can be made.

THE WORLDWIDE EXCHANGE SYSTEM

The hopeful possibility of reciprocity undergirds the worldwide exchange system. From the beginning reciprocity has loomed large in American economic thought. Over the history of United States trade relations, however, the term reciprocity has been used very ambiguously. Since it had a positive popular ring to it, it was frequently used inappropriately as a catchword to defend partisan and parochial preferences. Despite opportunistic usage, it, nevertheless, has been an important part of the trade vocabulary of the United States since the signing of its first commercial agreement. That first treaty with France, signed in 1778, provided for reciprocal trade concessions between the two nations. Between that early date and the entry of the U.S. into World War II in 1941, reciprocity in trade had been the watchword.

After World War II, a worldwide commercial exchange system was established. The General Agreement on Trade and Tariffs (GATT) was set up as a reciprocal, multilateral trading system. The road to peace and harmony among nations was seen to follow along the trade routes of commercial exchange.

GATT was replaced by the World Trade Organization (WTO) in 1995. Reciprocity and multilateralism continued to be the foundational principles. The WTO, in fact, claims among its top benefits to humankind the promotion of world peace. WTO objectives are to serve the benefit of all and allow the exploitation of none. Such principles reveal clearly an extended expression of our neural dynamic, the tug-and-pull of ego and empathy, respect for self and others. Worldwide exchange, like social exchange at all levels, is propelled by human brains interacting with like human brains.

THE DIFFUSE RECIPROCAL VS. SPECIFIED RECIPROCAL

In earlier chapters (8 through 10) I traced the evolution of social exchange as driven by the neural dynamic. In the family and small groups of our primitive ancestry the reciprocal to a sharing or giving act was diffuse. That is, it created generalized bonds underpinned by affectional and ego circuitry that held us together for mutual protection, nurture, and survival.

As we evolved larger social exchange units, what has been called the gift economy emerged. In gift exchanges the reciprocal lost some of its diffused character and became anticipated. An even exchange maintained equal status in social relationships, unequal exchanges lead to inequalities of status. The social bonding effect of obligation remained. As the transactional market emerged, we came to exchange or trade with strangers. Social bonding was neither necessary nor desired. The reciprocal became specified or quantified, leaving no residual social bonding or obligation. Market exchange, however, still operated by the same reciprocal algorithms of our neural architecture.

The sourcing of reciprocity in the dynamic of neural architecture provides a solid foundation for understanding its appeal in exchange relations among nations. Reciprocity is driven by and a necessary response to behavioral tension. When reciprocity fails in trade, there is always behavioral tension. When reciprocity works— that is, when it moves toward dynamic balance or equilibrium—it tends to produce harmony or peace among nations as hoped for by the WTO.

Previously, in the literature on reciprocity and international trade, the motivational source of reciprocity has been begged. That is, its motivational source has been assumed, intuited, or taken for granted. But it has not been explained. Discussion has centered not on reciprocity's source, but on how it should be defined.

RECIPROCITY IN INTERNATIONAL RELATIONS THEORY

Robert Keohane, a political scientist at Harvard University, has given considerable thought to the question of reciprocity in international relations. In a work published in 1989 he broke the general concept of reciprocity down into two forms: specific reciprocity and diffuse reciprocity.[55]

Without attempting to source reciprocity he described the two types in terms that we can equate with the transition from the exchange practices of family and gift economies to the exchange practices of market economies.

Keohane identified specific reciprocity with prisoners' dilemma or tit for tat exercises in game theory. Such games allow two players, who might seek maximum gain by defecting in a single game, to develop cooperation for maximum total payoffs

---

[55] In his *After Hegemony* (1984), Keohane counterpoises egoism and empathy as conflicting motives practiced in international relations. He makes no connection with neuroscience and makes no effort to source either egoism or empathy in human nature. Nevertheless the writing of the book is clearly motivated by the neural dynamic, the tug-and-pull of ego and empathy. There would be no point in writing the book if that were not so (see especially pp.120–132).

over a series of continuing games. Reciprocals are clearly specified for each individual transaction and are cumulative over the series. The prisoners' dilemma represents a highly simplified, idealized exchange situation. It is divorced from reality, and rarely if ever, found in real life situations. It, nevertheless, by some considerable stretching of one's imagination, can be seen to approximate roughly a series of market transactions between two individuals.

Keohane finds it hard to apply specific reciprocity so defined to actual bilateral international trade situations. He finds it even more difficult to apply it to multilateral trade relations. This situation led him to suggest diffuse reciprocity as the more appropriate principle for international trade. Diffuse reciprocity requires a general commitment to a set of rules and practices, rather than a case by case response to a series of transactions.

Such a conclusion is tantamount to suggesting reversion to a form of pre-market reciprocity—that of the family or the gift economy—as the foundation for global trade. Keohane, in effect, found specific reciprocity, grounded in game theory, inadequate as a standard in international trading relations. As a consequence, he went to an intuited but related concept of diffuse reciprocity to fill the need. Without knowledge of the neural algorithms and their shaping role in the evolution of exchange, it is impossible, however, to see the relation between the two concepts. Keohane, thus, has difficulty accounting for why this should be or for what is actually going on.

A second major conceptual problem with reciprocity in the social sciences rests in the artificial dichotomy between egoistic and empathetic (altruistic) behavior. Such a dichotomy obscures the evolved linkage between the two—the fact that behavior is an ego/empathy spectrum, not a polar set of extremities. The reciprocal outcome shows respect for the interests of self and others. Such is the essence of the ego/empathy dynamic. Reciprocity can never be *just* self-interested as claimed by some. Nevertheless, it is always inclusive of self-interest.

Peter Blau, a prominent sociologist who wrote on power and exchange (1964), refused to associate reciprocity with norms. He did so on the ground that such association would make reciprocity inconsistent with self-interest. Keohane expressed agreement with Blau. He asserted that a concept of reciprocity, to be valuable, must be consistent with self-interested practice. Keohane, then, attempted to resolve the dilemma of Blau's statement by adding to the confusion. He changed the definition of norms, which included a moral component, to include standards of behavior to which even egoists could sometimes conform. This concession, in effect, grants that egoists could sometimes express empathy. Such tortuous devices show how distorted arguments can become in the absence of a grasp of the underlying neural dynamic.

But back to diffuse reciprocity.

MULTILATERALISM AS A REVERSION
TO THE FAMILY OR GIFT ECONOMY

According to Keohane the transition from specific reciprocity to diffuse reciprocity depends on sequential rather than simultaneous or one-shot exchange. He sees diffuse reciprocity as desirable for an effective global system. Diffuse reciprocity means that subscribing nations seek not balanced trade reciprocity on a nation by nation basis, but balanced reciprocity in the overall system of global exchange. Such a position allows for the principle of comparative advantage to work effectively. Comparative advantage requires that each nation do what it does best in contributing to the global trading system.

From the broad perspective of economic history, it is interesting, if not ironical, to watch what is going on here. Diffuse reciprocity characterized pre-market or pre-modern societies. This was pointed out by Harvard sociologist Talcott Parsons several decades ago in a set of so-called pattern variables that he thought up to contrast such societies (1960). Anthropologists have long known that diffuse reciprocity pervaded pre-market or so-called primitive societies. Such diffuseness is also characteristic of family exchange, probably from the beginning of time. It still pervades family giving and sharing to this day.

Now, as we proceed to globalization of exchange, we see the clear call for a return to an earlier principle of social exchange. A reverse movement from the modern market principle of specificity to pre-market diffuseness of reciprocal obligation.

And the call has been heeded—even if without conscious intent. If you visit the website of the World Trade Organization at the turn of the present century, you will see the institutionalization of diffuse reciprocity implicit in its objectives and its proclaimed benefits for international society. The ten benefits provide for: (1) promoting peace among nations, (2) resolving disputes, (3) rules for proper exchange behavior, (4) reducing cost of living, (5) making more choices available to world-wide consumers, (6) raising incomes in poorer countries, (7) promoting growth and jobs, (8) improving efficiency, (9) reducing lobbying of governments by special interests, and (10) promoting good government in general. In principle, if not always in practice, the WTO exemplifies the promotion of diffuse reciprocity as integral to the global exchange system. Not just the WTO, but the World Bank has, also, recognized the essential importance of reciprocity. Business scholars Robert Wood and Gary Hamel report on that institution's recent efforts to confront the persistent problem of global poverty through innovative market procedures (Wood & Hamel, 2002).

THE WORLDWIDE HUMAN FAMILY?
A HOKEY TERM OR A HOPEFUL IDEAL?

These days we hear a lot about the global village and other one-world concepts proceeding from the information age. Technology has made face to face real-time relations a virtual if not tangible reality. We can look down on our planet from space and see its isolation, its fragility, and its unity.

At such times we turn naturally to such thoughts as the worldwide human family. In doing so the concept of stranger vanishes before our very eyes. We extend the neural dynamic, which evolved originally in small family units, to now include all people and nations.

Such thoughts are surely ideal, but they are neither hokey nor softheaded. They rest solidly on what we are—they rest upon the very affectional and self-preserving core dynamic that prescribes our humanity.

In the present global situation, any international organization, claiming to represent all nations, must reflect this common core of our humanity in both its principles and conduct. That is, if it is to be acceptable and successful in the long-term. Immanuel Kant (1724–1804), the great German philosopher of the 18th century, with no knowledge of brain science, saw such acceptable common principles based upon a categorical imperative that all thinking humans would inevitably come up against through careful retrospection. In the absence of brain science, the categorical imperative was the bedrock of just and equitable behavior. More modern scholars fall back, instead, on the poorly grasped concept of reciprocity.

In 1978, social historian Barrington Moore, Jr. in his *Injustice: The Social Basis of Obedience and Revolt* wrote as follows:

Without the concept of reciprocity—or better, mutual obligation…it becomes impossible to interpret human society as the consequence of anything other than perpetual force and fraud…such an interpretation would be a manifest exaggeration (1978: 506).

Moore went on to say that only a pure form of reciprocity could serve as a universal code for the organization of society if all authority were removed (1978: 510).

Much has been written on the subject of reciprocity and the writing continues to this day. I do not intend to review the literature or acknowledge every worthy contributor and contribution. The centrality of the concept of reciprocity in trade among nations has been fully established. No international organization, no international statesperson, can avoid its foundational implications.

If the global economic system as well as the global political system truly evolves toward greater freedom on principles of mutual benefit, balanced reciprocity will emerge ever more clearly. Such reciprocity is the only principle, minimally acceptable by all, upon which a long-term global system vested in freedom can hope to exist. It is the only system fully consonant with the common core of humanity. It is as close to natural law as we can get. It is the balanced expression of our human nature—our evolved neural architecture.

The equation of our social brain is a mathematical tool for estimating how close we get to, or how far we depart from, matching the demands of the common core of our humanity. When we achieve the assent of all nations, the principles adopted will invariably reflect the dynamic of our neural architecture—the balance of self- and other-interest, ego and empathy, which is the essence of reciprocity in its fullest sense.

PART V

THE NEURAL FOUNDATIONS
OF JUSTICE, MORALS, AND ETHICS

26

THE CONCEPT OF JUSTICE

In this chapter the dynamic of the consilient social brain directly confronts the concept of justice. Much of what we have covered so far relates to justice. Reciprocity, for example, implies justice. Equality and inequality imply justice. Since the time of written history, humans have expressed concerns about what is just and what is not. Justice is, in fact, one of the most central of all human concerns.

Let's take examples from the ancient world, the first from Greece, the second from China.

HARMONY AND FAIRNESS IN ANCIENT GREECE

In the *Republic*, Plato (427–347 BC) has Socrates working to properly define justice. The first protagonist confronting Socrates contends that justice always serves the interests of the rulers of society. Justice, in that case, only amounts to might makes right. Socrates quickly dispatches this first cynical definition. The next protagonist proposes that people follow the social conventions of justice in order to avoid punishment—that is, for their own self-interest. This explanation, Socrates rejects after treatment at some length. He sees that justice is neither merely vulgar self-interest nor simply social convention.

If not, then, what is it? Plato, or Socrates, never does get to a clear cut standard for justice. Nevertheless, he argues that justice is desirable in itself—and that justice follows the rule of reason. Further, justice leads to harmony in the self as well as in society. Plato's idea of society is, of course, not an egalitarian one, but rather a hierarchical one with the philosophers as rulers based on reason. Others fit in as appropriate to their qualities. Justice is seen by Plato as the harmonious outcome of each person playing his proper part within Plato's concept of society as it should be.

Plato is preoccupied with reason, which he considers the highest human faculty. He holds that reason must control the emotions or passions that are the source of tension and conflict in society. He likewise sees the ideal society structured accordingly. Thus, he derives the concept of the philosopher king as the proper ruler with other members occupying their lesser appropriate roles.

Plato's concern is, thus, mainly with the management by reason of the behavioral tension emanating from the more animal-like (i.e., self-preservation and affection) qualities of man.

HARMONY AND FAIRNESS IN ANCIENT CHINA

Confucius (551–479 BC) set the standard for thinking about justice in Ancient China. For Confucius the just order for society sprang from the character and virtue of the prince and his subjects. It was similar to Plato's concept in this respect. The ideal ruler was just and the ideal subjects were loyal and obedient in return. The result was a harmonious society. He introduced the ideas of *li* meaning rules of conduct and *ren,* meaning agape or benevolent love. These two, proper conduct and benevolence, working together, produced justice and social harmony in practice.

Confucius's follower, Mencius (c. 372–c. 298 BC) was roughly contemporary with Plato. Mencius believed that one could govern the entire world easily based upon the principle that is common to all mankind—that one cannot bear to see others suffer. This is very similar to Adam Smith's statement made in *Theory of Moral Sentiments* quoted in Chapter 10.

Mencius held the feeling of distress at the suffering of others to be the first sign of humanity. This, of course, amounts to the emergence of empathy. He further said that every child in his mother's arms knew about love for his parents. Such love, extended first as love and respect to elders, ends with one having love and respect for everyone (Mencius, 1970 [298 BC]; cf. Shun, 1997: 145–146).

Mencius, then, saw the origin of justice in society as stemming from love and respect for others. This is, in effect, the balance of self and others, ego and empathy. Mencius seems to have intuited the dynamic of the neural architecture rather well.

THE COMMON ELEMENTS FROM WEST AND EAST

From both Plato in West and from Confucius and Mencius in the East, justice is seen as leading to individual and social harmony. When justice breaks down, things go wrong both within the self and in society. The central issue from both viewpoints, however their details vary, is to avoid disharmony or conflict and achieve harmony or balance. This, of course, reflects the essence of the motivating reciprocal algorithms of our neural architecture—the tug and pull between self-interest and other-interest, and the desirable tendency to dynamic balance, equilibrium or harmony as indexed by the social brain dynamic.

JUSTICE IN THE MODERN WORLD

The literature on justice continued in religious context through the middle ages. Beginning with the renaissance, the discussions of justice took a more secular turn. Thomas Hobbes (1588–1679), John Locke (1632–1704), and later Jean-Jacques Rousseau (1712–1778) brought the concept of the social contract to center stage as the foundation for concepts of justice. Social contract theory has remained at the center of discussions of justice up to modern times.

The present popular idea of the social contract is that governments are legitimate when formed by the agreement and support of the citizens and illegitimate to the extent they are not. Even tyrannies feel obligated to recognize this principle when they hold single party, single candidate elections to falsely validate their legitimacy.

Social contract theory acknowledges the fundamental social nature of humankind. How best to deal with that social nature and bring it into harmonious balance in society is the overriding question on which a concept of justice turns. What is actually being addressed at bottom is none other than the management of behavioral tension driving our social neural architecture. A look at some of these more recent writings is enlightening.

JOHN RAWLS

John Rawls (1921–), of Harvard University, is one of the most influential modern thinkers on equality, morality and justice. In his *Theory of Justice* (1971), he sees society as a cooperative venture for mutual advantage typically marked by conflict as well as identity of interests. In Rawls' view, conflict of interest comes from the fact that people are not indifferent to the distribution of benefits resulting from their cooperative effort.

Rawls develops the idea of a social contract based upon the hypothetical device of a beginning or *original position* behind a *veil of ignorance* from which each member proceeds. Behind the veil of ignorance no one knows of her/his circumstances in life and must decide on rules of working together that would be acceptable regardless of fate or fortune. This device allows for rules and working conditions that are universally acceptable and applicable to emerge. Rawls sees this as the way to justice and harmony in society on a universal basis.

Rawls' motivated objective is the same as the ancients—Plato, Confucius, and Mencius. It is social balance or harmony. The context is, of course, quite different.

In a later work (1985) Rawls goes to a definition of justice as fairness. He distills two principles of justice which read as follows:

1. Each person has an equal right to a fully adequate scheme of equal basic rights and liberties, which scheme is compatible with a similar scheme for all.
2. Social and economic inequalities are to satisfy two conditions: first, they must be attached to offices and positions open to all under conditions of fair equality of opportunity; and second, they must be to the greatest benefit of the least advantaged members of society (1999: 292).

Rawls' acknowledged purpose in developing the above rules is to find a shared basis for deciding the best institutional forms for liberty and equality. In other words, he is shooting for social harmony within a particular context—that of the liberal economic society. The inequalities permitted are justifiable only by real equal opportunity and the end result of greatest benefit to the least advantaged. The least advantaged, of course, are those bagging the most behavioral tension, threatening the stability of society, and creating the most behavioral tension through empathetic engagement in such sensitive scholars as Rawls and all the rest of us empathetic members of humankind.

Rawls position and contextual solution both ride upon the dynamic of our neural architecture, the tug and pull of ego and empathy as they tend toward dynamic balance.

SUSAN MOLLER OKIN

Okin, a Stanford University scholar, criticizes Rawls from a feminist perspective. In her *Gender, Justice, and the Family* (1989), she see Rawls' concept of an original position behind a veil of ignorance being set at the level of head of household. At that level, she objects that the dynamic within the family is obscured. This obscuring is significant because the dynamic within the family is the foundation for society. A gender-structured family, which is pervasive in modern society, will contribute to a gender-structured society. A non-gender-structured, democratic family structure will, accordingly, contribute to a non-gender-structured, democratic social structure. Although differing contextually and supporting a different version of family and social structure, Confucius and Mencius also acknowledged the importance of the family dynamic for supporting the preferred social structure.

Okin clearly expresses the natural behavioral tension behind the exclusion of women from full consideration in a gender-structured society. She suggests that a fully human moral or political theory can be developed only with the full participation of both sexes. And, she claims that only children who are equally mothered and fathered can fully develop the psychological and moral capacities that presently seem to be unevenly distributed between the sexes.

A MODERN EUROPEAN PERSPECTIVE: HABERMAS

Justice has been a special concern of the prominent German philosopher Jürgen Habermas. Habermas was, until his retirement in the early 1990s, the most influential representative of the Frankfurt School which has long been associated with a humanistic Marxist approach. Throughout his writing Habermas seems to draw on an intuitive assumption of a tendency toward justice or equality in human nature.

Like Rawls, Okin, and other modern thinkers, he avoids specific claims for human nature, but tries to set up ideal conditions for justice to emerge from the consent of all in a social contractual relationship.

Habermas, like Rawls, tries to set up a hypothetical method that will allow justice to emerge within the social context. He calls this method *discourse ethics*. Basic to discourse ethics is the "ideal speech situation"(Habermas, 1990: 196–198, Warren, 1984: 175). The conditions of the ideal speech situation are as follows:

1. Only those norms may claim to be valid that could meet with the consent of all affected in their role as participants in a practical discourse (Habermas 1990: 197).

2. Justice, or morality, is seen as demanding equal respect and equal rights for the individual as well as empathy and concern for the well-being of one's neighbor (Habermas 1990: 200).

Discourse ethics is aimed at developing norms of justice and morality under assumed conditions of full and complete knowledge of all effects and side effects, through the participation of all concerned freely participating, without force or domination of any kind, except the force of the better argument (Habermas, 1990: 198–203).

In effect Rawls and Habermas are aiming at the same conditions albeit through different approaches. Rawls, with his original position and veil of ignorance is trying to draw out the universal conditions for justice and harmony in society. Habermas, from positions as they now exist, tries through the structure of discourse ethics to get *back* to the universal conditions for justice and harmony.

BUT WHY THE QUESTION?

Modern thinkers on social justice mostly avoid making statements about human nature. This avoidance is a probable hangover of the emphasis of modern science on externalities. In an attempt to proceed from a seeming position of objectivity, it is safer to just try to set up conditions, ideal or otherwise. Then, observe what emerges. Based on such observation, one can lay claim to objectivity or empirics.

But such a posture misses an essential point—the necessary subjectivity that must motivate even the very asking of the question. That is, why is the question of justice important to begin with? Why do we care about it? Indeed, why is it central to human concerns over history? And why are the distinguished thinkers taking the time and effort to dream up conditions for the expression of justice and equality in society? In short, what motivates them?

Discussions on justice, despite techniques of avoidance, invariably have assumptions about human nature. Sometimes these assumptions seem explicit. Sometimes they are implicit. The most fundamental, pervasive assumption of such discussions, however, is the social nature of humankind. Without the assumption of our social nature, there would be no reason whatsoever to study justice. Justice is inevitably social and basically concerns the harmonizing of individual interests within a social context. That is, the harmonizing of self-interest with other-interest, ego with empathy, self-preservation with affection. Without our mammalian neural circuitry, there would be no question of justice, no discussion of justice.

The concept of justice is always motivated by the behavioral tension driving the choices of our neural architecture. The essential questions of justice concern how best to manage that tension, mitigate social conflict, and achieve social harmony or, as is said more recently, to achieve what is called social solidarity.

Justice is, in short, an attempt to find a satisfactory institutional solution to the dynamic equation of our social brain. The equation, the dynamic, is always the same, even if intuited only poorly or even erroneously. The solutions inevitably are contextual. They are, in effect, verbal models. Like their cousins, the more formal mathematical models with their precise assumptions, conditions, and axioms, the verbal models are also structured attempts to direct the movement of the neural architecture toward dynamic balance, unity, or harmony within a social context.

Viewed from the perspective of sociophysiology, concepts of justice are active attempts, motivated by the selfsame homeostatic physiological neural dynamic, to find the proper homeostatic set points to keep our social architecture within social survival limits while trying optimally to set conditions that assist its movement toward dynamic balance or harmony within the social context. In effect, concepts of social justice concern the management of behavioral tension—or conflict management, if you choose. In each case, the dynamic and the objective are the same. The particular social context that the dynamic is being squeezed into is what differs. And the particularity of social context creates the differing questions of appropriate institutions.

What is often overlooked is that the dynamic itself, rooted in brain structure or human nature, is the shaping force behind it all. It is that very shaping force that is motivating the thinkers to ask the questions which edge the force itself forward in historical expression.

Again, whatever the social context, the dynamic operation of our social brain is the guiding framework. To the extent that the ratio approaches dynamic balance or plus or minus one, we approach social justice or harmony. To the extent that the ratio diverges we will have behavioral tension, inequality, conflict—and injustice.

27

OUR MORAL CONSCIOUSNESS

Reciprocity, driven by the tug-and-pull of ego and empathy, shapes our entire social lives. Our social lives are a panoramic expression of give-and-take, social exchange of myriad forms.

We must understand the neural reward systems and the internal dynamic of our evolved brain structure to fully appreciate the depths of our human social life. Why? Because the dynamic of these reward systems provides the *subjective motivational basis* for our choices in behavior as well as the *entire texture and meaning of our lives*. It is also the foundation for our ethical and moral behavior so important to our economic and political relations, both domestic and global.

This subjective motivation and experience, although it is the most important aspect of our lives, has, of course, been almost completely ignored by the externalized positivistic perspective that has dominated science since the days of Newton. The time has now come for science to acknowledge more fully this *subjective motivation* along with its *objective manifestations* and give it its due place in our lives.

THE INEVITABILITY OF CONFLICT
AND THE EMERGENCE OF MORAL CONSCIOUSNESS

The reciprocal algorithms of our neural architecture not only underpin the inevitability of conflict and the tendency to reciprocity that we discussed in earlier chapters. They also, underpin the accompanying emergence in self-awareness of moral consciousness. Reciprocity, and the subjective experience of it, are the outcome of the conflict—the tug-and-pull of ego and empathy as they approach dynamic balance. We go through conflict to get to reciprocity. The CSN model of our social brain captures this well.

Looking back over history we see that there has never been a human society without conflict. Some have more, some have less. None are without it. And the central and indelible presence of conflict in human life has not been lost on our greatest thinkers or systems of thought.

Socrates saw human nature as made up of two winged steeds, one noble, one ignoble, harnessed to a single chariot and struggling against the control of a charioteer.

Hillel, experiencing tension between two opposing promptings in his life, wrote, "if I am not for me, who will be? But if I am only for me, who am I?"

Christ, acknowledging the conflict, admonished us to struggle to love our neighbor as ourselves.

Religions have projected the struggle between good and evil upon the cosmos. From Taoism to Buddhism, from Judaism to Islam and Christianity, our central moral themes have arisen from and examined the dualities posed by the tug-and-pull between preservation of self and affection for others. Conflict, then, and the resolving tendency toward reciprocity, is in the nature of humankind, pervasive and inevitable.

The eternal moral and ethical dilemma—Hillel's question: Do I serve myself or others?—is wired irrevocably into our human nature and carried with us into almost every aspect of our daily lives.

I AND YOU:
THE INNER AND OUTER DYNAMIC
OF THE RECIPROCAL ALGORITHMS

The reciprocal algorithms are the basis as well as the dynamic of our social life and moral consciousness as the highest mammalian life form. The energy-driven algorithms keep us in almost constant internal conflict as ego and empathy tug-and-pull against each other in our daily, moment-by-moment, living, as we interact with each other.

The *dynamic* which originates *internally* within each of us becomes *externalized* in our social interactions because of the effects of the behavioral tension produced in each of us and between each of us as a result of these interactions. These are the mechanisms of our social evolution (which interact with other variables when we shift academic perspectives). We evolved through millions of years of social interaction with these mechanisms becoming increasingly sensitive and refined in foraging societies that demanded sharing and reciprocity.

The outcome is that each of us, who has a fully-formed, developed, human brain, has what may be thought of as the equivalent of two persons within us—an *I* (ego) and a *YOU* (empathy). The *I* within us pushes us to respond first to our own needs; the *YOU* within us impels us to respond to the needs of others.

The CSN model illustrates well this *I* and *YOU* within us. Egoistic behavior is *I* behavior. Empathetic behavior is *YOU* behavior. Wherever empathy is engaged through its roots in affection, we subjectively experience the warmth of feeling, the caring, the attachment that flows from our mammalian affectional circuitry. Where *I* and *YOU*, ego and empathy, come into dynamic balance or close thereto, we may experience both the subjective feelings and the objective expressions of what is called *love*. We, in effect, may achieve the maxim of love your neighbor as yourself.

Of the numerous 20th century thinkers who sensed and worked to articulate this internal and external struggle, which I have defined as the reciprocal dynamic, the most perceptive was arguably Martin Buber (1878–1965), whose work had profound influence on postwar Europe.

BUBER: I AND THOU

Buber's best known work, translated into English as *I and Thou,* was first published in 1922. The German title *Ich und Du,* however, means simply I and You. The German pronoun *Du* is the second person familiar form used among family members and friends. It does not carry the lofty, abstract connotation of the English pronoun *thou.*

Buber, then, came to English already somewhat misrepresented. His intent was to communicate simply, intimately. This intent got muddled, if not lost, in the translation. As a result readers have tended to see Buber primarily as a somewhat abstract mystic with the lofty *thou* being construed as a mystical term implying the Deity even when it referred to relations among ordinary folk.

According to Buber our interactions with the world are all driven by dialectical (in my terms, behavioral) tension within and without. The two primary ways to interact with the world are from positions of I–It and I–You. Both hyphenated word combinations are seen as a word-pair entity. There is a tension or dynamic that binds them.

Buber sees the I–It word pair as the position we take when we relate to nature, other creatures, and people as objects—objects to be utilized. On the other hand Buber sees the word combination I–You as establishing the world of relationship. One does not exploit or utilize in such relationship, but connects and experiences.

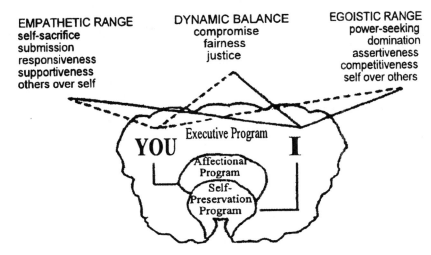

Figure 8. The major ranges of behavior reflecting Buber's I–Thou concept.

The I–You relationship occurs in three spheres or at three levels.

1) When with the I–You we look to nature—animals, trees, rivers, mountains, and the like we do not use them as objects. Rather we connect with them in relationship.

2) When with the I–You, we turn to other humans, who like us, share speech and concepts, we also connect with them in relationship. And we can speak to each other using the terms I and You.

3) When with the I–You, we approach the spiritual level, we communicate not with words, but become non-verbally aware of *relationship* to which we respond with thoughts and acts.

Buber's is plainly a dialectic driven by tension. And since he sees love as the experience of meeting between the I and You, in a state of tension, he is clearly describing the same process that I have described as the algorithms of reciprocity.

THE RECIPROCAL ALGORITHMS IN THE THEOLOGY OF PAUL TILLICH: LOVE, POWER, AND JUSTICE

The theology of Paul Tillich (1886–1965), like that of Buber, shows very clearly the dynamic of the reciprocal algorithms. One of his later works, *Love, Power, and Justice*, published in 1954, is the clearest exposition of algorithms' elements and dynamic.

Love, Power, and Justice, by its very title reveals the intuitive perception of the tug-and-pull of ego and empathy as they tend toward dynamic balance. From the perspective of our neural algorithms, power is an expression of ego, which incorporates or appropriates things to itself. Love, as conceived by Tillich, comes out of affectional circuitry and expresses the concern for others. As ego and empathy tug-and-pull toward a dynamic balance of self- and other-interest, what we describe as justice emerges.

Justice, in Figure 9, emerges at the confluence of power and love, of ego and empathy, or I and Thou. This again follows the graph of the major ranges of behavior. Where ego and empathy approach dynamic balance, they produce respect for self and others, fairness, equality, and, of course, the motivation for the *concept of justice* in our behavior, subjective experience, as well as in our legal and ethical thought, as discussed in the previous chapter.

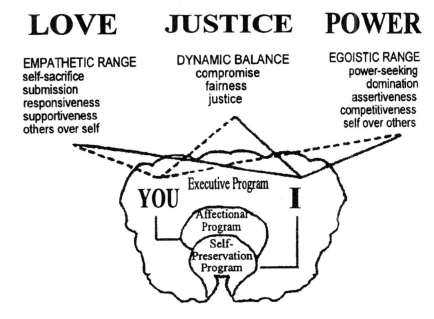

LOVE   JUSTICE   POWER

EMPATHETIC RANGE
self-sacrifice
submission
responsiveness
supportiveness
others over self

DYNAMIC BALANCE
compromise
fairness
justice

EGOISTIC RANGE
power-seeking
domination
assertiveness
competitiveness
self over others

YOU   Executive Program   I

Affectional
Program

Self-
Preservation
Program

Figure 9. Tillich's concept of the interaction of power, love, and justice as expressed. by the major ranges of behavior. Note the difference between this figure and Figure 8 which represents the I and Thou of Buber. Although there are minor differences in the definitions of love, the warmth, comfort, nurturing, and caring of the mammalian affectional circuitry characterizes virtually all descriptions of love, and the experience is dependent on that programming.

TOWARD FORGIVENESS AND SPIRITUAL REACH

The tug-and-pull of ego and empathy, proceeding from our earlier brain complexes, driven by behavioral tension, represented in and negotiated by the frontal cortex, may seem mechanistic—leaving no room for free will and the higher reaches of morality and spirituality. Is our only hope, then, to move from inevitable conflict to a condition of relative mechanical and drab reciprocity?

I think not. The dialogue that takes place in the neural network architecture of the frontal cortex is one of choices. Choices imply a measure of free will. The concept of a *theory of mind,* favored today by many researchers, requires both a theory of a mind of self (ego) and a theory of mind of others (empathy).[56] The emergence and development

---

[56] The term *theory of mind* was originally coined by primatologist David Premack (Premack & Woodruff, 1978) researching the question of whether chimpanzees had a concept of other minds existing in their fellow primates. It has since been used in an attempt to account for the deficit of relatedness to others presumed to be central to the condition of autism (Frith, 1997, 1989; Baron-Cohen, 1995; Brother's 1995). It has been applied to child development, where the standard account is concerned with the child's grasp of others' attention, beliefs, and false beliefs (Astington, et al., 1988) and to persons with frontal lobe damage such as the much discussed case of Phineas Gage (see Damasio, 1994). Attention has also been directed toward how the child contructs the meaningful intention and evaluative attitudes of others (Fridlund, 1991; for a critique of some current issues, see

of both aspects of mind, as well as their dynamic balance, are tuned neuronally and enhanced by moral socialization and education.

The theory of mind is inevitably linked somatically to its self-preservation and affection emotional substrates of neural architecture, including the physiological activities of hormones and neurotransmitters. From conscious management may well emerge the all-important quality of *forgiveness*. Forgiveness facilitates the release of behavioral tension, enhancing personal well-being and the resolution of conflict, both internal and interpersonal, at a higher moral, if not spiritual level.

Drawing upon the known amplifying qualities of the thalamocingulate gateway bridging subcortical circuits and the frontal cortex,[57] we may consciously blend and amplify the essentially conflicting motives into an experience of love of self and others that may be extended to all humanity. Indeed to all creation.

Such is the direction that all our great teachers East and West have beckoned us toward. Mencius of ancient China saw the progressive extension of love from parents, to elders, and ultimately to everyone as the mark of true humanity. It is the dynamic that such recent thinkers as Buber and Tillich also strived to articulate. If the conflict were not there, in our human nature, our evolved neural structures, there would be no virtue, no challenge, no moral or spiritual achievement in transcending it.

IN SUM

MacLean's emphasis on subjective experience in his exposition of the interconnected, modular triune brain concept provides the foundation in brain science, for the study and explication of the all-important human characteristic of moral consciousness. The extrapolation of the three-level brain concept into the realm of psychology by the subjective/behavioral CSN model defines the basic reciprocal dynamic of ego and empathy as driven by behavioral tension. This reciprocal dynamic of our neural architecture, enhanced by elaboration of the neocortex and the development of language, allows us to account for the emergence of moral consciousness (cf. MacLean, 1990: 561–562).

Moral consciousness is reflected in the universal norm of reciprocity covered in earlier chapters. It is also reflected in the concept of justice so central to human concerns. As well, it is reflected in humankind's loftier philosophical and spiritual abstractions and expressions.

When we consciously, intentionally, work to equilibrate and transcend the dual algorithmic dynamic, we respond to the exhortations of Socrates, Mencius, Hillel, Christ, and other great figures of humanity to value and love self and others as one. This

---

Grossman, et al., 1997). Any adequate theory of mind would have to have to allow, either explicitly or implicitly, for a generalized concept of self or ego as well as a similarly generalized concept of empathy or other interest—or else it would be utterly meaningless. That is, to have a theory of the mind of others, you must first have an idea of a mind of self.

[57] The thalamocingulate gateway can be viewed as a set of neural structures that bridge the lower and higher brain centers. It is known to gate subcortical inputs into the higher cortex. It may also amplify or diminish the inputs (see Sherman & Guillery, 2001; Devinsky & Luciano, 1993).

is, further, the moral and spiritual challenge facing our species in the quest for a subjectively experienced and objectively manifested world of unity in diversity that inclusively affirms all humankind.

Again the dynamic of our social brain represents this dynamic in mathematical terms. To the extent that ego and empathy diverge to the extremes, we are increasingly in conflict within ourselves and with society. On the other hand, as they move toward dynamic balance, tapping the deepest levels of the emotional circuitry—of personal well-being and caring—we achieve the emotional inclusiveness necessary to our personal moral health and the future of our species.

28

THE CSN MODEL VS.
THE MASLOW HIERARCHY

In this chapter I compare the Maslow hierarchy with the CSN model built upon the evolutionary neuroscience of Paul MacLean. In case the reader is has forgotten the details from the discussion in Chapter 2, let's take a quick review.

THE MASLOW HIERARCHY

Maslow had arranged his hierarchy from bottom to top in the form of a pyramid, staircase, or stepladder. He put the physiological needs such as hunger and thirst at the base. On top of these basic needs he stacked the safety needs; then, the belonging or social needs; and next, the esteem or ego needs in ascending order. At the very top of the pyramid or stepladder he put what he called the need for self-actualization.

Maslow theorized that these needs were emergent: That is, as we satisfied our basic needs of hunger and thirst, our safety needs would then emerge. Accordingly as we satisfied our newly emerged safety needs, the next level, the belonging or social needs, would come into play. Next came the esteem needs, and finally, as these were satisfied, the self-actualizing need at the top of the hierarchy emerged. In self-actualizing we were projected to become all that we could be.

Maslow's hierarchy has appeared in every basic text on psychology and behavior for the past five or so decades. It also appears in most texts on organizational behavior and business management. Its influence has been widespread as a behavioral scheme of ready and easy reference. It has also been popularized in casual and popular writing about motivation. The Maslow need hierarchy represents one of the earliest comprehensive efforts to develop a model of the human biological inheritance.

SHORTCOMINGS OF THE MASLOW MODEL

The Maslow hierarchy has, however, serious shortcomings that limit its usefulness for thinking about our evolved brain structure. For one thing, it lacks an evolutionary perspective. The hierarchy of needs is presented as a given, disconnected from the evolutionary process which produced it.

Secondly, Maslow put the concept together in the days before the full emergence of evolutionary neuroscience. It, therefore, makes no connection with neural architecture. The needs are asserted from informed intuition more than solid science or reliable empirical research.

Thirdly, the concept of hierarchy is not fully developed. Maslow did not adequately spell out the interaction of the levels of hierarchy nor did he satisfactorily account for those cases that violate the proposed normal priority of needs.

The hierarchy has also been criticized for being culture bound. That is, it fit neatly with particularly the U.S. concept of material achievement and success as a steady stair step progression of higher development (Yankelovich, 1981). It thereby tends to ignore or diminish the great accomplishments in thought, morality, and service to humanity of many of the great figures of human history (Maddi, 1989). Maslow's hierarchy, with its almost exclusive focus on the individual, affords little insight into the dynamics of social interaction. In other words it is not an interactive model. In fact it turned us away from social interaction.

Maslow's focus on a staircase-like hierarchy of inner needs tended to turn us inwardly away from the social environment. Co-opted and blended with the prevailing view of self-interest as the sole primary human motive in American business and economics, Maslow's theory of self-actualization, with its lofty connotations of self-fulfillment and creative expression became reduced, especially in the decades of the 70s and 80s, to a license for indulgent self-interest.

In blaming Maslow's concept for the excesses of that self-indulgent time, well-known pollster Daniel Yankelovich, writing in 1981, dubbed it the Maslow escalator. This isolated, indulgent version of self-interest, as expressed in our social and business experience, earned the labels of "narcissistic" and "me first." One of the great popular appeals of the Maslow hierarchy is that it could be interpreted to fit so well with the prevailing emphasis on self-interest in our everyday as well as academic thinking on economics, business, and politics.

CONFLICT, NOT EMERGENCE

But inward focus and simplistic hierarchy were not the only problems with Maslow's hierarchy. It allowed us to be drawn excessively toward our inner selves and away from society because it missed a point central to human behavior—that conflict, not emergence, is behavior's most definitive characteristic.

Maslow placed the social or relatedness needs (empathy) lower on the escalator than esteem and self-actualization needs (ego). His theory contains the clear suggestion that we pass through these social needs or rise above them in the trek up the hierarchical ladder. This was a fundamental error, resulting in a considerable distortion of our view of human social nature. The two sets of needs, social and self-interested, although hierarchical to some extent, are wired together in the same brain to produce the tug-and-pull, conflictual dynamic of interpersonal or social behavior. We are not autonomous, but at best semiautonomous creatures, completely immersed in a pervasive social context, which is, at this point in our evolution, both demanded and made possible by our evolved brain structure.

FOR ME? FOR YOU? OR FOR US?
IT'S ALWAYS THE SAME!

The dynamic of our neural architecture shows that the tug-and-pull of ego and empathy drives interpersonal behavior not only at the levels of Maslow's social and esteem needs, but at all levels. The basic questions of interaction are the same anywhere in the hierarchy.

These questions are: Do I do it or take it for myself (ego)? Do I do it for or give it to others (empathy)? Or do I do it for both myself and others? (dynamic balance).

It is enlightening to try out these questions at each level of Maslow's staircase.

Take the physiological needs first. I can see myself lost in the desert with a friend. I have one remaining canteen of water. It's half full, and I don't know if or when we'll find more. My interpersonal choices are three: Do I keep it all for myself (ego)? Do I give it all to my friend (empathy)? Or do we share it (dynamic balance)? I would face the same choices if my companion were a spouse, child, friend, or enemy.

These three questions would likewise apply to the next level of needs, those of safety. Suppose we are threatened by a wild beast? Or a natural disaster? An intruder? A terrorist? Do I protect myself? Others? Self and others? The conflict is more or less evident depending on the urgency of what is happening, but it is always present.

At the next level the social needs are directly related to affection and empathy—while above them, the esteem needs are related to ego. But as we have seen, ego and empathy and their inexorable conflict pervade all levels of Maslow's hierarchy. In evolutionary terms, the conflict did not exist prior to the appearance of affectional circuitry in the mammalian brain; but ever since it appeared, it has influenced all needs and all behaviors.

The ego-empathy conflict even pervades Maslow's highest need level—self-actualization. Behaviorally speaking, the need for self-actualization has more to do with ego rather than empathy, but again the choices are the same as at all the other need levels. Do I put my own priorities, feelings, and objectives first? Or do I first consider the priorities, feelings, and objectives of my parents, spouse, children, friends, company, church, nation, or worldwide humanity itself? Or do I struggle to achieve a balance?

The self reference perspective of Maslow's hierarchy fit well with the self-reference perspective of economics. And it had the same distorting effects that I have noted in earlier chapters.

There is, however, a general hierarchical quality to human behavior as Maslow proposed. The triune modular brain structure is itself hierarchical. The basic self-preservational circuitry is more ancient and lies below the more recent mammalian and neocortical structures. And sometimes the basic circuitry overrides over the newer. At such times ancient, often socially undesirable behaviors burst forth, disrupting our civilized social interaction.[58] On the other hand there are also clearly times when the affectional circuitry overrides the earlier self-preservational circuits in favor of pro-social, caring behavior.

THE EVOLUTION OF BEHAVIORAL CHOICE

The tug-and-pull of these circuitries, when connected to the frontal executive leads to the capacity for behavioral choice. Normally the wiring between the levels and their input to the frontal cortex allows the subcortical circuits of self-preservation and affection to function at a roughly equal level in the tug-and-pull of ego and empathy. This is not a deterministic process, however. Through experience, education, discipline, and practice, we may strengthen the control circuitry of the frontal cortex to manage more effectively the dynamic tug-and-pull between the conflicting programs.

This capacity to manage, to choose, emerged with the development of general purpose neural network architecture which was connected with but not dedicated to the service of earlier life-preserving and affectional circuitry. This general purpose six-layered frontal circuitry located in the neocortex allowed us to partially escape the blind instinctual tyranny of the earlier circuits.[59]

We became, thus, creatures of choice. That is, we can be said scientifically to have an element of free will. The exercise of this free will—the making of choices—may, however, involve varying degrees of emotional and motivational intensity as the significance of the choices to the fundamental self-preservation and affectional circuitry varies.

SO WHAT, THEN, IS ACTUALIZATION?
THE SYNTHESIS OF OUR DUAL CIRCUITRY

If Maslow's hierarchy is in error, what does the CSN Model of our neural architecture offer to replace the previously highly valued and popular concept of self-actualization? How do we express the highest and best of our behavioral potential?

Here's how. We blend ego and empathy in dynamic balance or unity as we saw it in the previous chapter on moral consciousness and spirituality. At the highest levels of emotional abstraction—in philosophical terms—we synthesize the two powerful motives

---

[58] Kent Bailey (2002) describes cases such as those of serial killer Ted Bundy and the teenagers who executed the Columbine school massacre in terms of downshifting under stress to subcortical, more primitive circuitry.

[59] Although the neocortex can be divided into a number of specialized areas based on structure and function, there is also increasing evidence of structural and functional consistencies from one area to the other. In other words, the cortical mechanisms underlying the varied functions and structures of our higher cognitive circuitry seem less specific and more generalized and flexible than previously thought. Findings strongly indicate that the cortex is composed of building blocks which are to some degree equipotential and can be made to serve other functions. Experiments have shown that tissues from one area of the cortex transplanted to a second area take on the functional properties of the second area (see O'Leary, 1989; Eccles, 1984; Mountcastle, 1978).

in unconditional love for self and others, extending the synthesis even to the universe. At the practical level we affirm ourselves, our ego, with an empathic contribution or gift of our very best to society.

Rarely, such experiences occur spontaneously—beyond our control. Circumstances may unexpectedly release the fully synthesized expression of the dual circuitry. Maslow called such moments *peak experiences*. Such peak experiences happen only occasionally in our lives and seem illusive. We can, however, develop the ability to induce them. We can through disciplined exercise, for instance in meditation, concentration, or visualization, learn to tap and release the emotional power of the dual circuitry.

Such a release requires the full and unconditional acceptance of self and others, self-preservation and affection, ego and empathy, in dynamic synthesis. It is a powerful experience and difficult to maintain at high intensity for long periods. But with practice and relaxation we may come to tap the synthetic experience at lower levels of intensity fairly regularly in our daily lives at home, work, and play. Such synthesized, or dynamically-balanced experience is expressed by the social dynamic as it approaches equilibrium. Likewise the behavioral conflict, tension, and ultimate stress of our daily lives may be indexed by the social equation as the ratio diverges to the extremities of ego and empathy circuitry.

THE SOCIAL DYNAMIC, ACTUALIZATION, AND OUR SUBJECTIVE ESSENCE

The dynamic equation of our social brain captures our subjective essence, our actualization. But it does so only in mathematical abstraction—in rarefied detachment from the powerful forces it represents. This is true of all mathematics. Austere and icyly beautiful, math only represents what its symbols can never feel or truly convey the experience of. Mathematics is neither essence nor reality and never can be.

We experience our subjective essence—we actualize it—when we engage fully the dynamic circuitry of self-preservation and affection with intensity, clarity, and purity. In approach to dynamic equilibrium—in the continuing effort to so express our inner dual selves more fully—we become the best that we can be while contributing to the betterment of our world.

The neural social equation confirms, in mathematical detachment, the dynamic maxim to love one's neighbor as one's self. It encompasses the totalization of Jesuit philosopher, Teilhard de Chardin—Buber's meeting of the I and You—the unity of Brahmin—the essence of the compassionate Buddha—the full humanity of Mencius—the life-affirming experiences and visions of mystics and great teachers from all times and all places.

The subjective essence the equation represents is an individual experience inclusive of all others. A dynamic resolution of opposites, contradictions. The resolution of the ultimate Zen koan. I would call it dynamically-balanced actualization. It is the total affirmation of self or ego in total empathic unity with all that is. It is made possible by the conflict-resolving powers of our higher neural network architecture as it blends the impulses of our basic circuitries into a seemingly infinite expression of unifying love of self and others. It expresses the best that we can be.

29

CONCLUSION

The chapters of this book have covered the dynamic of our consilient social brain from a number of different perspectives. The social brain dynamic was represented by the graph of the major ranges of behavior of the CSN model, the descriptive algorithms of reciprocal behavior, and the dynamic social equation. The three forms of representation depict the reciprocal global-state variables of our self-preserving and affectional neural circuitry, ego and empathy. Each representative form is useful in making clear the neural network dynamic. I will rely mainly on the dynamic equation in making this summary.

The terms inserted into the dynamic equation changed when we shifted from one discipline to another. This vocabulary shift underscored one of the main problems in the division of sciences into separate domains in our university system. We often lose sight of linkages across disciplinary boundaries because of mere changes in terminology. When we say the same things differently, we have an all too human tendency to think that we've said something new or entirely different. Perhaps it is an unconscious defense mechanism of our remarkable brain. Perhaps it is even a strategem of that most superb organ of the universe to avoid boring itself to death.

The unifying power of the consilient social brain and its dynamic equation, thereby, can easily be overlooked. The unmistakeable linkages, if not isomorphisms, can pass unnoticed across our intellectual field of vision unless we grasp the fact that the various alternative expressions are really getting at the same homeostatic algorithmic dynamic of our neural architecture. Although the list is not exhaustive, the various forms of the equation covered in this book are presented below. In each case, the equation, as represented, is expressed as approaching balance or equilibrium. As the equation approaches equilibrium or dynamic balance, behavioral tension is minimized. As the ratio diverges from dynamic balance, behavioral tension increases.

From Neuroscience:

$$\text{Behavioral Tension} = \frac{\text{Ego}}{\text{Empathy}} \quad \text{or} \quad \frac{\text{Empathy}}{\text{Ego}} = \pm 1 \quad \text{(approx. equilibrium, unity, or dynamic balance)}$$

This first form of the social equation was developed in the early chapters directly from the evidence newly emerging in evolutionary neuroscience. It could just as easily been written as self-preservation/affection rather than ego/empathy, to reflect the basic homeostatic tug and pull of the two circuitries which all alternative forms of the equation represent. It is, of course, an organic algorithm, derived from but differing in structuring power from the usual algorithms we find in physics.

In the first example, I represented both ego and empathy alternately as numerator and denominator. I did this because the dynamic is a homeostatic tug-and-pull rather than a simple reciprocal. This reversibility also avoids the unnecessary use of fractions and keeps the magnitudes essentially in the form of whole numbers. This dual form is assumed but not expressed in the variants that follow. You can always turn the equation upside down to avoid fractions without affecting its accurate representation of the neural dynamic. Also, for brevity's sake I will abbreviate the ever present behavioral tension as BT.

From Social Psychology:

$$BT = \text{Interpersonal Tension} = \frac{\text{Ego}}{\text{Empathy}} = \pm 1 \quad \text{(approx. equilibrium, unity or dynamic balance)}$$

This second form of the equation maintains the continuity between neuroscience and social psychology. It represents the dynamic that pervades all our interpersonal relations from simple dyadic person-person relations, to relations within the family, the group, the workplace, as well as our relationships with society as a whole. The equation could also be written as take/give or give/take to express the well-appreciated fact that our interpersonal lives are characterized at all levels by give-and-take. Of course, as give-and-take approach dynamic balance we have the all-important human quality of sharing which responsible parents encourage so assiduously in their children.

From Economics:

$$BT = \text{Equilibrium Price} = \frac{\text{Demand}}{\text{Supply}} = \pm 1 \quad \text{(approx. equilibrium, unity or dynamic balance)}$$

This third form of the social equation represents the transactional market level of the all-pervasive social exchange relationships that characterize social organization at every level. At the market level, the terminology, but not the dynamic changes. At the market level, the reciprocals become specified or quantified. The social exchange process is formalized. Beyond that, only the terms change, the underlying neural algorithmic dynamic remains the same.

From Sociology and Political Science:

$$BT = \text{Socio-Political Tension} = \frac{\text{Domination}}{\text{Subordination}} = \pm 1 \quad \text{(approx. equilibrium, unity or dynamic balance)}$$

   This fourth form of the social equation captures the dynamic of social and political differentials of wealth and power. Social and political structure become important at this point. Differentials in wealth and power, combined with the institutions, customs, and ideologies that support them, become *structured* behavioral tension, *structured* inequalities, or *structured* dominant-submissive relationships. As these approach dynamic balance, the behavioral tension levels of the society become minimized. As the ratio diverges, it indexes the tensions and stresses within the society. This form of the social equation can index both the health, threats, and challenges a socio-political society faces.

Invisible Hand
Of economics:
Of politics:

$$BT = \frac{Ego}{Empathy} = \pm 1 \text{ (approx. equilibrium or unity)}$$
$$\text{dynamic balance}$$

   I repeat the original, generic, form of the social equation in this context to point out that the long sought and variously sourced invisible hand has its origin not in the hand of Deity, Newtonian mechanics, or other inappropriate physical dynamic, but in a pervasive dynamic of our evolved neural architecture. The tug-and-pull of ego and empathy, when unobstructed by excessive differentials of wealth and power or problems of complexity and distance, tends toward a dynamic balance or roughly equal distribution of goods and services.

   When the tendency fails, because of the many possible obstructing factors, we may choose—again, motivated morally by the same dynamic—to assist the natural tendency to achieve its end. This form of the social equation tells us that in the face of inevitable obstructions resulting from complexity, distance, and other factors, the maintenance of political, economic, and social democracy will require at times, pragmatic, intelligent, situational, and limited assistance.

Of Moral Consciousness (Buber's I-Thou)

$$BT = \text{Dialectical Tension} = \frac{YOU}{I} = \pm 1 \text{ (equilibrium, unity}$$
$$\text{or dynamic balance)}$$

   This fifth form of the social equation takes us into the issues of justice, ethics, and moral consciousness. I venture here into areas where scientists traditionally fear to tread. It is a great failure, if not tragedy, of modern science that it has so long refused to enter fully into this most important aspect of human life. Instead modern science, with some notable exceptions, has focused mainly on the negative side—fear, aggression, and human nastiness in general.

   The largely ignored, if not denied part—our subjective, conscious experience of the tug-and-pull of our self-preservation and affectional circuitries, with their powerful reward systems—however, makes up the entire meaning and texture of our lives.

Without them we would lack the essence of what it means to be human—to experience the humanity of ourselves and others. The extent to which we connect with others with minimal behavioral tension, in harmony and solidarity, is a measure of the quality of our lives and our moral development. To the extent that the ratio diverges, our sense of justice and our moral development suffer and we live in tension, stress, and disharmony. The equation can also be written alternatively, as the ratio of Love of Self/Love of Others. As the ratio approaches dynamic balance, we begin to approximate the various forms of the golden rule as well as the maxim to love one's neighbor as one's self.

Actualization

$$BT = \frac{Ego}{Empathy} = \pm 1 \text{ (dynamic balance extended to infinity))}$$

Finally, the generic form of the social equation represents the synthesis of the dual circuitries expressed in the outcomes of a lifetime. In the face of our mortality, the dynamic moves us to leave our best contribution or gift to society.

This may be phrased in many ways. It is well captured in the often heard wish to leave the world a better place. As the synthesis of these dynamic and powerful reward systems emerges spontaneously, we get what may be called peak experiences. As we concentrate upon these reward mechanisms in meditation or relaxation, allowing their full release to infinity—that is, to the limits of our neural network architecture—we may release the sensations of all-encompassing unity that characterize so-called mystical or peak experience.

THE CHOICES BEFORE US

With the demonstrated pervasiveness of our social neural architecture, our choices are now clear. Our essential human nature is no longer a matter of philosophical speculation but a fact of science. We have two major sets of neural circuitries, functioning as global-state variables, that define our essential social life. We cannot fall back on our egoistic, aggressive, greedy, self-seeking behaviors that split us apart into Hobbesian warring individual units—justifying it with the saying that "it's just human nature." No, it is a matter of choice and we cannot escape responsibility for it.

We are social creatures by our neural architecture. We are, in fact, dual creatures. Each with an *I* and *You* within us. The actualization or full expression of this dynamic circuitry is a full, blended expression of ego and empathy. Not one set of circuits amplified at the expense of the other. The full expression of our dual circuitry amplified through gating limbic portals into the executive of the frontal cortex carries a powerful emotional experience with far reaching social and political implications.

It is the full affirmation of our ego and empathy expressed as a personal contribution, our personal best to society. We find our meaning, our significance, perhaps even the intimations of our immortality in unity of self with others from the lowest levels of abstraction to the highest levels that our neural network architecture will permit.

The equation—the dynamic it represents—applies across the spectrum of our social activities from one-on-one interpersonal activities to all forms of social and economic exchange, to the very operation of our larger political systems. The equation applies, not by some imaginative stretch, but because all these seemingly separate areas of social expression are only artificially delimited aspects of our social lives.

There was a time in our primitive beginnings when all these disparate aspects were collapsed into one often conflicting, yet overall sharing, supporting, nurturing social unit—the nuclear, then, extended family. This primitive family seems the social analog to the big bang that initiated our physical universe.

In the primitive family the contentious, yet deeply binding, interactive dynamic of our self-preserving and affectional instincts preserved us against odds from one early generation to the next. Then, like the big bang of physics, the singularity of the nuclear family burst forth into history to shape our still evolving social forms. Our societies, our markets, and our political systems are still propelled by the same powerful algorithmic dynamic represented by the equation of our social brain—that sets our choices for survival as well as our potential for the future.

In the crucible of the primitive mammalian human family, then, were forged, refined, and selected the DNA, RNA, and amino acid sequences that assure the continuation and development in each of us of the neural circuitries that drive and shape our social lives. The same genes, the same gene-created circuitries, provide our potential, in the maturity of our species, to at last harness these dynamic forces and to return in essence to our origins—one family. By proof of science—by the evidence of the newly sequenced human genome—we are truly all the dispersed and variegated prodigal sons and daughters of the all-inclusive human family.

APPENDICES

APPENDIX I.

THE MISMEASURE OF PAUL MACLEAN

APPENDIX II.

A NEW PARADIGM FOR THINKING ABOUT GLOBAL ECONOMICS AND POLITICS

I

THE MISMEASURE
OF PAUL MACLEAN

INTRODUCTION

Paul D. MacLean is a scientific thinker well ahead of his time. Following his deeply held interest in the larger questions of human life, he started out studying philosophy. Being unable to find satisfactory answers to questions such as the origin and meaning of life—why humans in spite of their unrivaled intelligence often behaved in seemingly irrational ways threatening their individual as well as species survival—he turned to medicine and the study of the human brain. He anticipated the brain, as the biological substrate of these behaviors, held the key to better understanding of these fundamental questions as well as hopefully their answers,

MacLean was, for many years, chief of the Laboratory of Brain Evolution and Behavior of the National Institute of Mental Health. In 1952, drawing upon the nineteenth century French scientist Paul Broca's designation of the great limbic node that surrounded the brain stem of mammals, he introduced the conceptual term "limbic system" into the neuroscientific literature. In 1968 he introduced the concept of the triune brain, which became widely popularized after the publication of Carl Sagan's rather overly dramatic and simplified discussion of it in *The Dragons of Eden* (1977). MacLean, further developing the triune brain concept, which aroused great interest in psychiatry, education, and the lay public, produced his detailed and highly documented volume, *The Triune Brain in Evolution: Role in Paleocerebral Functions* in 1990.

THE TRIUNE BRAIN CONCEPT AND ITS CRITICS

MacLean's triune brain concept has been acknowledged the single most influential idea in neuroscience since World War II (e.g., Durant in Harrington, 1992: 268). Nevertheless, following the publication of his 1990 opus, MacLean received highly critical reviews in two prominent science periodicals, *Science* (October 12, 1990: 303–305) and *American Scientist* (September–October 1992: 497–498). Both reviews were written by neurobiologists who claimed that MacLean's triune brain concept has had limited acceptance or been largely ignored by professional neurobiologists.[60]

Anton Reiner, at that time a recent graduate, wrote the *Science* review, the more extensive of the two. After initially recognizing MacLean as a trailblazer of neuroscience, whose triune brain concept has been well-received outside the field of brain research, as the centerpiece of Sagan's popular, *The Dragons of Eden*, and frequently as the only discussion of brain evolution in psychiatry and psychology textbooks, Reiner makes several points critical of the triune brain concept.

He notes firstly that since MacLean introduced the concept, there has been tremendous growth in neuroscientific research that has greatly extended our knowledge of brain function and evolution. This statement carries the general implication, which Reiner later makes explicit, that the concept is out of date.

Second, in initiating a criticism of MacLean's concept of the limbic system, Reiner writes: "MacLean's presentation of the role of the hippocampus in limbic functions is not well reconciled with the current evidence that the hippocampus plays a role in memory"(1990: 304).

Third, Reiner contends that current research indicates that MacLean's reptilian complex is not a reptilian invention but seems to be present in vertebrates all the way back to jawless fishes.

Fourth, Reiner asserts that MacLean overreaches the evidence when he claims that the basal ganglia are the neural seat for the control of species-typical types of behaviors.

Fifth, Reiner states that the limbic system, a widely used term MacLean authored as a pioneer neuroresearcher, is not properly represented by MacLean. Contrary to MacLean, as Reiner would have it, the limbic system did not appear first in early mammals. Amphibians, reptiles, and birds also have limbic features such as the septum, amygdala, a different-looking hippocampal complex, and maybe even a cingulate cortex.

Sixth, Reiner maintains that MacLean assigns the functions of parental behavior, which Reiner claims that MacLean regards as uniquely mammalian, to the mammalian cingulate cortex, ignoring the fact that some reptiles (crocodiles), all birds, and possibly even some extinct reptiles (dinosaurs) also engaged in parental behavior.

Seventh, Reiner makes a couple of other criticisms of MacLean concerning (a) his preference for correspondence over the more evolutionarily appropriate concept of homology and (b) his apparently uncritical acceptance of Haeckel's idea that ontogeny recapitulates phylogeny.

Finally, although Reiner praises MacLean's motives and acknowledges the appeal of the triune brain concept for dealing with "big" behaviors that we are all interested in, such as: "How does our animal heritage affect our behavior? Why do we do the things we do? Why can we not live together more harmoniously?," he feels that there are some telling shortcomings, as recited above, in MacLean's scholarship. He concludes that "neuroscience research *can* (emphasis mine) shed light" on these important human questions, "though *perhaps* (emphasis mine) not in as global and simple a way as MacLean has sought"(1990: 305).

---

[60] A highly favorable review of MacLean's 1990 book was written by Emre Kokmen, M.D., of the Mayo Clinic, Rochester, Minnesota, in *Journal of Neurosurgery*. V. 75, Dec, 1991, p. 998. In this chapter I focus on the reviews in *Science* and *American Scientist* because they have reached a wider audience and have become red flag reviews unjustifiably inhibiting the thoughtful application of the triune brain concept in related fields as well as in the psychological and social sciences.

CRITIQUING THE *SCIENCE* CRITIQUE

Book reviews because of their very nature are usually overly brief and usually cannot deal in depth with the points they take issue with. Reviewers, then, are often themselves guilty of the same kinds of oversimplifications and misinterpretations that they seek to expose in their reviews. When Reiner states "I strongly believe the triune-brain idea to be wrong," he is caught up in the same oversimplifying tendency that he claims unjustifiably to find troublesome in MacLean.

The triune brain concept may be wrong in some of its particulars, right in others, but still be very useful and valid in its more general features. After all, at this stage of our knowledge of the brain, although it is quite advanced over the 1960s and 1970s, there are not a great number of things we can say with absolute confidence—very few generalizations that are without arguable interpretations of more detailed research data. Further, Reiner takes apart but does not offer a replacement generalization. His analysis is destructive, not constructive. This type of analysis is the easy part of the job. Almost anybody can do it.

However in his apparent eagerness to discredit and take apart MacLean's useful generalization, Reiner also fails to study his subject closely and therefore engages in some very careless scholarship. He makes significant omissions, outright errors, and substantial misrepresentations of MacLean's work. Let's look at the points Reiner raises one by one.

1. Reiner blatantly misstates the facts when he claims that the triune brain concept as well as MacLean's book are outdated and lack up-to-date documentation. Reiner's first point (i.e., that there has been a great growth in knowledge about the brain since MacLean first announced his triune brain concept in the 1960s and 1970s) implies that MacLean has left the concept untouched and undocumented since that time and has therefore not considered any of the more recent findings. The implications of this statement are belied by the currency of research cited by MacLean and included in his discussions. To back up his case for the alleged outdated ideas and data in the book, Reiner baldly states "only a handful of papers from the '80s' are cited" (Reiner, 1990: 305). This categorically false statement is easily contradicted by a count of bibliographic items. The bibliography of this work contains over 180 entries (a big handful indeed!) that date from 1980 to at least 1988 and over 220 entries that date between 1975 and 1979. This amounts to at least 400 entries of rather recent documentation—keeping in mind that the publication date of MacLean's book and Reiner's review was for both 1990.

2. Reiner misstates or ignores the facts when he says, "MacLean's presentation of the role of the hippocampus in limbic functions is not well reconciled with the current evidence that the hippocampus plays a role in memory." The phrasing of this statement implies that MacLean is unaware of or fails to report on the extensive research indicating the role of the hippocampus in memory. Such an implication is totally unwarranted. MacLean devotes fully two chapters to reporting and discussing such research. These chapters even have "memory" in their titles. Chapter 26 is titled *Microelectric Study of Limbic Inputs Relevant to Ontology and Memory* (emphasis mine). Chapter 27 is titled *Question of Limbic Mechanisms Linking a Sense of Individuality to Memory* (emphasis mine) *of Ongoing Experience*. These chapters deal at length with the role of the hippocampus in memory and propose an integrative role for the hippocampus in tying

learning to affect or emotion (For a summary of MacLean's discussion on these matters, consult 1990: 514–16).

3. Claiming that the reptilian complex is not a reptilian invention, Reiner misrepresents MacLean's position. On this third point, Reiner contends that current research indicates that MacLean's reptilian complex is not a reptilian invention but seems to be present in vertebrates all the way back to jawless fishes. This is largely a taxonomic question. At what point do we declare something to be a fish, an amphibian, an amniote, a reptile, or a mammal? And do we view mammals as branching off from the amniote tree before we have distinct reptiles in the line of descent? Or do we prefer the more likely probability that mammals descended in a line from the ancient mammal-like reptiles of the predinosaur Permian-Triassic periods called therapsids, who represent a branching of the ancient reptile line (cotylosaurs). Therapsids appeared approximately 230 millions years ago, and approximately 50 million years before the emergence of the great dinosaurs of the Jurassic and Cretaceous periods.

MacLean knows these facts and clearly acknowledges them, while supporting in a lineage for mammals that traces back to the therapsids, of the synapsida subclass that branched off from the diapsida line that eventually produced the great dinosaurs many years later. This is the standard position in evolutionary theory today. One might wish to compare the phylogenetic tree in MacLean (1990: 34) with Butler and Hodos (1996: 72), Strickberger (1996: 396), and Hickman, et al. (1984: Fig. 27.1). And it is the accepted position of standard zoology texts (e.g., Miller & Harley, 1992; Hickman, et al., 1984, 1990). Mammals, and ultimately us humans, then, did not evolve from dinosaurs but from a parallel lineage that split much further back in geologic time.

If the term reptilian brain or reptilian complex causes confusion with modern reptiles, and because the reviewers don't wish to read MacLean's work closely, the reptilian Complex could be thought of, and perhaps redesignated, as the ancient amniote complex or even the early vertebrate complex. And, of course, as MacLean acknowledges thoroughly, this early brain complex is *not* the reptilian brain of modern reptiles but it is also not the same as that of the early vertebrates, amniotes, or therapsids. At several points in his book, MacLean makes this unequivocally clear by his reference to stem reptiles (cotylosaurs) (MacLean, 1990: 33, 82), those early reptiles from which both the diapsid and synapsid lines branched off. To ensure the proper evolutionary context, MacLean also uses the term "protoreptilian" in his initial definition and adds the clarifying comment that he refers to the reptilian complex (or R-complex) only for brevity's sake (see MacLean, 1990: 15–16, 244, 519). This protoreptilian, or stem reptile brain has been altered by modifications that include those produced by differentiation and elaboration of earlier structures (e.g., see MacLean 1990: 243). These modifications, to include differentiations and elaborations, provide, in addition to their previous maintenance and behavioral functions, neural circuitry in support of the enhanced limbic structures of mammals. These enhanced mammalian limbic structures necessarily engage and enhance prior circuitry in the brain stem. And together these enhanced limbic and brain stem circuits provide support for the greatly enhanced neocortex (or isocortex) which eventually got modifications sufficient to permit language and the development of complex technological societies.[61]

---

[61] The use of the term "additions" is deliberately avoided here because it has been the source of some confusion (see Butler & Hodos, 1996: 86). New brain structures do not spring de novo out of nowhere but rather evolve from the differentiation of previously existing structures. When differentiations become sufficiently established,

4. Reiner misrepresents MacLean's position on the basal ganglia. Reiner says he knows of no one other than MacLean who believes the basal ganglia to be the neural seat for the control of species-typical types of behaviors (1990: 305). This statement is a misrepresentation of MacLean's position as well as an admission of ignorance on the part of Reiner. In the first place, MacLean never uses the inclusive term "neural seat." Further, MacLean is not talking about all species-typical behavior but only some. He specifically excludes from this discussion such mammalian class/species-typical behavior as maternal nursing and play, which are attributed primarily to other brain parts and treated in other chapters of the book.

In Part II on the *Striatal Complex with Respect to Species-Typical Behavior*, MacLean repeatedly emphasizes that the traditional view that the striatal complex is primarily involved in motor functions represents an oversimplification. He writes that the purpose of the present investigation is to test the hypothesis that the striatal complex plays an "essential" role in certain species typical behaviors as well as certain basic forms of behavior common to both reptiles and mammals (MacLean, 1990: 243). At one point after reciting the evidence, MacLean says that the results "suggest that the medial globus pallidus (a structure of the basal ganglia) is a site of convergence of neural systems involved in the species-typical mirror display of gothic-type squirrel monkeys" (MacLean, 1990: 189). Also, a little further on, MacLean tells us that "findings indicate that in animals as diverse as lizards and monkeys, the R-complex is *basically involved* (emphasis mine) in the organized expression of species typical, prosematic communication of a ritualistic nature" (1990: 189).

Additional research, some predating others postdating Reiner's review and of which Reiner is apparently ignorant, adds further support to MacLean's hypothesis. For example, J. Wayne Aldridge and colleagues from the University of Michigan in a research report titled "Neuronal Coding of Serial Order: Syntax of Grooming in the Neostriatum,"(1993) conclude that there is "direct evidence that the neostriatum *coordinates the control* (emphasis mine) of rule-governed behavioral sequences." This study builds upon a series of earlier studies of species-typical grooming behavior of the rat (e.g., Berridge & Fentress, 1988; Berridge & Whishaw, 1992; Cromwell & Berridge, 1990). These earlier and more recent studies certainly support MacLean's hypothesis that the striatal complex plays an essential role in some species typical behaviors of a ritualistic nature.

And, of course, there is the growing body of clinical evidence, going well back into the 1970s and 1980s, that neurological disorders in humans (such as Parkinson's, Huntington's, and Tourette syndromes) that involve damage to the neostriatum produce specific deficits in the sequential order of movement, language, and cognitive function (e.g., Holthoff-Detto, et al., 1997; Cummings, 1993; Benecke, et al., 1987; Marsden, 1982, 1984; Oberg & Divac, 1979). Such serial order patterns in behavior are phylogenetically old as well as pervasive and often constitute the basis of identifying so-called species-typical behaviors. Greenberg (2002) who did early work with MacLean, provides a comprehensive update of the research on the striatum.

---

they are often referred to loosely as "additions." This does not deny that seemingly new additions may possibly and occasionally arise, but the intent here is to emphasize the phylogenetic continuity that underpins the concept of homology.

5. Reiner misrepresents the facts when he claims that MacLean says the limbic system first appeared in mammals. MacLean does not claim that the limbic system first appeared in early mammals. He acknowledges that limbic features appear in fishes, reptiles, and birds, but are rudimentary and poorly developed when compared with those of mammals (MacLean, 1990: 247, 287). According to MacLean's view, then, it is not the presence or absence of limbic features themselves in ancestral amniote or reptilian vertebrates, but rather the significant and prominent development of limbic features in mammals that is appropriately of interest in understanding the evolution of characteristically and uniquely mammalian behavior. Further, care must be exercised in making comparisons across existing modern species. We can only infer that the structures and undeveloped and/or rudimentary homologues of such structures in modern species were also present in ancestral lines. Brains do not fossilize, so the point cannot be made conclusively. The currently accepted inferential position in neuroscience is that there are homologues of limbic structures going well back into vertebrate history, although these homologues in modern species are often difficult to establish and sometimes downright dubious (Striedter, 1997; Veenman, et al., 1997).[62]

6. Reiner displays careless scholarship and misrepresents the facts of neuroscience, evolution, and animal behavior as well as MacLean's position on parental behavior and

---

[62] The accuracy and utility of the concept and term "limbic system" has itself been a separate topic of some disagreement in recent years. Some authors state that it does not represent a truly functional system and that the term should be discarded. Others defend its use. Most texts continue to find the term useful and because of its longtime usage it will probably remain in the literature. Some recent and prominent scholars illustrate the controversy well. Pierre Gloor of the Montreal Neurological Institute, McGill University, in his thoroughgoing work *The Temporal Lobe and Limbic System*, by the very use of the term in the title indicates his position. Further on in the text, while acknowledging the controversy he writes that this system in mammals exhibits an organization that is sufficiently different from that characterizing other areas of the cerebral hemisphere to merit such a designation (Gloor, 1997: 106).

And well-known neurologist Richard Restak tells us that based upon a large body of experimental work, it is appropriate to conclude that, "depending on the areas stimulated, the limbic system serves as a generator of agreeable-pleasurable or disagreeable-aversive affects" (1994: 143). Nevertheless, there is little agreement among neuroscientists concerning the contributions of the different components, and their mutual influence on each other (1994: 149).

On the other hand William Blessing, a neuroscientist at Flinders University, in his study of the lower brain stem, feels that emphasis on the limbic system has detracted from the study of brain stem mechanism, that it has been "plagued by its anatomical and physiological vagueness and by the lack of precision with which the term is used" (Blessing, 1997: 15). Further, he thinks the term should be dropped from the literature (Blessing, 1997: 16).

A third recent author, neuroscientist Joseph LeDoux (1997: Ch. 4) argues that because the limbic system is not solely dedicated to the single global function of emotion, a claim that MacLean fully recognizes in his chapters on memory (1990: Chs: 26 & 27), that the concept should be abandoned. LeDoux apparently prefers a single functional criterion for the definition of a system, whereas MacLean seems to prefer a combination of functional and anatomical criteria. Le Doux concludes his argument by stating: "As a result, there may not be one emotional system in the brain but many" (1997: 103). Compare this with the concluding line of the definitional description by Kandel et al., authors of the most widely used textbook on neuroscience and behavior: "The limbic system contains neurons that form complex circuits that play an important role in learning, memory, and emotion"(1995: 708).

The use and value of the conceptual term "limbic system," then, seems to depend on one's research focus and how one chooses to define a system. It might be added that the definition of what constitutes a system is controversial in all disciplines, not just in neuroscience.

the cingulate cortex. He claims that MacLean assigns the functions of parental behavior to the cingulate cortex and that MacLean regards parental behavior as uniquely mammalian. According to Reiner, MacLean's alleged position "ignores the fact that some reptiles, such as crocodiles, and all birds engage in parental behavior, not to mention the possibility suggested by paleontological data that some extinct reptiles, namely dinosaurs, also engaged in parental behavior"(Reiner, 1990: 305).

Such a blanket claim makes one wonder if Reiner felt it worth his while to even consult the book he is reporting on. First, MacLean does not "assign" parental behavior to the cingulate cortex. Instead he reports the recent (at that time) research on maternal mechanisms in the septal or medial preoptic area (MacLean, 1990: 351–353) and indicates that this area may have provided the initial potentiality for full scale mammalian maternal behavior (MacLean, 1990: 354), that would include play and the development of empathy. The very title of his Chapter 21 is *Participation* (emphasis mine) *of Thalamocingulate Division in Family-Related Behavior*. Participation is participation not unilateral and unequivocal assignment. And MacLean uses the systemic term "thalamocingulate" to indicate intra-limbic nuclei and cortical connections, not simply cingulate cortex as Reiner states. MacLean cites good evidence for thalamocingulate participation in "nursing, conjoined with maternal care"(MacLean, 1990: 380). After all, lesions in certain portions of the cingulate cortex interfere with nursing and other maternal behavior (Stamm, 1955; Slotnick, 1967), not with blanket parental care as Reiner asserts.

Perhaps it may be too early or simply erroneous in neuroscience to assign anything specifically and finally to any exclusive part of the limbic area. More likely there is some localization of minor function, but for most behaviors of any scale there seems to be fairly wide-ranging neural circuitry that may be inter-rupted by lesions at many different points. For example, recent research on maternal behavior (nursing, retrieval, nestbuilding) in rats has focused on the medial preoptic area with its connections to other limbic structures and the brain stem (Numan, 1990). Alison Fleming and her colleagues (1996), summarize what we know about the neural control of maternal behavior. Not only the medial preoptic area with its brain stem projections, but also other limbic sites are involved, including the amygdala (Numan, et al., 1993; Fleming, et al., 1980), hippocampus (Terlecki & Sainsbury, 1978; Kimble, et al., 1967), septum (Fleischer & Slotnik, 1978), and cingulate cortex (Slotnik, 1967; Stamm, 1955).

Most emotions, emotional behaviors, and emotional memories seem to be distributed, involving multiple pathways. Specific behaviors and categories of behaviors can be interrupted by lesions at varying points in these multiple pathways. More recent research has again confirmed that the cingulate cortex is involved in emotion and motivation (Stern & Passingham, 1996). In a recent research report John Freeman and colleagues conclude that the neural circuitry formed by interconnected cingulate cortical, limbic thalamic, and hippocampal neurons has fundamentally similar functions in the affective behaviors of approach and avoidance (Freeman, et al., 1996).

Like any good scientist with an open mind, MacLean, at the close of his chapter on participation of the thalamocingulate division in family-related behavior, calls for more neurobehavioral research to explore the extent of this participation (MacLean, 1990: 410). It is also noteworthy that MacLean is one of the few thinkers in neuroscience who shows concern for the neural substrate of such family-based behavior, characteristic of mammals, as play and the underpinning but illusive quality of empathy. Although such characteristics have been reported on behaviorally (e.g., for play, see Burghardt, 1988,

1984; Fagen, 1981), they have largely been ignored in the search for neural substrates, not because they are unimportant, but because of the extreme difficulty in defining and objectifying them. But the evidence clearly points to neocortical as well as limbic cortical and subcortical representation (e.g., see Fuster, 1997: esp. 169; Frith, 1997: 98; Frith, 1989: 154–155). Recent reports by Damasio (1999), Panksepp (1998) and Carter, et al. (1997) provide hope that mainstream neuroscience will direct more serious research toward a better understanding of these difficult and ignored questions which are so critical to a full understanding and appreciation of humanity.

Reiner also indiscriminately uses the blanket term "parental behavior" coupled with attributing that same blanket usage to MacLean. In this usage, Reiner shows a remarkable deficit of scholarship, naivete, or both. MacLean is not discussing all parental behavior. He is discussing those nurturing behaviors that are the most distinguishing characteristic of mammals and a fundamental part of their taxonomic classification and differentiation from birds and reptiles. These behaviors must be found in either new structures or modifications to existing structures. As Butler and Hodos point out, new structures may be added to organ systems, but modification of existing structures appears to be more common (1996: 86). The jury is still out on the neurophysiology of these defining mammalian behavioral features. What is more, with the emphasis on cognition in neuroscience, until very recently surprisingly little attention has been paid to the extensive work on the neural and hormonal basis of the motivational and emotional aspects of maternal care. This is openly acknowledged by leading scholars in the brain science field (e.g., Rosenblatt & Snowden, 1996; LeDoux, 1997: 68; Kandel, Schwartz & Jessell, 1995). The previously cited work by Panksepp (1998) and Carter, et al. (1997) represent a step in the right direction.

The blanket term "parental care" as used by Reiner in his criticism of MacLean amounts to condemnation by indiscriminate generalization. Parental care has been defined by a leading authority as "any kind of parental behavior that appears likely to increase the fitness of the parent's offspring" (Clutton-Brock, 1991: 8). This very broad and inclusive term includes even nest and burrow preparation. The very production of eggs is included. This kind of "parental care" is found in the earliest vertebrates with very primitive brains indeed. If the all-inclusive definition of parental care can be stretched to include the production of eggs and digging a hole to place them in, perhaps it could conceivably be stretched to include even the sharing of cellular membranes during asexual reproduction by single-celled organisms.

But specifically, what about parental care in modern reptiles? Contrary to Reiner's claim, MacLean reports on parental care in crocodiles (MacLean, 1990: 136–137) and also in some species of skink lizards (MacLean, 1990: 136, 248–249). A recent review article on parental care among reptiles by Carl Gans of the Department of Biology, University of Michigan, brings us up to date. Gans claims that the most spectacular example of reptilian parental care takes place among crocodiles. Both parents respond to the call of hatchlings who vocalize underground while emerging from the eggs. The adults dig them up and transport them to water in their large buccal pouch (Pooley, 1977). The young are then washed and stay shortly in association with the adults. After a relatively brief period, however, the juveniles' response to the adults reverses. The juveniles disperse suddenly into small, nearby channels where they may dig themselves tunnels. Gans notes: "In view of the fact that crocodylians may be *cannibalistic* (emphasis mine), there seems to be both an inhibition of cannibal-is in the parents and an inhibition of a possible adult avoidance reaction in the neonates" (1996: 153).

This kind of short-lived parental care during which the cannibalism of parents is inhibited may be impressive in reptiles, but it is a far, far cry from the highly developed family-related behavior in mammals; behavior that is so further developed in the human species that it extends often throughout an entire lifetime and becomes the basis for a vastly extended social life. The *equating* of parental care in reptiles with parental care in mammals is simply ludicrous. It is this mammalian family behavior that concerns MacLean, and the neural substrate is appropriately sought in the brain modifications that became prominent with the appearance of mammals.

7. Reiner's further inaccuracies: recapitulation, homology, and correspondence, and so on. Near the end of his review Reiner makes the following isolated statement: "MacLean also errs in his apparent sweeping acceptance of Haeckel's idea that ontogeny recapitulates phylogeny" (1990: 305). Again, Reiner distorts and misrepresents. From a close review of the book it is by no means clear that MacLean "sweepingly" accepts Haeckel's concept. In fact he only refers to it once (MacLean, 1990: 46), while at the same time noting the well-known exceptions. Haeckel's concept has been largely superceded in neuroscience today by the principles of von Baerian recapitulation. The von Baerian version holds that while ontogeny does not recapitulate phylogeny in the thoroughgoing Haeckelian sense, it does recapitulate the features of an organism in terms of the organism's general to more specific classification. In other words, the von Baerian principles state that the more general features of an organism develop before the more specific features do (Butler & Hodos, 1996: 51–52). The issue, however, is still not so clearly settled. The emergent discipline of evolutionary developmental biology is looking more closely into such questions (Hall, 1992; Thomson, 1988). For instance, evolutionary biologist Wallace Arthur, in summarizing the main themes of this emerging discipline, writes: "No single comparative embryological pattern is universally found or can be described as a 'law'. Von Baerian divergence, its antithesis (convergence) and a broadly Haeckelian (quasi-recapitulatory) pattern can all be found, depending on the comparison made"(1997: 292).

On the additional point that MacLean prefers to think in terms of correspondence rather than homology probably reflects his functional-behavioral orientation. In fact it is specifically in discussing the issue of the relationship between structure and behavior that (MacLean, 1990: 37) makes this comment. Later, he returns to a more standard use of homology (MacLean, 1990: 228). There is, in fact, presently no sure-fire way of demonstrating that homologues have the same one-to-one functions or produce the same one-to-one behaviors across species. In reporting that MacLean, at one point, expresses preference for the term "correspondence" because of the confusion in the definition of homology, Reiner shows what can only be considered a misplaced and sophomoric "gotcha" exuberance. He writes that MacLean's comment "should leave Stephen J. Gould, not to mention all other students of evolution, aghast," adding that such a comment constitutes a "very critical misjudgment to make in a work on evolution."(Reiner, 1990: 305).

This is truly a naive, if not preposterous statement by Reiner. Could it be that Reiner is not aware of the long history of the pervasive problems associated with the definition of homology? For example, Leigh Van Valen, of the biology department of the University of Chicago, in the first sentence of his frequently referenced article on homology and its causes, writes: "Homology is the central concept of anatomy, yet it is an elusive concept."(1982: 305). Further on, in view of the persistent definitional ambiguities, Van Valen practically equates the two terms "homologue" and "correspondence" when he writes: "In fact, homology can be defined, in a quite general way, as *correspondence* (emphasis mine) caused by a continuity of information," although in a footnote Van Valen admits that correspondence itself needs further definition beyond the scope of his paper (305: fn. 1; cf. Roth, 1994). Although there has been some sharpening of the concept of homology, with emphasis on phyletic continuity, the ambiguities have by no means been adequately resolved (Gehring, 1998; Trevarrow, 1998; Striedter, 1998; Arthur, 1997: 171–177; Hall, 1994, 1996). The study of molecular biology and the genome is adding further insights into the conservation of homologues from very early life forms indeed (e.g., see Gehring, 1988; C.U.M. Smith, 2002).

And there remains the haunting question that is still wide open for research and investigation: Do most homologous behaviors share a homologous structural basis or can homologous behaviors be rooted in nonhomologous structures? (see Hall, 1996: 29: fn. 23). The recent report by William Blessing on the lower brain stem emphasizes the question of multiple neural representations of body parts and behavior, in that behavior originally represented and controlled in the brain stem of an earlier vertebrate may maintain its brain stem representation, but be controlled by an added representation in the frontal cortex of a more highly developed mammal. Such multiple representations at different levels as the brain became more complex would certainly confuse the issue of a straightforward homologous match of structure and function (1997: 1–18; see also, Brown, 1977).

Research on very limited aspects of function is often suggestive but far from conclusive even on such limited function. Establishing homologues of the prefrontal cortex can be particularly vexing. A recent research article by Gagliardo and colleagues, "Behavioural effects of ablations of the *presumed* (emphasis mine) 'prefrontal cortex' or the corticoid in pigeons" (Gagliardo, et al., 1996), indicates, not only in its discussion and conclusions, but in the very title itself, the uncertainty, ambiguity, and cautions that currently characterize such research efforts (see also Fuster, 1997: 7–11).

An awful lot of assuming goes on in some quarters of neuroscience on this issue, which simply cannot be settled at this time based on the empirical evidence. This is one of the problems and cautions that must be acknowledged when generalizing across species, say from rats to humans. In maternal behavior, for example, can we say factually that the medial preoptic area plays the same part in the maternal behavior of humans that it does it the rat brain? No, we cannot. At least not yet. But neuroscientists, after first hedging themselves, and following homologous logic, seem inclined to think so. Nevertheless, it is entirely within the realm of possibility that we may find that it does so only in part or not at all. As neuroresearcher Joseph LeDoux notes: "Some *innate* (emphasis mine) behavioral patterns are known to involve hierarchically organized response components" (1997: 120). And further on he adds: "Species differences can involve any brain region or pathway, due to particular brain specializations required for certain species-specific adaptations or to random changes"(1997: 123). And neurologist Richard Restak points out that in the case of animals, multiple limbic areas may increase, modify or inhibit aggression. He notes further that even the same area may increase or inhibit responses under different experimental conditions and depending on the animal selected for experiment. As an example, he points out that the destruction of the cingulate gyrus (a limbic component) increases aggressive behavior in cats and dogs, whereas, on the contrary, such an operation has a calming effect in monkeys and humans (1994: 149).

Or perhaps, as Blessing notes, there are multiple representations. Then we might have to go to correspondence rather than homology (even homoplasy might not apply, since homoplasy, or parallel evolution, would probably not apply in such closely related species) to account for the behavioral circuitry. In other words, the corresponding neural circuitry—that circuitry controlling maternal behavior—may be found in the same, slightly differing, multiple, or perhaps (though highly unlikely) even totally different structural homologues or modifications.

In fact, if homology is correct and functionally, to include behaviorally, uniform—that is, the same structures account for the same functions and behaviors across classes, orders, and species—this finding would support the triune brain concept as set out by MacLean, which says generally that the protoreptilian complex common to both reptiles and mammals functions largely the same in both classes. This finding would also support MacLean's position that the expanded circuitry areas of the mammalian complex bear characteristically mammalian functions and are the circuitry for characteristically mammalian behaviors, such as nursing; a defining taxonomic feature of mammals (which, in part distinguishes them from reptiles and birds).

In a final series of somewhat gratuitously negative comments, Reiner writes about some of MacLean's legitimate speculations. For example, Reiner states "and mathematical skill (he thinks the cerebellum could be involved)"(Reiner, 1990: 305).

And why not? See MacLean's discussion on the subject (MacLean, 1990: 548–552). Recent research indicates that the cerebellum is not just a motor mechanism, but is also likely involved in higher cognitive and perhaps even language function. Especially relevant is the rather well-supported hypothesis that indicates a cerebellar mechanism involved in all tasks that require precise temporal computations. This could well suggest an involvement in mathematical processes. True, the evidence is insufficient to permit firm conclusions as to the cerebellar role in higher cognitive processes, but it is a research direction that needs further refinement and is currently pursued by a number of neurobiologists (Daum & Ackermann, 1995; Dimitrov, et al., 1996; Altman & Bayer, 1997: esp. 749–751).

Overall, given the outright errors, careless scholarship, misrepresentations, and sophomoric, prejudicial tone of Reiner's review, it probably should never have been allowed to appear in a publication of the stature and influence of *Science*. Such reviewing should perhaps raise questions of standards in the academic-scientific community.

REVIEW BY CAMPBELL IN AMERICAN SCIENTIST

The review by Campbell in *American Scientist* (1992) is a much shorter review than that of Reiner. It brings up some of the same points, but is less prejudicial in its tone. Since it is less detailed it expresses primarily the preferences and value judgments of the reviewer. Campbell repeats Reiner's erroneous charge about outdatedness. He writes: "that except for a very few papers, most of the references were published prior to 1980" (1992: 498). I have already noted that this "handful" of items amounts to more than 180 citations. One suspects that Campbell proceeded from his preconceptions and found what he expected to find. Campbell ends his review with the statement: "Unfortunately, the data presented are, *to some degree* (emphasis mine), outdated, and the evolutionary reasoning is unsophisticated" (1992: 498). The use of the term "unsophisticated" by the reviewer is totally unwarranted. For anyone who has closely read MacLean's detailed and thoughtful work, the evolutionary reasoning is, on the contrary, quite thoughtful, well-presented, and sophisticated. Such blanket judgments tell us more about the sociology of neuroscience and neuroscientists that they do about the subject matter of the discipline itself.

COMMENTS OF BUTLER AND HODOS

In their recent comprehensive and overall admirable work on comparative vertebrate anatomy, Butler and Hodos attempt to formalize the assignment of MacLean's work to the relics of history. Their comments reflect the standard oversimplified criticisms, misrepresentations, and errors that have become popular to repeat ever more unreflectively. Butler and Hodos assign the triune brain concept, inaccurately and indiscriminately, to a category they call "theories of addition." And without any detailed discussion or analysis of the very significant, indisputable points of accuracy in MacLean's concept, they write that the past three decades of work in comparative neurobiology "unequivocally" contradicts MacLean's theory (1996: 86).

How incredible that two such qualified authors should accept the same flagrant misrepresentations, inaccuracies, and oversimplifications of MacLean's work that have become commonplace in some sectors of neurobiology over the past decade. They seemingly merely parroted the errors and misrepresentations of Reiner and others rather than reading MacLean's 1990 work closely and open-mindedly. There is no point in repeating the responses given earlier to Reiner's review. The same points hold for Butler and Hodos' comments. The rebuttal points are clearly made and easily accessible to verification by anyone who chooses to make the effort. The categorical statement by Butler and Hodos that the extensive body of work in comparative neurobiology over the past three decades unequivocally contradicts MacLean's theory, which they apparently have not read, constitutes on that point poor, if not irresponsible, scholarship.

MACLEAN'S TRIUNE BRAIN CONCEPT: UTILITY AND VALIDITY

The triune brain concept may have its limitations. But its shortcomings have been patently misrepresented in some cases and grossly exaggerated in others. Whatever its faults may ultimately prove to be, the triune brain concept gets at a fundamental evolutionary pattern. The mammalian modifications, differentiations, and elaborations to the early vertebrate and ancestral amniote brains had the effect of introducing endothermy (warmbloodedness), maternal nursing, enhanced mechanisms of skin contact and comfort, as well as enhanced visual, vocal, and other cues to bond parents to offspring and serve as the underpinning for the extended and complex family life of humankind. The mammalian modifications, therefore, added greatly enhanced affectional, other-interested behavior to the primarily (although not exclusively) self-preservational, self-interested behaviors of ancestral amniotes and early vertebrates (not necessarily their modern representatives).

The simplistic representation and attempted demolition of MacLean's triune brain concept is not good science. Reiner's review, where it has any validity at all, is like discovering a termite or two in the bathroom wall, and then proceeding to pronounce a full alarm that the house is full of termites, only to find that it is necessary to treat a few boards in the subflooring. Further, in his deconstructive, analytic fervor, Reiner has offered no alternative higher level generalization. The review represents a dysfunction common to a lot of scientific practice, that of an analytical approach that takes apart but can't put back together. Perhaps we should call it analytic myopia. Uninterested in the bigger questions of humanity that we so desperately need help on, and lacking an interest in therapy, these analytic myopics continue their fine-grained focus. Fine-grained focus is fine, laudable, and very much needed. It becomes analytically myopic, however, when it fails to place in context what it finds and defines, when it employs sloppy scholarship, and when it attempts prejudicially to destroy or deconstruct that which it lacks the imagination and courage to put together.

On the other hand, the theories of brain evolution that Butler and Hodos review favorably and the synthesis that they present at the end of their book focus on the immunohistological, hormonal, and morphological mechanics (1996: 463–473). They say, in fact, almost nothing at all about behavior or the significance for behavioral evolution of the various mechanisms of evolution they identify. And they make no attempt whatsoever to confront the larger behavioral questions of humanity where we need help and guidance from neuroscience in defining the neurobiological basis of human nature in order to establish links up the scale of generalization with the social sciences. The theories they present are only of interest to the technical aspects of neuroscience. They are not, however, incompatible, but tend to support MacLean's concepts when these concepts are accurately and thoughtfully considered.

The key point in comparing these theories with that of MacLean's is that they are comparable, at best, only in part. They ask and respond to different questions. MacLean tries to address the larger questions of human nature and behavior. The others show no interest in such questions but address the fine- grained technical questions of anatomical and functional evolution. At the level where they meet, they do not contradict each other but are largely compatible. At the point where they diverge, they primarily address different questions. This is, I think, the root of the tension between the two. MacLean's concept facing up the scale of integration is useful and has been appropriately well received in the therapeutic sciences, and is also very useful for the social sciences. On the other hand, it has not been, but may yet become, more useful and better received in other quarters of neuroscience, especially when subjective experience is eventually given its due in the study of consciousness. There are, in fact, recent signs that the importance of subjective experience, which is of great interest to MacLean, is gaining fuller recognition in the newer studies of consciousness (Damasio, 1994, 1999; Smith, 1996: 471–474; Searle, 1997; Edelman & Tononi, 2000; Cory, 2000a,b).

The triune brain concept may need modification, then, as the body of neuroscience grows—but certainly not outright rejection. With appropriate clarifications, it is still by far the best concept we have for linking neuroscience with the larger, more highly integrated concepts of the social sciences. This is true even if its level of integration has limited utility for some neuroscience researchers who are doing ever more fine-grained research into neural architecture and function.

The transitions from early vertebrate to amniote to synapsid reptile to mammal were in behavioral effect transitions from nearly exclusively self- preserving organisms with relatively little or less complex social life to, at least in part, a nurturing, "other-maintaining," "other-supporting," or "other-interested" organism. And that makes all the difference in the world for human evolution. Our other-maintaining mechanisms combined with our self-preserving ones provide the biological glue as well as the dynamic for our remarkable behavioral evolution, our social life, and ultimately the crucial social and political factor of our moral consciousness.

The qualitative differences between the familial and social behaviors of even the most caring of reptiles (say, modern crocodiles), birds or social insects and the mammal we call human are overwhelmingly evident. Humans with their social, cognitive, and language skills, for better or for worse, dominate the planet and no other species comes close. Any neurobiologist who cannot see or appreciate the difference suffers from analytic myopia or some form of misplaced species egalitarianism (cf. Butler & Hodos, 1996: 3–4). The proper study of humans is humans and to some extent their lineal ancestors. The triune brain concept integrates some fundamental patterns out of much that is yet unknown and uncertain in neuroscience. And this generalization, when properly understood, appreciated, and applied, is the most useful bridging link, thus far articulated, between neuroscience and the larger and pressingly critical questions of humanity's survival, as well as the hoped for transformation of humanity into a truly life-supporting, planet-preserving and enhancing custodial species.

When other neuroscience researchers reach the conceptual point in their grasp of the discipline that they feel an increasing obligation to take a more integrative view and proceed to move up the scale of generalization in order to confront the larger questions of human life, they will likely produce concepts closely resembling the triune brain. Homology and behavioral evolution will almost inevitably take them in that direction. Frankly, despite its current lack of popularity in some quarters of neurobiology, I think that the triune brain concept will continue to be influential, and with appropriate modifications as research progresses, provide an important underpinning for interdisciplinary communication and bridging. The chapters constituting this volume amply demonstrate its heuristic value and it integrative utility.

II

A NEW PARADIGM FOR THINKING
ABOUT GLOBAL ECONOMICS AND POLITICS

WHAT IS A PARADIGM SHIFT?

A paradigm shift is a shift in scientific perspective. The most famous paradigm shift in history was the shift from the Ptolemaic geocentric theory of the solar system to the Copernican heliocentric system.

WHAT DOES A PARADIGM SHIFT DO?

A paradigm shift may be considered to do at least four essential things:

1. It makes necessary accommodation with new scientific findings.

2. It allows us to see old things in a new, more accurate way.

3. It allows us to see things we could not see before.

4. It allows us to explain things we could not explain before.

The first table contrasts the current paradigm with the new paradigm made possible by a proper grasp of the dynamic of our neural architecture. The following tables show the relevance of the new paradigm for global free enterprise as well as for mathematical modeling.

Table 1. Paradigm Shift Made Possible by New Findings in Neural Architecture

<u>Current Paradigm</u>	<u>Suggested New Paradigm</u>
Ethnocentric View of Economics & Free Enterprise Theory 1776–2000	Global View of Economics & Free Enterprise Theory 2001----→
1. Based on sole self-interest motive	1. Based on dynamic tug and pull of ego (self-interest) & empathy (other-interest)
2. Psychological model of Maslow Pyramid	2. Conflict Systems Neurobehavioral (CSN) Model
3. Demand & Supply based on self-interest as sole primary motive (Empathy hidden/implicit)	3. Demand & Supply based on interaction of dual motives of ego/empathy
4. No equation linking economics with human nature	4. $BT = EP = \dfrac{EGO}{EMP} = \dfrac{DEM}{SUP} = \pm 1$

Table 2. Relevance of New Shift for Global Business/Society

Traditional Paradigm	**New Paradigm**
Disadvantages	Advantages
1. Inaccurate scientifically	1. Scientifically accurate
2. Inherent selfishness Can breed and justify greed	2. Golden Rule Justifies responsible behavior Respect for self & others
3. Supports & justifies inequality	3. Supports & justifies equality

Table 2. continued.

4. Bad global press for Free Enterprise System (as selfish, materialistic system)	4. Supports moral basis for Global Free Enterprise (as caring, responsible system)
5. Builds behavioral tension	5. Mitigates behavioral tension
6. Encourages conflict	6. Encourages conflict resolution
7. Basis for national centeredness Seeking national self-interest	7. Basis for global centeredness Global respect for self/others
8 Domination, exploitation in trade & business	8. Reciprocity in trade & business
9. Ethnocentric	9. Global or universal

Table 3. New Paradigm: Differences in Mathematical Modeling

1.   Demand and supply curves: Makes explicit the role of empathy as a primary motive with self-interest. This is presently obscured or denied from the self-reference perspective in economics which distorts the real nature of the market.

2.   Establishes price as an endogenous variable (one that can be explained). Presently, price is treated as exogenous (it cannot be explained).

3.   All points on supply and demand curves outside of the equilibrium point represent points of behavioral tension. Behavioral tension is what motivates buyers and sellers to change the price toward equilibrium. This is not explained in present economics.

4.   Provides an equation that links economic theory (laws of supply and demand) with neuroscience.

5.   Equilibrium price is expressed as approximate (dynamic) balance of supply/demand or ego/empathy—driven by behavioral tension.

REFERENCES

Aldridge, J., Berridge, K., Herman, M., and Zimmer, L. 1993. "Neuronal Coding of Serial Order: Syntax of Grooming in the Neostriatum." *Psychological Science.* V. 4, N. 6 (Nov): 391–395.

Alexander, R. 1987. *The Biology of Moral Systems.* Hawthorne, N.Y.:Aldine de Gruyter.

Allsopp, V. 1995. *Understanding Economics.* London: Routledge.

Alt, J. and Shepsle, K., eds. 1990. *Perspectives of Positive Political Economy.* Cambridge University Press.

Altman, J, and Bayer, S., 1997. *Development of the Cerebellar System: In Relation to Its Evolution, Structure, and Functions.* NY: CRC Press

Appadurai, A., ed. 1986. *The Social Life of Things.* Cambridge University Press.

Aristotle. 1985 [c 322 B.C.] *Nicomachean Ethics.* Trans. by T. Irwin. Indianapolis IN: Hackett.

Arndt, H. 1984. *Economic Theory VS Economic Reality.* Trans. by W. Kirby. Michigan State University Press.

Arrow, K. 1987. in *Arrow and the Ascent of Modern Economic Theory.* Ed. by Feiwel, G., London: Macmillan.

Arrow, K. 1963 (1951*). Social Choice and Individual Values.* Yale University Press.

Arrow, K. and Debreu, G. 1954. "Existence of a Equilibrium for a Competitive Economy." *Econometrica,* 22: 265–290.

Arrow, K. and Hahn, F. 1971. *General Competitive Analysis.* NY: North-Holland Publishing.

Arthur, W. 1997. *The Origin of Animal Body Plans: A Study in Evolutionary Developmental Biology.* Cambridge University Press.

Astington, J., Harris, P., and D. Olson, D., eds. 1988. *Developing Theories of Mind.* Cambridge University Press.

Axelrod, R. and Hamilton, W. 1981. "The Evolution of Cooperation." Pp.1390 in *Science.*V. 211.

Ayer, A. J., ed. 1959. *Logical Positivism.* Glencoe, IL: The Free Press.

Baal, J. van. 1975. *Reciprocity and the Position of Women.* Amsterdam: Van Gorcum, Assen.

Baars, B. 1997. *In the Theatre of Consciousness.* Oxford University Press.

Baars, B. 1988. *A Cognitive Theory of Consciousness.* Cambridge University Press.

Bachevalier, J. 2000. "The Amygdala, Social Cognition, and Autism." Pp. 509–543 in *The Amygdala: A Functional Analysis.* ed. by J. P. Aggleton. Oxford University Press.

Bailey, Kent. 2002. "Upshifting and Downshifting the Triune Brain: Roles in Individual and Social Pathology." In G. Cory and R. Gardner, eds. *The Evolutionary Neuroethology of Paul MacLean: Convergences and Frontiers.* Westport, CT: Praeger.

Barfield, T., ed. 1997. *The Dictionary of Anthropology.* Blackwell.

Barkow, J. Cosmides, L. and Tooby, J. eds. 1992. *The Adapted Mind: Evolutionary Psychology and the Generation of Culture.* Oxford University Press.

Baron-Cohen, S. 1995. *Mindblindness.* The MIT Press.

Bartlett, R. 1989. *Economics and Power: An Inquiry into Human Relations and Markets.* Cambridge University Press.

Bates, R. 1997. "Area Studies and the Discipline: A Useful Controversy." Pp. 166–169 in *PS: Politics and Political Science.* V. XXX, N.2.

Batson, C. 1991. *The Altruism Question: Toward a Social-Psychological Answer.* Hillsdale, NJ: Lawrence Erlbaum Associates.

Becker, G. 1987. "Economic Analysis and Human Behavior." Pp. 3–17 in *Advances in Behavioral Economics* V. 1. Ed. by L. Green and J. Kagel. Norwood, NJ: Ablex Publishing.

Becker, J.; Breedlove, S.; and Crews, D. eds. 1992. *Behavioral Endocrinology.* MIT Press.

Becker, L. 1986. *Reciprocity.* Boston, MA: Routledge and Kegan Paul.

Beitz, C. 1979. "Bounded Morality: Justice and the State in World Politics." Pp. 405–424 in *International Organization.* V. 33.

Bendor, J. and Swistak, P. 1997. "The Evolutionary Stability of Cooperation." Pp. 290–303 in *American Political Science Review.* V.91. N.2.

Benecke, R.; Rothwell, J.; Dick, J.; Day, B.; and Marsden, C. 1987. "Disturbance of Sequential Movements in Patients with Parkinson's Desease." *Brain.* V. 110: 361–380.

Berlinski, D. 2000. *The Advent of the Algorithm.* NY: Harcourt.

Berridge, K. and Fentress, J. 1988. "Disruption of Natural Grooming Chains after Striato-pallidal Lesions." *Psychobiology.* V. 15: 336–342.

Berridge, K. and Whishaw, I. 1992. "Cortex, Striatum, and Cerebellum: Control of Serial Order in a Grooming Sequence." *Experimental Brain Research.* V. 90: 275–290.

Bianchi, M. 1993. "How to Learn Sociality: True and False Solutions to Mandeville's Problem." *History of Political Economy.* Vol. 25. N. 2 (summer), 209–240.

Birtchnell, J. 1999. *Relating in Psychotherapy.* Westport, CT: Praeger.

Birtchnell, J. 1993. *How Humans Relate.* Westport, CT: Praeger.

Blau, P. 1964. *Exchange and Power in Social Life.* NY: John Wiley.

Blaug, M. 1980. *The Methods of Economics: or how economists explain.* Cambridge University Press.

Blessing, W. 1997. *The Lower Brainstem and Bodily Homeostasis.* Oxford University Press.

Boehm, C. 1999. *Hierarchy in the Forest: The Evolution of Egalitarian Behavior.* Harvard University Press.

Bohannon, P. 1963. *Social Anthropology.* NY: Holt, Rinehart, and Winston.

Boulding, K. 1950. *A Reconstruction of Economics.* NY: John Wiley.

Bowlby, J. 1988. *A Secure Base: Parent-Child Attachment and Healthy Human Development.* NY: Basic Books.

Bowlby, J. 1969. *Attachment.* Vol.1. NY: Basic Books.

Bowles, S. and Gintis, H. 1998. *Recasting Egalitarianism.* London: Verso.

Bromley, D. 1989. *Economic Interests and Institutions: The Conceptual Foundations of Public Policy.* NY: Basil Blackwell.

Brothers, L. 1995. "Neurophysiology of the Perception of Intentions by Primates." Pp. 1107–1115 in *The Cognitive Neurosciences.* Ed. by M. Gazzaniga. MIT Press.

Brothers, L. 1989. "A Biological Perspective on Empathy." *American Journal of Psychiatry,* 146, 10–19.

Brown, J. 1977. *Mind, Brain, and Consciousness.* NY: Academic Press.

Brownell, H. and Martino, G. 1998. "Deficits in Inference and Social Cognition: The Effects of Right Hemisphere Brain Damage on Discourse." Pp. 309–328 in *Right Hemisphere Language Comprehension: Perspectives from Cognitive Neuroscience.* Ed. by M. Beeman and C. Chiarello. Mahwah, NJ: Lawrence Erlbaum Associates.

Buber, M. 1958. *I and Thou.* 2nd Ed., Trans. By R. Smith. NY: Scribner's.

Buchanan, J. 1991. *The Economics and the Ethics of Constitutional Order.* University of Michigan Press.

Buchanan, J and Tullock, G. 1962. *The Calculus of Consent: Logical Foundations of Constitutional Democracy.* University of Michigan Press.

Burghardt, G. 1988. "Precocity, Play and the Ectotherm–Endotherm Transition." Pp. 107–148 in *Handbook of Behavioral Neurobiology.* V. 9. Ed. by E. Bass. NY: Plenum.

Burghardt, G. 1984. "On the Origins of Play." Pp. 5–41 in *Play in Animals and Humans.* Ed. by P. Smith. NY: Basil Blackwell.

Buss, D. 1999. *Evolutionary Psychology.* Boston: Allyn and Bacon.

Butler, A. and Hodos, W. 1996. *Comparative Vertebrate Neuroanatomy.* NY: Wiley-Liss.

Butler, E. 1985. *Hayek: His Contribution to the Political and Economic Thought of Our Time.* NY: Universe Books.

Caldwell, B. 1982. *Beyond Positivism: Economic Methodology in the Twentieth Century.* London: George Allen & Unwin.

Campbell, C. 1992. "Book Review (MacLean: The Triune Brain in Evolution)". Pp. 497–498 in *American Scientist,* V. 80 (Sept-Oct 19 1992)

Cannon, W. B. 1932. *The Wisdom of the Body.* NY: Norton.

Cannon, W. B. 1929. *Bodily Changes in Pain, Hunger, Fear, and Rage.* NY: D. Appleton & Co.

Carter, C., Lederhendler, I., and Kirkpatrick, B. eds. 1997. *The Integrative Neurobiology of Affiliation.* NY: New York Academy of Sciences, Vol. 807.

Chalmers, D. 1997. "The Puzzle of Conscious Experience." Pp.30–37 in *Scientific American: Mysteries of the Mind*. Special Issue V. 7, N.1.

Cheal, D. (1988). *The Gift Economy*. London: Routledge.

Chertow, M. and Esty, D. 1996. *Thinking Ecologically: The Next Generation of Environmental Policy*. Yale University Press.

Churchland, P. and Sejnowski, T.. 1992. *The Computational Brain*. MIT Press.

Clutton-Brock, T. H. 1991. *The Evolution of Parental Care*. Princeton University Press.

Coase, R. 1960. "The Problem of Social Cost." *Journal of Law and Economics*, 3: 1–44.

Coase, R. 1937. "The Nature of the Firm." *Economica*. 4 (November): 386–405.

Coe, C. 1990. Psychobiology of Maternal Behavior in Nonhuman Primates." Pp. 157–183 in *Mammalian Parenting: Biochemical, Neurobiological, and Behavioral Determinants*. Ed. by N. Krasnegor and R. Bridges. Oxford University Press.

Coleman, J. 1990. *Foundations of Social Theory*. Cambridge, MA: Belknap Press of Harvard University Press.

Cook, K., O'Brien, J., and Kollock, P. 1990. "Exchange Theory: A Blueprint for Structure and Progress," Pp. 158–181 in *Frontiers of Social Theory: The New Synthesis*, ed. by G. Ritzer. Columbia University Press.

Cook, K., ed. 1987. *Social Exchange Theory*. Newbury Park, CA: Sage.

Corning, P. 1996. "The Cooperative Gene: On the Role of Synergy in Evolution." Pp. 183–207 in *Evolutionary Theory*. V.11.

Corning, P. 1983. *The Synergism Hypothesis*. NY: McGraw-Hill.

Cory, G. 2001a. "Neural Network Theory and Neuroscience: Applications to Socio-Economic Theory." *Paper presented at the 13th Annual Meeting on Socio-Economics*, University of Amsterdam, June 28–July 1, 2001.

Cory, G. 2001b. "Transaction Costs, the Firm and Evolved Neural Architecture." *Paper presented at the 76th Annual Conference of the Western Economic Association International*, San Francisco, July 4–8.

Cory, G. 2000a. "From MacLean's Triune Brain Concept to the Conflict Systems Neurobehavioral Model: The Subjective Basis of Moral and Spiritual Consciousness." *Zygon: Journal of Religion & Science*, Vol 35. No.2, pp. 385–414.

Cory, G. 2000b. *Toward Consilience: The Bioneurological Basis of Thought, Behavior, Language, and Experience*. NY: Kluwer Academic/Plenum.

Cory, G. 1999. *The Reciprocal Modular Brain in Economics and Politics: Shaping the Rational and Moral Basis of Organization, Exchange, and Choice*. NY: Plenum Press.

Cory, G. 1998. "MacLean's Triune Brain Concept: in Praise and Appraisal." Pp. 6–19, 22–24. in *Across-Species Comparisons and Psychopathology Society (ASCAP) Newsletter*. V. 11. No. 07.

Cory, G. 1992. *Rescuing Capitalist Free Enterprise for the Twenty First Century*. Vancouver, WA: Center for Behavioral Ecology.

Cory, G. 1974. *The Biopsychological Basis of Political Socialization and Political Culture*. Ph.D. Dissertation. Stanford University.

Cory, G. and Gardner, R., eds. 2002. *The Evolutionary Neuroethology of Paul MacLean: Convergences and Frontiers*. Westport. CT: Praeger.

Cosmides, L. and Tooby, J. 1989. "Evolutionary Psychology and the Generation of Culture, Part II." Pp. 51–97 in *Ethology and Sociobiology*. V. 10.

Cournot, A. 1929 [1838] *Researches into the Mathematical Principles of the Theory of Wealth*. Trans. N. Bacon. Homewood, Ill: Richard D. Irwin.

Cowan, W., Jessell, T., and Lipursky, S., eds. 1997. *Molecular and Cellular Approaches to Neural Development*. Oxford University Press.

Crawford, C. and Krebs, D., eds. 1998. *The Handbook of Evolutionary Psychology*. Mahwah, NJ: Lawrence Erlbaum.

Crews, D. 1997. "Species Diversity with the Evolution of Behavioral Controlling Mechanisms. Carter, C., Lederhendler, I., and Kirkpatrick, B. (Eds.). *The Integrative Neurobiology of Affiliation*. NY: New York Academy of Sciences, Vol. 807: 1–21.

Crick, F. 1994. *The Astonishing Hypothesis: The Scientific Search for the Soul*. NY: Charles Scribner's Sons.

Cromwell, H. and Berridge, K. 1990. "Anterior Lesions of the Corpus Striatum Produce a Disruption of Stereotyped Grooming Sequences in the Rat." *Society for Neuroscience Abstracts*. V. 16: 233.

Cummings, J. 1993. "Frontal-Subcortical Circuits and Human Behavior." in *Archives of Neurology* V. 50 (Aug): 873–880.

Cummins, D. 1998. "Social Norms and Other Minds: The Evolutionary Roots of Higher Cognition." Pp. 30–50 in *The Evolution of Mind*. Ed. by Cummins, D. and Allen, C. Oxford University Press.

Dahlman, C. 1980. *The Open Field System and Beyond*. Cambridge University Press.

Daly, H. E., ed. 1980. *Economics, Ecology, and Ethics*. San Francisco: W. H. Freeman.

Daly, H. E. and Cobb, J. 1989. *For the Common Good: Redirecting the Economy Towards Community, the Environment and a Sustainable Future*. Boston: Beacon Press.

Damasio, A. 1999. *The Feeling of What Happens*. NY: Harcourt.

Damasio, A. 1994. *Descartes Error: Emotion, Reason, and the Human Brain*. NY: Grosset/Putnam.

Darwin, C. 1964 [1859]. *The Origin of Species*. Facsimile of the First Edition with introduction by E. Mayr. Harvard University Press.

Daum, I. and Ackermann, H. 1995. "Cerebellar contributions to cognition." in *Behavioural Brain Research*. 67: 202–210.

Davidson, R. 1995. "Cerebral Asymmetry, Emotion, and Affective Style." Pp. 361–387 in J. Davidson & K. Hugdahl (eds). *Brain Asymmetry*. MIT Press.

Davies, J. 1991. "Maslow and Theory of Political Development: Getting to Fundamentals." Pp. 389–420 in *Political Psychology*. V. 12. N.3.

Davies, J. 1963. *Human Nature in Politics*. NY: Wiley.

Davis, L and North, D. 1970. "Institutional Change and American Economic Growth: a first step towards a theory of institutional innovation." Pp. 131–149 in *Journal of Economic History*. 30.

Davis, N. 2000. *The Gift in Sixteenth Century France*. University of Wisconsin Press.

Dawkins, R. 1976. *The Selfish Gene*. Oxford University Press.

Dennett, D. 1998. "Reflections on Language and Mind." Pp. 284–293 in *Language and Thought*. Ed. by P. Carruthers and J. Boucher. Cambridge University Press.

Devinsky, O. and Luciano, D. 1993. "The Contributions of Cingulate Cortex to Human Behavior." Pp. 527–556 in *Neurobiology of Cingulate Cortex and Limbic Thalamus: A Comprehensive Handbook*. Ed. by Vogt, B. and Gabriel, M. Boston: Birkhauser.

de Waal. F. 2002. "Evolutionary Psychology: The Wheat and the Chaff." Pp. 187–191 in *Current Directions in Psychological Science*. Vol. 11. N. 6.

de Waal, F. 1996. *Good Natured: The Origins of Right and Wrong in Humans and Other Animals*. Harvard University Press.

Dimitrov, M.; Grafman, J.; Kosseff, P.; Wachs, J.; Alway, D.; Higgins, J.; Litvan, I.; Lou, J.; and Hallett, M. 1996. "Preserved cognitive processes in cerebellar degeneration." *Behavioural Brain Research*. 79: 131–135.

Donnerstein, E and E. Hatfield. 1982. "Aggression and Inequity." Pp 309–329 in *Equity and Justice in Social Behavior*, edited. by J. Greenberg and R. Cohen. NY: Academic Press.

Douglas, M. 1990. "Foreword: No Free Gifts" in M. Mauss, *The Gift*. Trans. by W. Halls. NY: Norton.

Dugger, W. 1996. "Four Modes of Inequality." Pp. 21–38 in *Inequality: Radical Institutionalist Views on Race, Gender, Class, and Nation*. Ed. by W. Dugger. Westport, CT: Greenwood Press.

Durfee, E. 1993. "Cooperative Distributed Problem-Solving Between (and within) Intelligent Agents." Pp. 84–98 in *Neuroscience: From Neural Networks to Artificial Intelligence*. Ed. by P. Rudomin, et al., Heidelberg: Springer-Verlag.

Dworkin, R. 1973. "The Original Position." *University of Chicago Law Review*. 40: 500–533.

Ebenstein, A. 2001. *Frederich Hayek: A Biography*. NY: St. Martins.

Eccles, J. 1984. "The Cerebral Neocortex: A Theory of its Operation." Pp. 1–36 in Cerebral Cortex. V. 2: *Functional Properties of Cortical Cells*. E. Jones & A. Peters (eds). NY: Plenum Press.

Eckel, C. and Grossman, P. 1997. "Equity and Fairness in Economic Decisions: Evidence from Bargaining Experiments." Pp. 281–301 in *Advances in Economic Psychology*. Ed. by G. Antonides and W. F. van Raaij. NY: John Wiley & Sons.

Edelman, G. and Tononi, G. 2000. *A Universe of Consciousness*. NY: Basic Books.

Edelman, G. 1992. *Bright Air, Brilliant Fire*. NY: Basic Books.

Eggertsson, T. 1990. *Economic Behavior and Institutions*. Cambridge University Press.

Ehrlich, P. and Ehrlich, A. 1996. *Betrayal of Science and Reason*. Wash., D. C.: Island Press.

Ehrlich, P. and Ehrlich, A. 1990. *The Population Explosion*. NY: Simon and Schuster.

Ehrlich, P. 1969. *The Population Bomb*. NY: Ballentine Books.

Eibl-Eibsfeldt, I. 1989. *Human Ethology*. NY: Aldine de Gruyter.

Einstein, Albert. 1954. "Physics and Reality." Pp. 290–323 in *Ideas and Opinions*. NY: Crown.

Eisenberg, N. 1994. "Empathy." Pp. 247–253 in *Encyclopedia of Human Behavior*, edited by V. S. Ramachandran. NY: Academic Press.

Eisler, R. and Levine, D. 2002. "Nuture, Nature, and Caring: We are not Prisoners of Our Genes." Pp. 9–52. In *Brain and Mind*. Vol. 3, No.1.

Ekins, P., ed. 1986. *The Living Economy: A New Economics in the Making*. London: Routledge

Ekins, P. and Max-Neef, M., eds. 1992. *Real-Life Economics*. London: Routledge.

Erdal, D. and Whiten, A. 1996. "Egalitarianism and Machiavellian Intelligence in Human Evolution." Pp. 139–150 in *Modelling the Early Human Mind*. Ed. by P. Mellars and K. Gibson. Cambridge: The McDonald Institute.

Eslinger, P. 1996. "Conceptualizing, Describing, and Measuring Components of Executive Function." Pp. 367–395 in *Attention, Memory, and Executive Function*. Ed. by Lyon, G. and Krasnegor, N. Baltimore: Paul H. Brookes Publishing Co.

Etzioni, A. 1988. *The Moral Dimension: Toward a New Economics*. NY: MacMillan.

Etzioni, A. 1986. "The Case for a Multiple-Utility Conception." *Economics and Philosophy*, 2: 159–183.

Fagen, R. 1981. *Animal Play Behavior*. Oxford University Press.

Fehr, E. and Gachter, S. 2000. "Fairness and Retaliation: The Economics of Reciprocity." *Journal of Economic Perspectives*. V. 14, N. 3: 159–181.

Feiwel, G., ed. 1987. *Arrow and the Ascent of Modern Economic Theory*. London: Macmillan Press.

Fennell, L. 2002. "Unpacking the Gift." Pp. 85–101 in *The Question of the Gift*. Ed. by M, Osteen. London: Routledge.

Feyerabend, P. 1975. *Against Method: outline of an anarchistic theory of knowledge*. London: New Left Books.

Fleischer, S. and Slotnik, B. 1978. "Disruption of maternal behavior in rats with lesions of the septal area." *Physiological Behavior*. 21: 189–200.

Fleming, A., Morgan, H., and Walsh, C. 1996. "Experiential Factors in Postpartum Regulation of Maternal Care." Pp. 295–332 in *Parental Care: Evolution, Mechanisms, and Adaptive Intelligence*. Ed. by Rosenblatt, J. and Snowden, C. NY: Academic Press.

Fleming, A., Vaccarino, F., and Leubke, C. 1980 "Amygdaloid inhibition of maternal behavior in the nulliparous female rat."Pp. 731–743. in *Physiological Behavior*, 25.

Frank, R., Gilovich, T., and Regan, D. 1993. "Does Studying Economics Inhibit Cooperation?" Pp. 159–171 in *Journal of Economic Perspectives* 7. No. 2 (Spring).

Frank, R. 1988. *Passions Within Reason: The Strategic Role of the Emotions*. NY: Norton.

Frederick, W. 1995. *Values, Nature, and Culture in the American Corporation*. Oxford University Press.

Freeman, J.; Cuppernell, C; Flannery, K; Gabriel, M. 1996. "Limbic thalamic, cingulate cortical and hippocampal neuronal correlates of discriminative approach learning in rabbits." Pp. 123–136 in *Behavioural Brain Research* 80.

Frey. B. 1992. *Economics as a Science of Human Behavior*. Boston: Kluwer Academic Publishers.

Fridlund, A. 1991. "Evolution and Facial Action in Reflex, Social Motive, and Paralanguage." Pp. 3–100 in *Biological Psychology*. 32.

Friedman, M. 1953. *Essays in Positive Economics*. University of Chicago Press.

Friston, K. 2002. "Beyond Phrenology: What Can Neuroimaging Tell Us About Distributed Circuitry?" *Annual Review of Neuroscience*. 25: 221–250.

Frith, U. (1993) 1997. "Autism." Pp. 92–98 in *Scientific American: Mysteries of the Mind*. Spec.Issue V. 7, N.1.

Frith, U. 1989. *Autism: Explaining the Enigma*. Cambridge, MA: Basil Blackwell.

Fukuyama, F. 1992. *The End of History and the Last Man*. NY: Free Press.

Fukuyama, F. "The End of History." *The National Interest*. Summer 1989, pp. 3–18.

Furubotn, E. and Richter, R 1991. "The New Institutional Economics: An Assessment." Pp. 1–32 in *The New Institutional Economics*. Ed. by Furubotn and Richter. Texas A&M University Press.

Fuster, J. 1999. "Cognitive Functions of the Frontal Lobes." Pp. 187–195 in *The Human Frontal Lobes*. Ed. by B. Miller and J. Cummings. NY: The Guilford Press.

Fuster, J. 1997. *The Prefrontal Cortex: Anatomy, Physiology, and Neuropsychology of the Frontal Lobe*. Third Edition. NY: Lippincott-Raven.

Gans, C. 1996. "An overview of Parental Care among the Reptilia." Pp. 145–157 in *Parental Care: Evolution, Mechanisms, and Adaptive Intelligence*. Ed. by Rosenblatt, J. and Snowden, C. NY: Academic Press.

Gardner, R. 2002. "MacLean's Paradigm and Its Relevance for Psychiatry's Basic Science." Pp.85–105 in G. Cory & R. Gardner, eds. *The Evolutionary Neuroethology of Paul MacLean: Convergences and Frontiers*. Westport, CT: Praeger.

Gardner, R. 1982. "Mechanisms in Major Depressive Disorder: An Evolutionary Model." *Archives of General Psychiatry*. 39. 1436–1441.

Gauthier, D. 1977. *The Social Contract as Ideology*. Princeton, NJ: Princeton University Press.

Gehring, W. 1998. *Master Control Genes in Development and Evolution: The Homeobox Story*. Yale University Press.

Gérard-Varet, L.-A, Kolm, S.-C., and Ythier, J. eds. (2000). *The Economics of Reciprocity, Giving, and Altruism*. NY: St. Martin's Press.

Gilbert, P. and Bailey, K., eds. 2000. *Genes on the Couch: Explorations in Evolutionary Psychotherapy*. Philadelphia, PA: Taylor & Francis.

Gloor, P. 1997. *The Temporal Lobe and the Limbic System*. Oxford University Press.

Godelier, M. 1999. *The Enigma of the Gift.* NY: Polity Press.

Goldberg, E. 2001. *The Executive Brain: Frontal Lobes and the Civilized Mind.* Oxford University Press.

Goodall, J. 1986. *The Chimpanzees of Gombe: Patterns of Behavior.* Harvard University Press.

Goudie, A., ed. 1997. *The Human Impact Reader.* Blackwell Publishers.

Gouldner, A. 1960. "The Norm of Reciprocity; a Preliminary Statement." *American Sociological Review* 25: 161–178.

Granovetter, M. and Swedberg, R. 2001. *The Sociology of Economic Life.* Boulder, CO: Westview.

Greenberg, N. 2002. "Adaptive Functions of the Corpus Striatum." Pp. 45–81 in G. Cory and R. Gardner, eds. *The Evolutionary Neuroethology of Paul MacLean: Convergences and Frontiers.* Westport, CT: Praeger.

Greenough, W. and Chang, F. 1989. Plasticity of Synapse Structure and Pattern in the Cerebral Cortex." In A. Peters & E. Jones (eds.), *Cerebral Cortex:* V. 7: 391–440. NY: Plenum Press.

Gregory, C. 1982. *Gifts and Commodities.* NY: Academic Press.

Groenewegen, J., ed. 1997. *Transaction Cost Economics and Beyond.* Boston: Kluwer Academic.

Grossman, J., Carter, A., Volkmar, F. 1997. "Social Behavior in Autism." Pp. 440–454 in *The Integrative Neurobiology of Affiliation.* Ed. by C. S. Carter, I. Lederhendler and B. Kirkpatrick. NY: Annals of the NY Academy of Sciences (Vol. 809).

Gutnick, M. J. and Mody, I., eds. 1995. *The Cortical Neuron.* Oxford University Press.

Habermas, J. 1990 *Justification and Application: Remarks on Discourse Ethics.* Trans. by C. Cronin. Cambridge, MA: MIT Press.

Habermas, J. 1989. J. *Habermas on Society and Politics: A Reader.* Ed. by S. Seidman. Boston: Beacon Press.

Hall, B. 1996. "Homology and Embryonic Development." Pp. 1–37 in *Evolutionary Biology.* V. 28. Ed. by M, K., Hecht, R. MacIntyre, and M. Clegg. NY: Plenum Press.

Hall, B., ed. 1994. *Homology: The Hierarchical Basis of Comparative Biology.* San Diego: Academic Press.

Hall, B. 1992. *Evolutionary Developmental Biology.* London: Chapman & Hall.

Hameroff, S; Kaszniak, A.; Scott, A., eds. 1996. *Toward a Science of Conciousness: The First Tuscon Discussions and Debates.* MIT Press.

Hameroff, S. and Penrose, R. 1996. "Orchestrated Reduction of Quantum Coherence in Brain Microtubules: A Model for Consciousness." Pp. 507–539 in Hameroff, S., Kaszniak, A., Scott, A., eds., 1996. *Toward a Science of Consciousness: The First Tuscon Discussions and Debates.* MIT Press.

Hamilton, W. 1964. "The Genetical Evolution of Social Behavior, I & II." Pp. 1–16, & 17–52 in *Journal of Theoretical Biology.* V. 7.

Hamilton, W. 1963."The Evolution of Altruistic Behavior." *American Naturalist* 97, 354–356.

Hampden-Turner, C. and Trompenaars, A. 1993. *The Seven Cultures of Capitalism.* NY: Doubleday.

Harel, D. 1987. *Algorithmics: The Spirit of Computing.* Reading, MA: Addison-Wesley.

Harlow, H. 1986. *From Learning to Love: The Selected Papers of H. F. Harlow.* Ed. by C. Harlow. NY: Praeger.

Harlow, H. and Harlow., M. 1965. "The Affectional Systems." Pp. 386–334 in *Behavior of Non-Human Primates.* Ed. by A. Schrier, H. Harlow, and F. Stollnitz. New York: Academic Press.

Harrington, A., ed. 1992. *So Human a Brain.* Boston: Birkhauser.

Harris, J. 2002. "Empathy, Autism, and the Integration of the Triune Brain." Pp. 155–166 in G. Cory & R. Gardner (eds.). *The Evolutionary Neuroethology of Paul MacLean: Convergences and Frontiers.* Westport, CT: Praeger.

Harth, E. 1997. "From Brains to Neural Nets." Pp. 1241–1255 in Neural Networks. V. 10, N.7.

Hatfield, E. and Traupmann, J. 1981. "Intimate Relationships: A Perspective from Equity Theory." Pp. 165–178 in *Personal Relationships. 1: Studying Personal Relationships.* Ed by S. Duck and R. Gilmour. NY: Academic Press.

Hayek. F. 1991. *Economic Freedom.* Oxford: Basil Blackwell.

Hayek. F. 1988. *The Fatal Conceit.* University of Chicago Press.

Hayek. F. 1973, 1976, 1979. *Law, Legislation, and Liberty.* 3 vols. University of Chicago Press.

Hayek. F. 1945. "The Use of Knowledge in Society." Pp. 519–530 in *American Economic Review* (Sep).

Hayek. F. 1944. *The Road to Serfdom.* University of Chicago Press.

Hayek. F. 1937. "Economics and Knowledge." Pp. 33–54 in *Economica* (February).

Heilbroner, R. 1997. "The Embarrassment of Economics." Pp. 18–21 in *Microeconomics 98/99.* Guilford, CT: Dushkin-McGraw-Hill.

Heilbroner, R. and Galbraith, J. 1990. *The Economic Problem.* Englewood Cliffs, NJ: Prentice Hall.

Heller, W; Nitschke, J. and Miller, G. 1998. "Lateralization in Emotion and Emotional Disorders." Pp. 26–32 in *Current Directions in Psychological Science,* Vol. 7. N.1.

Hempel, C. 1966. *Philosophy of Natural Science.* Englewood Cliffs, NJ: Prentice-Hall.

Herbert, J. and Schulkin, J. 2002. "Neurochemical Coding of Adaptive Responses in the Limbic System." Pp. 659–689 in *Hormones, Brain and Behavior.* Ed. by D. Pfaff, A. Arnold, S. Fahrbach, A. Etgen, and R. Rubin. NY: Academic Press.

Hickman, C.; Roberts, L.; & Hickman, F. 1990. *Biology of Animals.* Fifth Edition. St. Louis: Times Mirror/Mosby.

Hickman, C.; Roberts, L.; & Hickman, F. 1984 *Integrated Principles of Zoology.* Seventh Edition. St. Louis: Times Mirror/Mosby.

Hicks. J. 1939. *Value and Capital: An Inquiry into Some Fundamental Principles of Economics.* Oxford University Press.

Hirschman, A. 1982. *Shifting Involvements: Private Interest and Public Action.* Princeton University Press.

Hobbes, T. 1977 [1651]. *Leviathan.* Ed. by C. MacPherson. NY: Penguin.

Hobhouse, L. [1906] 1951. *Morals in evolution: A Study in Comparative Ethics.* London: Chapman & Hall.

Hoffman E., McCabe, K., and Smith, V. 1998. "Behavioral Foundations of Reciprocity: Experimental Economics and Evolutionary Psychology." Pp. 335–352 in *Economic Inquiry.* V. 36. N. 3.

Hoffman, M. 2000. *Empathy and Moral Development.* Cambridge University Press.

Hoffman, M. 1981. "Is Altruism Part of Human Nature?" Pp. 121–137 in *Journal of Personality and Social Psychology.* 40.

Hofstader, D. 1995. *Fluid Concepts and Creative Analogies.* NY: Basic Books.

Holthoff-Detto, V.; Kessler, J.; Herholz, K.; Bonner, H.; Pietrzyk, U.; Wurker, M.; Ghaemi, M.; Wienhard, K.; Wagner, R.; Heiss, W. 1997. "Functional Effects of Striatal Dysfunction in Parkinson Desease." *Archives of Neurology.* V. 54 (Feb): 145–150.

Homans, G. 1961. *Social behavior: Its Elementary Forms.* NY: Harcourt Brace and World.

Homans, G. 1950. *The Human Group.* NY: Harcourt Brace Jovanovich.

Humphrey, N. 1976. "The Function of the Intellect." Pp. 303–317 in *Growing Points in Ethology.* Ed. by P. Bateson and R. Hinde Cambridge University Press.

Hunt, R. 2002. "Economic Transfers and Exchanges: Concepts for Describing Allocations." Pp. 105–118 in *Theory in Economic Anthropology.* Ed. by J. Ensminger. NY: Altamira Press.

Ingrao, B. and Israel, G. 1990. *The Invisible Hand: Economic Equilibrium in the History of Science.* Trans. by Ian McGilvray. The MIT Press.

Isaac, G. 1978. "The Food-sharing Behavior of Protohuman Hominids." Pp. 90–108 in *Scientific American.* V. 238.

Jaffé, W. 1983. *William Jaffé's Essays on Walras.* Edited by D. Walker. Cambridge University Press.

Jencks, C. 1990 "Varieties of Altruism." pp. 53–67 in *Beyond Self-Interest.* Edited by J. Mansbridge. University of Chicago Press.

Jevons, W. S. 1888. *The Theory of Political Economy.* London: MacMillan and Co.

Jevons, W. S. 1905. *Essays of Economics.* London: MacMillan and Co.

Johnson, C. 1997. "Perception vs. Observation, or the Contributions of Rational Choice Theory and Area Studies to Contemporary Political Science." *PS: Politics and Political Science.* V. XXX. N.2: 170–174

Johnson, D. 1991. *Public Choice: An Introduction to the New Political Economy.* Mountain View, CA: Mayfield Publishing.

Johnson, G. 1986. *Research Methodology for Economists.* New York: Macmillan.

Kahneman, D., Diener, E., and Schwarz, N., eds. 1999 *Well-Being: The Foundations of Hedonic Psychology.* NY: Russell Sage Foundation.

Kandel, E., Schwartz, J., and Jessell, T. 2000. *Essentials of Neural Science and Behavior.* Fourth Edition. NY: McGraw-Hill

Kandel, E., Schwartz, J., and Jessell, T. 1995. *Essentials of Neural Science and Behavior.* Third Edition. Norwalk, CT: Appleton & Lange.

Kant, I. 1964 [1797]. *The Doctrine of Virtue and Part II of Metaphysics of Ethics.* Trans. By M. Gregor. University of Pennsylvania Press.

Keohane, R. 1990. "Empathy and International Regimes." Pp. 227–236 in *Beyond Self-Interest.* Ed. by J. Mansbridge. University of Chicago Press.

Keohane, R. 1989. *International Institutions and State Power.* Boulder, Co: Westview Press.

Keohane, R. 1984. *After Hegemony.* Princeton University Press.

Kimble, D., Rogers, L., and Hendrickson, C. 1967. "Hippocampal lesions disrupt maternal, not sexual behavior in the albino rat." Pp. 401–405 in *Journal of Comparative Physiological Psychology.* 63.

Knauft, B. 1991. "Violence and Sociality in Human Evolution." *Current Anthropology,* 32: 391–428.

Knauft, B. 1994. "Culture and Cooperation in Human Evolution." Pp. 37–67 in L. Sponsel and T. Gregor, eds. *The Anthropology of Peace and Nonviolence.* Boulder, CO: Lynne Rienner.

Knutson, J. 1972. *The Human Basis of the Polity.* New York: Aldine-Atherton.

Koch, C. 1999. *Biophysics of Computation: Information Processing in Single Neurons*. Oxford University Press.

Kohlberg, L. 1984. *The Psychology of Moral Development*. Vol. 2. San Francisco: Harper & Row.

Kohler, H. 1992. *Economics*. Lexington, Mass: D. C. Heath and Company

Kohler, H. 1968. *Scarcity Challenged: An Introduction to Economics*. NY: Holt, Rinehart and Winston, Inc.

Kokmen, E. 1991. "Book Review (The Triune Brain in Evolution)." *Journal of Neurosurgery*. Vol. 75 (December): 998.

Kolb, B. 1995. *Brain Plasticity and Behavior*. Mahwah, NJ: Erlbaum.

Kolb, B.; Gibb, R. and Robinson, T. 2003. Brain Plasticity and Behavior." *Current Directions in Psychological Science*. V. 12, N1 (February): 1–5.

Kolb, B.; Forgie, M.; Gibb, R.; Gorny, G. & Rowntree, S. 1998. "Age, Experience, and the Changing Brain." *Neuroscience and Biobehavioral Reviews*. 22: 143–159.

Krasnegor, N. and Bridges, R., eds. 1990. *Mammalian Parenting: Biochemical, Neurobiological, and Behavioral Determinants*. Oxford University Press.

LaBerge, D. 1995. *Attentional Processing: The Brain's Art of Mindfulness*. Harvard University Press.

Landsburg, S. 1992. *Price Theory and Applications*. NY: The Dryden Press.

Langlois, R. 1986a."The New Institutional Economics: An introductory essay." Pp. 1–15 in *Economics as a Process: Essays in the New Institutional Economics*. Ed. by R. Langlois. Cambridge University Press.

Langlois, R. 1986b. "Rationality, Institutions, and Explanation." Pp. 225–255 in Economics as a Process: *Essays in the New Institutional Economics*. Edited by R.N. Langlois. Cambridge University Press.

Lapeyre, P. and Lledo, P-M. 1994. "Homeostasis." Pp. 517–528 in *The Encyclopedia of Human Behavior*. Ed. by V. Ramachandran. San Diego, CA: Academic Press.

Lawrence, P. and Nohria, N. 2002. *Driven*. San Francisco, CA: Jossey-Bass.

LeDoux, J. 1997. *The Emotional Brain*. NY: Simon & Schuster.

Leven, S. 1994. "Semiotics, Meaning, and Discursive Neural Networks." Pp. 65–82 in *Neural Networks for Knowledge Representation and Inference*. Ed. by Levine, D. and Aparicio, M. Hillsdale, NJ: Lawrence Erlbaum Associates.

Levi-Strauss, C [1949] 1969. *The Elementary Structures of Kinship*. London: Eyre and Spottiwoode.

Levine, D. 1986. "A Neural Network Theory of Frontal Lobe Function." Pp, 716–727 in *Proceedings of the Eighth Annual Conference of the Cognitive Science Society*. Hillsdale, NJ: Lawrence Erlbaum Associates.

Levine, D. and Jani, N. 2002. "Toward a Neural Network Theory of the Triune Brain. In Cory, G. and Gardner, R., eds. *The Evolutionary Neuroethology of Paul MacLean: Convergences and Frontiers*. Westport, CT: Praeger.

Lieberman, P. 2000. *Human Language and Our Reptilian Brain*. Harvard University Press.

Lieberman, P. 1998. *Eve Spoke*. NY: Norton.

Lorenz, K. 1971. *Studies in Animal and Human Behavior*. Vol. 2. Trans. by R. Martin. Harvard University Press.

Lorenz, K. 1970. *Studies in Animal and Human Behavior*. Vol. 1. Trans. by R. Martin. Harvard University Press.

Losco, J. 1986. "Biology, Moral Conduct, and Policy Science." Pp. 117–144 in *Biology and Bureaucracy*. Ed. by E. White and J. Losco. Lanham, MD: University Press of America.

Loye, D. 2002a. "The Moral Brain." Pp. 133–150 in *Brain and Mind*. Vol. 3, No. 2.

Loye, D. 2002b. *Darwin's Lost Theory*. NY: Seven Stories Press.

Lusick, I. 1997. "The Disciplines of Political Science & Studying the Culture of Rational Choice as Case in Point." Pp. 175–179 in *PS: Politics and Political Science*. V. XXX. N. 2.

Lynne, G. 2000. "A Metaeconomics Look at the Case for a Multiple-Utility Conception." Prepared for *Roundtable at 12th Annual Meeting Society for the Advancement of Socio-Economics*, London School of Economics, July 7–11, 2000.

Lynne, G. 1999. "Divided Self Models of the Socioeconomic Person: The Metaeconomics Approach." *Journal of Socio-Economics* 28: 267–288.

MacLean, P. 1993. "Human Nature: Duality or Triality." Pp. 107–112 in *Politics and the Life Sciences*. V. 12. N.2.

MacLean, P. 1992. "Obtaining Knowledge of the Subjective Brain ('Epistemics')." p.57–70 in *So Human a Brain*. Ed. by A. Harrington. Boston: Birkhauser.

MacLean, P. 1990. *The Triune Brain in Evolution: Role in Paleocerebral Functions*. NY: Plenum.

Maddi, S. 1989. *Personality Theories*. 5th Edition. Chicago, IL: The Dorsey Press.

Malinowski, B. 1926. *Crime and Custom in Savage Society*. London: Kegan Paul.

Malinowski, B. 1922. *Argonauts of the Western Pacific*. London: Routledge & Kegan Paul.

Mansbridge, J., ed. 1990. *Beyond Self-Interest*. University of Chicago Press.

Margolis, H. 1982. *Selfishness, Altruism, and Rationality: A Theory of Social Choice.* Cambridge University Press.

Marsden, C. D. 1984. "Which Motor Disorder in Parkinson's Desease Indicates the True Motor Function of the Basal Ganglia?" Pp. 225–241 in *Functions of the Basal Ganglia* (Ciba Foundation Symposium 107). London: Pitman.

Marsden, C. D. 1982. "The Mysterious Motor Function of the Basal Ganglia: The Robert Wartenberg Lecture." *Neurology.* V. 32: 514–539.

Maslow, A. 1968. *Toward a Psychology of Being.* Second Edition. NY: Van Nostrand Reinhold.

Maslow, A. 1970. *Motivation and Personality.* Second Edition. NY: Harper & Row.

Maslow, A. 1943. "A Theory of Human Motivation." Pp. 370–396 in *Psychological Review.* V.50.

Masters, R. 1989. *The Nature of Politics.* Yale University Press.

Mauss, Marcel. 1990. *The Gift. Trans. By W. Halls.* NY: Norton

Mauss, Marcel. 1954. *The Gift.* Trans. by Ian Cunnison. NY: W. W. Norton.

Maxwell, G. and Ames, R. E. 1981. "Economists Free Ride: Does Anyone Else?" Pp. 295–310 in *Journal of Public Economists* 15.

Maynard Smith, J. 2002. "Equations of Life." Pp. 193–211 in *It Must be Beautiful: Great Equations of Modern Science.* Ed. by G. Farmelo. London: Granta Books.

Maynard Smith, J. 1982. "The Evolution of Social Behavior - a Classification of Models." Pp. 28–44 in *Current Problems in Sociobiology.* Ed by. King's College Sociobiology Group. Cambridge University Press.

Mazlish, B. 1998. *The Uncertain Sciences.* Yale University Press.

Mazur, L., editor. 1994. *Beyond the Numbers.* Wash, D. C.: Island Press.

Mencius. 1970 [298 B.C.]. *The Mind of Mencius.* Trans. By D. Lau. NY: Penguin.

Miller, B. and . Cummings,.J. eds.. 1999. *The Human Frontal Lobes.* NY: The Guilford Press.

Miller, E. 1996. "Seen through a Glass Darkly: Competing Views of Equality and Inequality in Economic Thought." Pp. 87–99 in *Inequality: Radical Institutionalist Views on Race, Gender, Class, and Nation.* Ed. by W. Dugger. Westport, CT: Greenwood Press.

Miller, S. and Harley, J. 1992. *Zoology.* Duberque, IA: Wm. C. Brown Publishers.

Mirsky, A. 1996. "Disorders of Attention: A Neuropsychological Perspective." Pp. 71–95 in *Attention, Memory, and Executive Function.* Ed. by G. Lyon & N. Krasnegor. Baltimore, MD. Paul H. Brookes Publishing.

Moore, B. 1978. *Injustice: The Social Bases of Obedience and Revolt.* White Plains, NY: M. E. Sharpe

Morgan, L. H. 1877. *Ancient Society: or, Researches in the Lines of Human Progress from Savagery through Barbarism to Civilization.* NY: Henry Holt.

Morishima, M. "General Equilibrium Theory in the Twenty-First Century" in *The Future of Economics,* ed. By J. Hey. Oxford: Blackwell (1992).

Mountcastle, V. 1978. "An Organizing Principle for Cerebral Function." Pp. 5–50 in *The Mindful Brain.* V. Mountcastle & G. Edelman. The MIT Press.

Myers, N. and Simon, J. 1994. *Scarcity of Abundance? A Debate on the Environment.* NY: Norton.

Nasar, S. 1998. *A Beautiful Mind.* NY: Simon & Schuster.

Nash, J. 1953. "The Two Person Cooperative Games " *Econometrica,* vol 21, 405–421.

Nash, J. 1951. "Non-Cooperative Games." *Annals of Mathematics,* vol 54, 286–295.

Nash, J. 1950. "The Bargaining Problem" *Econometrica,* vol 18, 155–162.

Nelson, R. 2000. *An Introduction to Behavioral Endocrinology.* Second Edition. Sunderland, MA: Sinauer.

Neumann, J. von and Morgenstern, O. 1947. *Theory of Games and Economic Behavior.* Second edition. Princeton University Press.

Newman, J.; Baars, B.; & Cho, S. 1997. "A Neural Global Workspace Model for Conscious Attention." Pp. 1195–1206 in *Neural Networks.* V. 10, N. 7.

Newmarch, W. 1861. "The Progress of Economic Science During the Last Thirty Years: An Opening Address [before Section F]." *Journal of the Statistical Society,* vol. XXIV, Part IV (December), pp. 451–467.

Noorderhaven, N. 1996. "Opportunism and Trust in Transaction Cost Economics." Pp. 105–128 in *Transaction Cost Economics and Beyond.* Ed. by John Groenewegen. Boston: Kluwer Academic.

North, D. 1990. *Institutions, Institutional Change and Economic Performance.* Cambridge University Press.

Numan, M. 1994. ""Maternal Behavior." Pp. 221–302 in *Physiology of Reproduction.* 2nd edition. Vol. 2. Ed. by Knobil, E. and Neill, J. New York: Raven Press.

Numan, M. and Sheehan, T. 1997. "Neuroanatomical Circuitry for Mammalian Maternal Behavior." Pp. 101–125 in *The Integrative Neurobiology of Affiliation.* Ed. by C. S. Carter, I. Lederhendler, and B. Kirkpatrick. NY: New York Academy of Sciences, Vol. 807.

Oberg, R. and Divac, I. 1979. "'Cognitive' functions of the Neostriatum." Pp. 291–313 in *The Neostriatum.* Ed. by I. Divac and R.G.E. Oberg. Oxford: Pergamon Press.

Okin, S. 1989. *Justice, Gender, and the Family.* NY: Basic Books.

O'Leary, D. 1989. "Do Cortical Areas Emerge from a Protocortex?" Pp. 400–406 in *Trends in Neuroscience* 12 (Elsevier Trends Journals)

Osteen, M. 2002. "Gift or Commodity." Pp. 229–247 in *The Question of the Gift*. Ed. by M. Osteen. London: Routledge.

Panksepp, Jaak. 2002. "Foreword." In *The Evolutionary Neuroethology of Paul MacLean: Convergences and Frontiers*. Ed. by G. Cory and R. Gardner. Westport, CT: Praeger.

Panksepp, Jaak. 1998. *Affective Neuroscience*. Oxford University Press.

Panksepp, Jaak and Panksepp, Jules. B. 2000. "The Seven Sins of Evolutionary Psychology." *Evolution and Cognition*, 6, 108–131.

Parsons, T. 1960. "Pattern Variables Revisited," Pp. 467–488 in *American Sociological Review*, 25.

Parsons, T. 1951. *The Social System*. New York: Free Press.

Penrose, R. 1994. *Shadows of the Mind*. Oxford University Press.

Perlman, M. and McCann, C. 1998. *The Pillars of Economic Understanding*. University of Michigan Press.

Peterson, S. 1983. The Psychobiology of Hypostatizing." Pp. 423–451 in *Micropolitics*. 2.

Peterson, S. 1981. "Sociobiology and Ideas-Become-Real." Pp. 125–143 in *Journal of Social and Biological Structures*. 4.

Pettman, R. 1975. *Human Behavior and World Politics. A Transdisciplinary Introduction*. London: The MacMillan Press

Piaget, Jean. [1932] 1965. *The Moral Judgement of the Child*. NY: Free Press.

Pinker, S. 2002. *The Blank Slate: The Modern Denial of Human Nature*. NY: Viking.

Pinker, S. 1997. *How the Mind Works*. New York: Norton.

Plant, R. 1992. "Enterprise in its place: the moral limits of market." Pp. 85–99 in *The Values of the Enterprise Culture: The Moral Debate*. Ed. by P. Heelas and P. Morris. London: Routledge.

Plato. 1982 [c 380 B.C.]. *The Republic*. Trans. by G. Grube Indianapolis, IN: Hackett.

Polanyi, Karl. 1957. *The Great Transformation*. Boston: Beacon Press.

Pooley, A.C. 1977. "Nest opening response of the Nile crocodile." Pp. 17–26 in *Journal of Zoology* (London), 182.

Porter, T. M. 1986. *The Rise of Statistical Thinking. 1820–1900*. Princeton University Press.

Power, T. 1996. *Environmental Protection and Economic Well-Being*. Second Edition. Armonk, New York: M. E. Sharpe

Premack, D. and Woodruff, G. 1978. "Does the Chimpanzee have a Theory of Mind?" Pp. 515–526 in *Behavioral Brain Science*. 1.

Pribram, K. 1994. "Brain and the Structure of Narrative." Pp. 375–415 in *Neural Networks for Knowledge Representation and Inference*. Ed. by Levine, D. and Aparicio, M. Hillsdale, NJ: Lawrence Erlbaum Associates.

Pribram, K. 1973. "The Primate Frontal Cortex—Executive of the Brain." Pp. 293–314 in *Psychophysiology of the Frontal Lobes*. Ed. by Pribram, K. and Luria, A. NY: Academic Press.

Price, J. 1967. "Hypothesis: The Dominance Hierarchy and the Evolution of Mental Illness." *Lancet* ii, 243–246.

Price, J., Sloman, L., Gardner, R. Rohde, P. 1994. "The Social Competition Hypothesis of Depression." *British Journal of Psychiatry*. 164, 309–315.

Przewlocki, R. 2002. "Stress, Opiod Peptides, and Their Receptors." Pp. 691–733 in *Hormones, Brain and Behavior*. Ed. by D. Pfaff, A. Arnold, S. Fahrbach, A. Etgen, and R. Rubin. NY: Academic Press.

Rawls, J. 1999a [1985]. "Justice as Fairness: Political Not Metaphysical." Pp. 388–414 in Rawls, John. *Collected Papers*. Ed. by S. Freeman. Cambridge, MA: Harvard University Press

Rawls, J. 1999b [1971]. "Justice as Reciprocity." Pp. 190–224 in Rawls, J. *Collected Papers*. Ed. by S. Freeman. Cambridge, MA: Harvard University Press

Rawls, J. 1971. *A Theory of Justice*. Cambridge, MA: Harvard University Press.

Reiner, A. 1990. "An Explanation of Behavior" (review of MacLean's The Triune Brain in Evolution). Pp. 303–305 in *Science*, V. 250 (Oct 12, 1990).

Restak, R. 1994. *The Modular Brain*. A Lisa Drew Book. New York: Charles Scribner's Sons.

Robbins, L. 1952. *An Essay on the Nature & Significance of Economic Science*. Second Edition. London: MacMillan and Co.

Rodan, S. 2002. "Innovation and Heterogeneous Knowledge in Managerial Contact Networks." *Journal of Knowledge Management*. V. 6, N.2: 152–163.

Rosenblatt, J. and Snowden, C. 1996. *Parental Care: Evolution, Mechanisms, and Adaptive Intelligence*. NY: Academic Press.

Sagan, C. 1977. *The Dragons of Eden*. NY: Random House.

Sahlins, M. 1972. *Stone Age Economics*. Chicago, IL: Aldine-Atherton.

Sahlins, M. 1963. "On the Sociology of Primitive Exchange." pp. 139–236 in *TheRelevance of Models for Social Anthropology*. Ed. by M. Banton. London: Tavistock Publications.

Salter, F. 1995. *Emotions in Command*. Oxford University Press.

Samuelson, P. 1947. *Foundations of Economic Analysis*. Harvard University Press.

Sapolsky, R. 1999. "The Physiology and Pathophysiology of Unhappiness." Pp. 453–469 in D. Kahneman, E. Deiner, & N. Schwarz (eds.). Well-Being: *The Foundations of Hedonic Psychology*. NY: Russell Sage Foundation.

Sapolsky, R. 1992. "Neuroendocrinology of the Stress Response." Pp. 287–324. in J. Becker, S. Breedlove, & D. Crews (eds.) *Behavioral Endocrinology*. The MIT Press.

Say, J-B. 1855 *A Treatise on Political Economy*. Trans. By C. Prinsep. Philadelphia: Lippincott, Grambo & Co.

Schmid, A. 1989. *Benefit Cost Analysis: A Political Economy Approach*. Boulder, Colo: Westview Press.

Schmid, A. 1987. *Property, Power, and Public Choice: An Inquire into Law and Economics*. Second Edition. NY: Praeger.

Schnider, A. and Gutbrod, K. 1999. "Traumatic Brain Injury." Pp. 487–505 in B. Miller & J. Cummings (eds.). *The Human Frontal Lobes*. NY: The Guilford Press.

Schotter, A. 1981. *The Economic Theory of Social Institutions*. Cambridge University Press.

Schumpeter, J. 1954. *History of Economic Analysis*. Oxford University Press.

Schumpeter, J. 1950 [1942]. *Capitalism, Socialism, and Democracy*. NY: Harper & Row.

Searle, J. 1997. *The Mystery of Consciousness*. New York: The New York Times Review of Books.

Sen, A. 1997. *On Economic Inequality*. Expanded Edition. Oxford: Clarendon Press.

Sen, A. 1979. "Rational Fools: A Critique of the Behavioral Foundations of Economic Theory." in *Philosophy and Economic Theory*. Ed. by F. Hahn and M. Hollis. Oxford University Press.

Seymour-Smith, C. 1986. *Dictionary of Anthropology*. Boston: G. K. Hall & Co.

Shaw, C. and McEachern, J. 2001. *Toward a Theory of Neuroplasticity*. NY: Taylor and Francis.

Sherman, S. and Guillery, R. 2001. *Exploring the Thalamus*. NY: Academic Press.

Shun, K. 1997. *Mencius and Early Chinese Thought*. Stanford University Press.

Simmel, G. 1950. *The Sociology of Georg Simmel*. Trans. by K. Wolff. Glencoe, IL: The Free Press.

Simon, H. A. 1948. *Administrative Behavior*. NY: The MacMillan Company.

Simon, H. A. 1972. "Theories of Bounded Rationality." Pp. 161–176 in *Decision and Organization*. Ed. by C. McGuire and R. Radner. Amsterdam.

Simon, J. 1981. *The Ultimate Resource*. Princeton University Press.

Skinner, B. F. 1971. *Beyond Freedom and Dignity*. NY: Knopf.

Slater, D. and Tonkiss, F. 2001. *Market Society and Modern Social Theory*. Cambridge, U. K.: Polity Press.

Sloman, L. 2002. "Involuntary Defeat Strategy as Backdrop for Depression." Pp. 120–132 in G. Cory & R. Gardner (eds.). *The Evolutionary Neuroethology of Paul MacLean: Convergences and Frontiers*. Westport, CT: Praeger.

Slotnik, B. M. 1967. "Disturbances of maternal behavior in the rat following lesions of the cingulate cortex." *Behavior*. 29: 204–236.

Smith, Adam. 1977[1740–90]. "The Correspondence of Adam Smith,(1740–90)", Mossner, E. and Ross, T. Eds., in Vol. 6 of *The Glasgow Edition of the Works and Correspondence of Adam Smith*. General editing by D Raphael and A. Skinner. Oxford: Clarendon Press.

Smith, Adam. 1911[1789]. *The Theory of Moral Sentiments*. New edition. London: G. Bell.

Smith, Adam. 1937[1776]. *The Wealth of Nations*. Ed. by Edwin Cannan. NY: Modern Library.

Smith, C. 2002. "Deep Time and the Brain: The Message of the Molecules." Pp.31–44 in Cory, G. and Gardner, R., eds. *The Evolutionary Neuroethology of Paul MacLean: Convergences and Frontiers*. Westport, CT: Praeger.

Smith, C. 1996. *Elements of Molecular Neurobiology*. 2nd Edition. NY: Wiley.

Smith, M. 1991. "Comments of Davies' Maslow and Theory of Political Development." Pp. 421–423 in *Political Psychology*. V.12. N. 3.

Solnick, S. 1998. *Stealing the State: Control and Collapse in Soviet Institutions*. Harvard University Press.

Somit, A. and Peterson, S. 1997. *Darwinism, Dominance, and Democracy*. Westport, CT: Praeger.

Spitz, R. 1965. *The First Year of Life*. NY: International Universities Press.

Stamm, J. S. 1955. "The function of the medial cerebral cortex in maternal behavior in rats." *Journal of Comparative Physiological Psychology*. 48: 347–356.

Stapp, H. 1972. "The Copenhagen Interpretation." Pp. 1098–1116 in *American Journal of Physics*. 40 (8).

Steiner, Kurt. (forthcoming). *The Tokyo Trials*.

Stern, C. and Passingham, R. 1996. "The nucleus accumbens in monkeys (Macaca fascicularis): II. Emotion and motivation." *Behavioral Brain Research*. 75: 179–193.

Stigler, G. 1961. "The Economics of Information." *Journal of Political Economy*. 69 (June): 213–215.

Stigler, S. 1986. *The History of Statistics: The Measure of Uncertainty Before 1900*. Harvard University Press.

Strickberger, M. 1996. *Evolution*. Second Edition. Boston: Jones and Bartlett.

Striedter, G. 1998. "Stepping into the Same River Twice: Homologues as Recurring Attractors in Epigenetic Landscapes." *Brain, Behavior, and Evolution*. 52: 218–231.

Striedter, G. 1997. "The Telencephalon of Tetrapods in Evolution." *Brain, Behavior, and Evolution*. 49: 179–213.

Strum, S. and Latour, B. 1991. "Redefining the Social Link From Baboons to Humans." Pp. 73–85 in *Primate Politics*, edited. by G. Schubert and R. Masters. Southern Illinois University Press.

Taylor, S. 2002. *The Tending Instinct*. NY: Time Books.

Terlecki, L. and Sainsbury, R. 1978. "Effects of fimbria lesions on maternal behavior of the rat." *Physiological Behavior*. 21: 89–97.

Teske, N. 1997. "Beyond Altruism: Identity-Construction as Moral Motive in Political Explanation." Pp. 71–91 in *Political Psychology*. V.18. N. 1.

Thomson, K. 1988. *Morphogenesis and Evolution*. Oxford University Press.

Thurnwald, R. 1932. *Economics in Primitive Communities*. Oxford University Press.

Tickell, C. 1993. "The Human Species: A Suicidal Success." Pp. 219–226 in *Geographical Journal*. Vol. 159.

Tillich, P. 1954. *Love, Power, and Justice*. Oxford University Press.

Titmuss, R. 1972. *The Gift Relationship: From Human Blood to Social Policy*. NY: Pantheon.

Toates, F. 2001. *Biological Psychology*. NY: Prentice-Hall.

Tooby, J. and Cosmides, L. 1989. "Evolutionary Psychology and the Generation of Culture, Part I." Pp. 29–49 in *Ethology and Sociobiology*. V. 10.

Tooby, J. and DeVore, I. 1987 "The Reconstruction of Hominid Behavioral Evolution through Strategic Modeling." in *Primate Primate Models for the Origin of Human Behavior*. Ed. by W. G. Kinsey. New York: SUNY Press.

Trevarrow, B. 1998. "Developmental Homologues: Lineages and Analysis." Brain. Behavior, and Evolution. 52: 243–253.

Trivers, R. 1981. "*Sociobiology and Politics*." Pp. 1–44 in *Sociobiology and Human Politics*, Ed. by E. White. Lexington, MA: D. C. Heath & Company.

Trivers, R. 1971. "The Evolution of Reciprocal Altruism." Pp. 35–57 in *The Quarterly Review of Biology*. V. 46.

Tucker, D; Luu, P.; and Pribram, K. 1995. "Social and Emotional Self-Regulation." Pp. 213–239 in *Annals of the New York Academy of Sciences*. Vol. 769.

Tullock, G. 1990. "The Costs of Special Privilege." Pp. 195–211 in *Perspectives of Positive Political Economy*. Ed. by Alt, J. and K. Shepsle. Cambridge University Press.

Tullock, G. 1992. *Economic Hierarchies, Organization and the Structure of Production*. Boston: Kluwer Academic Publishers

Udehn. L. 1996. *The Limits of Public Choice*. London: Routledge.

Van Valen, Leigh M. 1982. "Homology and Causes." *Morphology*. 173: 305–312.

Vaughan, Genevieve. 1997. *For-Giving*. Austin, TX: Plain View Press.

Veblen, Thorstein. 1948[1897]. "Why is Economics not an Evolutionary Science?" Pp. 215–240 in *The Portable Veblen*. Ed. by M. Lerner. Viking Press.

Veenman, C.; Medina, L.; and Reiner, A. 1997. "Avian Homologues of Mammalian Intralaminar, Mediodorsal and Midline Thalamic Nuclei: Immuno-histochemical and Hodological Evidence." *Brain, Behavior, and Evolution*. 49: 78–98.

Walras, L. 1954. *Elements of Pure Economics*. 4th Edition. Trans. by W. Jaffe. Homewood, IL: Richard D. Irwin, Inc.

Walster, E., G. Walster, and E. Bersheid. 1978. *Equity: Theory and Research*. Boston: Allyn & Bacon.

Warren, S. 1984. *The Emergence of Dialectical Theory*. University of Chicago Press.

Weatherford, J. 1988. *Indian Givers: How the Indians of the Americas Transformed the New World*. NY: Crown Press.

Weisfeld, G. 2002. "Neural and Functional Aspects of Pride and Shame." Pp. 193–214 in G. Cory and R. Gardner (eds.), *The Evolutionary Neuroethology of Paul MacLean: Convergences and Frontiers*. Westport, CT: Praeger.

White, E. 2001. *The Fratricidal Global Village*. Westport, CT: Praeger.

White, E. 1992. *The End of the Empty Organism: Neurobiology and the Sciences of Human Action*. Westport, CT: Praeger.

Wilber, C., ed. 1998. *Economics, Ethics, and Public Policy*. Lanham, MD: Rowman & Littlefield.

Williamson, O. 1996. *The Mechanisms of Governance*. Oxford University Press.

Williamson, O. 1991. "The Logic of Economic Organization." Pp. 90–116 in *The Nature of the Firm: Origins, Evolution, and Development*. Ed. by O. Williamson & S. Winter. Oxford University Press.

Williamson, O. 1985. *The Economic Institution of Capitalism.* NY: Free Press.

Williamson, O. 1975. *Markets and Hierarchies: Analysis and Anti-Trust Implications.* NY: Free Press.

Wilson, D. R. 2002. "The Evolved Basis of Mood and Thought Disorders." In Cory, G. and Gardner, R., eds. *The Evolutionary Neuroethology of Paul MacLean: Convergences and Frontiers.* Westport, CT: Praeger.

Wilson, D. R. 1993. "Evolutionary Epidemiology: Darwinian Theory in the Service of Medicine and Psychiatry," *Acta Biotheoretica* 41, 205–218.

Wilson, E. O., 1998. *Consilience: The Unity of Knowledge.* NY: Alfred A. Knopf.

Wispe, L. 1991. *The Psychology of Sympathy.* NY: Plenum Press.

Wood, R. C. and Hamel, G. 2002. "The World Bank's Innovation Market." *Harvard Business Review.* Vol. 80, N. 11 (November): 104–113.

Yankelovich, D. 1981. *New Rules: Searching for Self-Fulfillment in a World Turned Upside Down.* NY: Random House.

Zigler, E. and Child, I. 1973. *Socialization and Personality Development.* Reading, MA: Addison-Wesley.

INDEX

DATE DUE